SAILING DIRECTIONS
EAST & NORTH COASTS OF IRELAND

The Irish Cruising Club Ltd. also publishes a companion volume "Sailing Directions for South and West Coasts of Ireland." Both volumes obtainable from booksellers and chandlers or from the agents Imry, Laurie, Norrie & Wilson Ltd., St. Ives, Cambridge, England, for United Kingdom—excluding Northern Ireland and all overseas areas. Irish yachtsmen may obtain copies direct from Mrs. Barbara Fox-Mills, The Tansey, Baily, Co. Dublin, Republic of Ireland.

ISBN 0 9501717 4 3

Printed by The Greystone Press, Caulside Drive, Antrim, Northern Ireland.

IRISH CRUISING CLUB

SAILING DIRECTIONS

for the

EAST & NORTH COASTS
OF IRELAND

Compiled by members of the Club, together with information
supplied by many other yachtsmen who have enjoyed the Irish Coast
With a foreword by Ronnie Sharp, Commodore, Clyde Cruising Club.

"What joy to sail the crested sea and watch the waves beat white upon the Irish shore."
—*St. Columba, A.D. 563.*

FOREWORD

The Seventh Edition of the I.C.C.'s Sailing Directions for the East and North Coasts of Ireland reflects the Club's continuing search for perfection.

Trusted and proven pilotage information from previous editions has been updated, and this has been supplemented by additional detail gathered mostly from local sources. The resultant publication is a sound technical manual which no yachtsman using the waters can afford to be without. One cannot place too much importance on the additional benefit which will accrue to holders of the book in future years. The Club intend to publish annually a supplement listing minor amendments which may be made to lights, buoyage etc. We are thus assured of having a book fit for the 1990s.

I have sailed up and down the Irish coastline for more than thirty years, and with help from the I.C.C. Directions have visited areas and explored anchorages which I would never have considered approaching without them.

On reading a draft of this enlarged and updated edition I was reminded of long and lasting friendships which have been made in the past as I look forward to the future with anticipation. The welcome that one meets on coming ashore in Ireland whether in remote anchorage, Yacht Club, or village pub is world renowned, and is, in my experience unsurpassed!

I congratulate the Irish Cruising Club on the quality of their publication, and commend the Sailing Directions to all who share these waters, be they professional mariner or amateur yachtsman.

R. L. Sharp
Commodore, Clyde Cruising Club

Ardbeg,
Craigmillar Avenue,
Milngavie,
Glasgow.

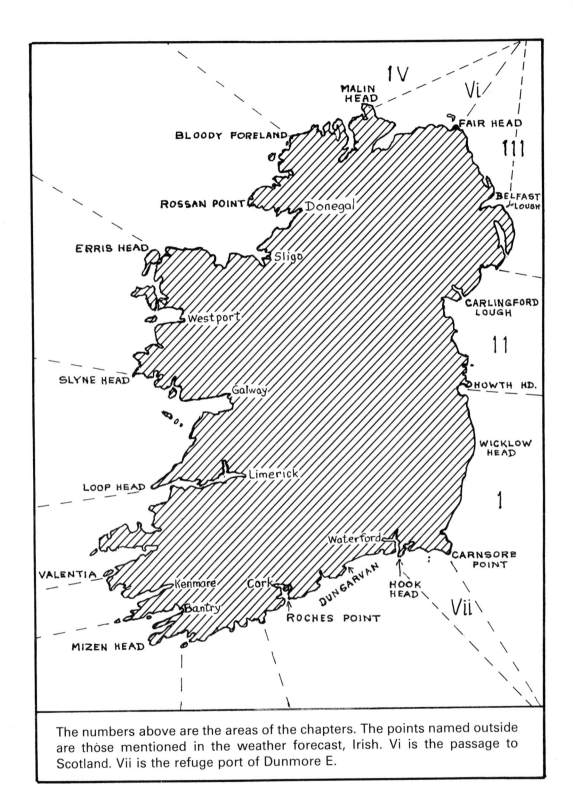

IV

Vi

MALIN
HEAD

FAIR HEAD

BLOODY FORELAND

III

BELFAST
LOUGH

ROSSAN POINT

Donegal

ERRIS HEAD

Sligo

CARLINGFORD
LOUGH

Westport

11

SLYNE HEAD

Galway

HOWTH HD.

WICKLOW
HEAD

LOOP HEAD

Limerick

1

Waterford

VALENTIA

Kenmare

Cork

DUNGARVAN

HOOK
HEAD

CARNSORE
POINT

Bantry

Vii

ROCHES POINT

MIZEN HEAD

The numbers above are the areas of the chapters. The points named outside
are those mentioned in the weather forecast, Irish. Vi is the passage to
Scotland. Vii is the refuge port of Dunmore E.

CONTENTS

Photographs, on Plates between Chapters III and IV preceded by a list of credits.

APPENDICES

Additions and Corrections

Any new information or corrections to these Sailing Directions are welcomed by the Club, and should be sent to either the Hon. Secretary, Cormac McHenry, 8 Heidleberg, Ardilea, Dublin 14, tel. (01) 884733, The Hon. Compiler, Arthur S. P. Orr, Evergreen, 11 Old Holywood Road, Belfast, BT4 2HJ, tel. Belfast (0232) 763601 or The Hon. Publications Officer, Mrs. Barbara Fox-Mills, The Tansey, Baily, Co. Dublin, tel. (01) 322823.

These Directions are not included in corrections by Admiralty Notices to Mariners and are therefore offered for sale for reference purposes only.

Introduction

When the Irish Cruising Club was founded, 50 years ago, one of its declared objects was to assemble and publish information about the coasts and anchorages of Ireland. Within a year the late Billy Mooney had written a detailed guide to the East coast; a moderate number of copies were stencilled and made available to members. In 1946, during his eight years as Commodore, Billy Mooney rewrote the book; it was elegantly printed and sold to visiting yachtsmen as well as to members. In 1956 a larger volume, "East & North Coast Sailing Directions," was produced; the North coast pilotage having been written by Wallace Clark. This edition was available through retail channels as at present. Further revised 4th and 5th editions were published in 1965 and 1970.

The 6th edition continued to contain nagivational advice from Billy Mooney; chapter IV was brought up to date by Wallace Clark. The late Paul Campbell was responsible for actual assembly and publishing of three editions in 1965, 1970 and 1979. The publication of this present edition has fallen on the shoulders of Arthur Orr. Many members and visiting yachtsmen continue to supply much of the information. Harbour Masters and Honorary Secretaries of yacht clubs along the section of the coast dealt with in this edition have been approached to give updated details of their patches, together with details of the availability of such mundane items as showers, launderettes, etc. Members have rewritten parts of the text to include local knowledge of their own areas.

A feature of this edition has been the amount of information coming from non-members of the club. This would point to a much wider readership of our publications. The setting up of the system whereby nominated members were made responsible for surveying small sections of the coast and reporting any changes through their area flag officers once a year has been moderately successful; some areas being more so than others, however, much knowledge has been obtained and the compiler is very grateful.

New plans of the marinas in the area have been included for the first time, also many of our photographs are now in colour; acknowledgement of the photographers is on page 48 immediately prior to the section. In some instances we have been able to include VHF channels in use and call signs.

Chapter V is new, it contains the old Appendix XI—Crossing to Scotland—basically to link up with the Clyde Cruising Club's Sailing Directions for the area. Included also in this chapter is the first part of Chapter I of ICC's South and West Coast Sailing Directions to help the many yachtsmen coming from the south of England or the Continent who, on a passage North may find it necessary or convenient to be West of Carnsore Point, and may wish to visit Dunmore East.

It is not possible here to thank individually all who have contributed and assisted. We feel confident that those who use the book will, be grateful to them, as well as to the original authors.

Three further appendices have been added. One giving a list of way points and particular attention is drawn to the introductory paragraph. The other two appendices are introduced for the benefit, mainly of strangers to our shores; the first is a list of places of historical interest, or beauty, or of interest to natural history, close to the coast which are worth visiting for various reasons if a yacht is held up by bad weather or for a general wish to see the sights and scenery. The second is a list of pubs and eating houses along the coast which have been visited by members who have enjoyed meals or drinks ashore and mentioned them in their logs. They are by no means comprehensive and further information is required if this particular aspect of the directions proves popular and is requested. The opening paragraph on page 155 should be read carefully before visiting any particular hostelry.

Our Sailing Directionis have always aimed to give information of particular use to small vessels visiting Ireland and have also included short descriptions of coastal and offshore features extracted from the Irish Coast Pilot. We advise that yachts should carry the Pilot for more detailed information about coasts, tides, etc. In our "Directions" each chapter commences with advice about charts, and a summary of coastal features and tides, then describes the coast and anchorages, starting from the SE and proceeding North and then West along the North Coast in Chapter IV. Inevitably it is less convenient to use the book when sailing in the opposite direction, but instructions have been included (where desirable) to help the clockwise cruiser.

ACKNOWLEDGEMENTS

Most of the plans in this book are based on British Admiralty Charts and Surveys and are Crown Copyright. Tidal information is based on the Admiralty Tide Tables, and other information is based on the Irish Coast Pilot. It is published with the permission of Her Majesty's Stationery Office. The remaining plans, individually acknowledged, are taken from the Irish Ordnance Survey by permission of the Minister of Finance, from the Department of Marine, and a few are based on the contractors' plans for the building of harbours or marinas.

Other sources supplying information include—The Cruising Association, Harbour Masters and Authorities, Secretaries of various yacht clubs, and many of our own members, to all of whom we are very grateful.

HUGH KENNEDY
Commodore
Irish Cruising Club

March 1991

Important Information

Please read these four pages before using this book as an aid to navigation. The information which follows is essential to proper understanding of the book and for the safety of your yacht and crew.

Breakers. On the charts many rocky patches and shoals with depths up to 20 to 30 m are marked "Breaker" or "Breaks in Gales". This means that in bad weather a whole sea may break and, of course, if a yacht were caught in one she would be knocked down, certainly be damaged and possibly be sunk; it would be lucky if no one were injured or drowned.

In the winter when the seas in the offing is often running high for long periods a storm or gale will quickly bring it into the coast where it may persist for days or weeks. The conditions on the coast can then become awesome and the strictest regard must be paid to these breaker warnings.

In summer the conditions are naturally far less severe, the seas rarely as big and big seas last for much shorter times. A yachtsman must judge from his own experience in what depths a sea is likely to break. There are no hard and fast rules and every case must be judged on its merits. Every few years in summer winds of strong gale force 9 or storm force 10 will be met with inshore on the coast and a yacht caught out in these conditions will experience very steep and breaking seas on any shoal waters and in wind against tide conditions in the open sea.

In general in normal fine to moderate summer weather and in semi-sheltered waters, anything with 4 m on it is unlikely to break except possibly at LW or a big swell. In the open sea the critical depths in moderate weather are somewhat greater, say 4 to 6 m or where there is any strong tide such as off the big headlands, 6 to 8 m. At all times, tide races or rips marked on the charts should be treated with caution, though in fine weather it is frequently possible to sail anywhere, such as Tory Island or close in to the Malin Head. Note that a rock may suddenly begin to break as the tide falls, the current changes direction or a larger sea than usual comes along. It may break intermittently, say every 5 to 10 minutes.

When a rock is on the point of breaking it will often form "blind" breakers, the sea building up into a steep pinnacle and then subsiding. These are very clear from leeward but almost impossible to see from windward.

In general it is best to err on the side of caution until much experience has been gained. It is very rare that a yacht gets caught in a breaker, normal commonsense and prudent seamanship keep them clear of trouble. However, even the very experienced sometimes get a surprise.

Drift Nets. In recent years there has been a huge increase in drift netting for salmon on the N and NW coasts of Ireland, the principal months being from May to the end of July. These nets are set off headlands, along straight lengths of coasts and in and off the bays and estuaries of salmon rivers. They are mostly set in daylight hours but this cannot be guaranteed, and in Donegal are frequently set by night and even unlit.

The common marking is by an orange float at each end and nothing in between except for the small floats which support the net. This means that in any sea they may not be seen until too late. Watch should be kept for 2 orange buoys ½ mile or more apart, usually extending out at right angles to to the shore with the inner buoy very close in to the land and the tending boat also at the inner end. This boat will, if it sees a yacht approaching its net, frequently get underway and steam fast along the line of the net waving to which side the yacht should go. It is often possible to make contact on VHF channels 16, 6 or 8 and get full details of the nearby nets.

If the worst happens it is considered safer to cross the net at right angles with engine and propeller stopped rather than turn away at the last moment and risk tangling with the net broadside on. A yacht with a traditional profile and propeller in an aperture will usually slide across safely. On a yacht with a separate rudder it would be worth carrying a "Y" end fitting which could attach to a spinnaker pole or long boathook or a hay fork with a long handle and possibly a sharp bread knife which could be firmly fixed to a pole. Watch should always be kept for a pair of coloured buoys ½ mile or so apart.

This menace has made it chancy to cruise close in to the coast at night. Scant regard is paid to the law or dates for salmon fishing, generally, so keep a good look out.

Hydrographic Surveys. Very little surveying of the coast of the Republic of Ireland has been done since 1914. In fact many of the surveys date back to the latter part of the last century. Yachtsmen are particularly warned about depths of water in river estuaries and of sandy bays where considerably less water than shown on the charts, may be encountered.

Lobster pots are numerous in suitable localities all along the coast. The inconspicuous corks of recent times are rapidly giving way to coloured plastic buoys, but floating plastic ropes are also used so it is safer to pass down-tide of a buoy. The same type of buoy is used for both pots and salmon nets so intense vigilance is necessary when one is sighted. A single buoy may be a pot or the end of a net. A number of buoys are usually pots. Two buoys up to a cable apart are probably a string of pots. Pots are most commonly set close inshore and in passages between outlying rocks.

Corrections. The Club proposes to issue an annual supplement to this book in April or May each year, bringing it up to date. Members will receive this automatically. Other users should apply to Mrs. Barbara Fox-Mills, The Tansey, Baily, Co. Dublin, enclosing a large self addressed envelope. The latest supplement will be found in the pocket inside the back cover in books purchased after 1991. Each supplement will include still current amendments from previous supplements so that only the latest need be carried. A subscription of £2.00 is now charged for these.

Should any member or reader discover any incorrect statement or important omission in the book please write to the Hon Secretary, Cormac McHenry, 8 Heidleberg, Ardilea, Dublin 14, with the facts. It is through this cooperation that we hope to keep the book up to date.

Tidal information. All heights and depths are in metres. Details of tidal streams appear in the text as required. Appendix 2 gives tidal constants for selected ports. Heights of tides have been adjusted to LAT for the whole coast as well as all depths given in the text and on the plans.

Lights and Buoys. The IALA System A is used on the coast and the changeover to this has now been completed and is included in this book. Buoys and lights are described in the text except for the upper reaches of commercial ports. Appendix 9 list the principal lights. In the text the visibility of lights given is the luminous range as stated on the charts. The luminous range is given in Appendix 9. A number of minor lights are maintained by local authorities, they are mostly in the approaches to small fishing quays, and are only switched on when it is known that local fishing boats are at sea, in these circumstances they are unreliable and should be checked with local harbour masters before sailing off the coast at night. Abbreviations for the type of buoy are as follows: Cardinal—Card, Conical—Cone, Can—Can.

Quite a number of lighthouses are being automated, as these become so amendments are made to their ranges and also their sound signals. A current edition of the Admiralty Light of Lights should be carried at all times.

The Commissioners of Irish Lights request mariners navigating around the coast of Ireland to exercise the greatest care to avoid damage to floating aids to navigation. The body of a "Lanby" (Large Automatic Navigational Buoy) is 40 feet in diameter and of low profile. This is not apparent either from the charted symbol or when seen at night and, because the direction of the tide flowing past them may not be as readily estimated as when approaching a light-float, mariners should take special care to give them a wide berth so as to avoid risk of collision.

However, should a collision take place with a Lanby, light-float or buoy (or damage to, or malfunction of any of these marks be observed) it is imperative that in the interest of safety of other shipping the fact be reported immediately to the nearest Coast Radio Station.

Mariners are also reminded that under section 666 of the Merchant Shipping Act 1894, a fine can be imposed on any person who wilfully or negligently runs foul of, or makes fast to, any light-float, buoy or beacon, in addition to the expense of making good any damage so occasioned.

Traffic Separation Zones. These are in existence at the SE corner of Ireland and in NE area. They are clearly marked on the Admiralty charts and should be crossed in the quickest possible way i.e. at right angles.

Radar Beacons. Mariners are advised that there may be occasions when a response is not received from a radar beacon. On these occasions Mariners should check that the appropriate radar set is in use. "X" band radar beacons can only be received on 3 cm radar sets, and "S" band radar beacons on 10 cm sets. Details are published in Admiralty List of Radio Signals, Vol. 2.

In addition, depending on range, the lack of response may be due to a fall off in the performance of the ship's radar or to a malfunction of the radar beacon itself.

Radar beacons should therefore be used with caution.

Depths. Both in the text and in plans the depths are given in metres and decimetres on shallow places. (Otherwise to the nearest metre.) They refer to LAT which is chart datum. They are based on information of varying age and reliability. In general depths on bars and in small harbours or alongside are believed to be accurate. Two and five metre lines (represented by dots and double dots respectively) are nearly all copied from the charts. There is a table for converting depths to fathoms in Appendix 20 at back of book.

Submarine Exercise Areas. In recent years some yachts and fishing boats have been damaged or sunk by submarines in the course of surfacing. As a submarine is visually blind until it actually raises its periscope, this is its most vulnerable manoeuvre as far as small boats are concerned. However, modern submarines have a very wide range of active and passive sensors which can "see" all types of noises and electronic transmissions, it therefore follows that vessels which are stopped in the water without engines running or underway with sails only, may not be "seen" by submerged craft. A good protection for such situations is to switch on your echo sounder when passage making in deep water.

Submarines of all nationalities are about the coasts in the deep water areas, and there is a large area of the Firth of Clyde and N. Channel designated on the Admiralty Charts as a Submarine Exercise Area in which particular care should be taken.

Naval Patrol. Off the coast of Northern Ireland there are a small number of Royal Naval Patrol vessels, these are on anti-terrorist duties. If sighted you should listen out on VHF 16 and obey any instructions. Sometimes yachts are boarded but more frequently it is only an enquiry of your last and next ports of call.

Abbreviations. These are those commonly used on Admiralty charts. Those unfamiliar with them are high recommended to obtain chart 5011, now in booklet form. Also see Appendix 19.

Customs. The international boundary line between the Republic of Ireland (Eire) and Northern Ireland is at the inner end of Carlingford Lough and again at the inner end of Lough Foyle. It is marked on the charts. Skippers should report to the Customs authorities at their next port of call after crossing the seaward extension of the boundary. Fly Q flag, if no customs are immediately available, report by phone to the nearest police station—Garda in the Republic and RUC in Northern Ireland. Courtesy ensigns are customary. See Appendix 14.

Names. In the metric charts many of the names differ from those on the old fathom charts. Where this difference is not immediately recognisable the new name is given in the text and when it appears for the first time the old fathom name is given after it in brackets.

Telephone numbers in this book are mostly preceded by an STD code. These codes are <u>incorrect</u> if phoning from the Republic of Ireland to Northern Ireland and vice versa. The local telephone directories give cross-border STD codes.

Appendices. Considerable further information is contained at the back of the book under various headings viz. Communications, Weather forecasts, Repairs, Sailmakers, Lists of Charts, Navigational Information, Distances, etc., etc.

Magnetic Variation is westerly and decreasing about 4' annually. From 1991 it may be assumed to be as follows:

Tuskar to St John Point	7°W
St. John Point to Malin Head	8°W
Malin Head to Bloody Foreland	9°W

BEARINGS THROUGHOUT ARE TRUE FROM SEAWARD.

Caution. These Sailing Directions are not intended for large craft but are written for yachts of moderate draft. Every effort has been made to avoid inaccuracy, but no responsibility will be accepted for damage or loss arising from any mistake or omission herein, or in correction sheets subsequently issued.

Part 1

EAST & NORTH COASTS

CARNSORE POINT to
BLOODY FORELAND

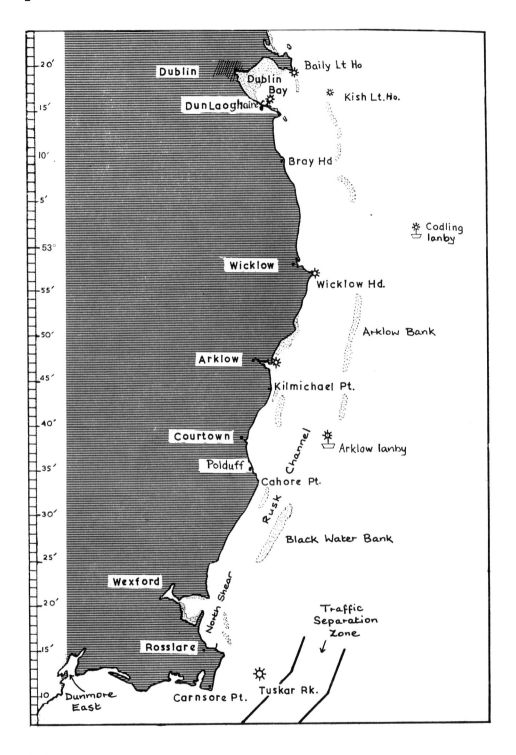

Dublin

Baily Lt Ho

Dublin Bay

Kish Lt.Ho.

DunLaoghaire

Bray Hd

Codling lanby

Wicklow

Wicklow Hd.

Arklow Bank

Arklow

Kilmichael Pt.

Courtown

Arklow lanby

Polduff

Cahore Pt.

Rusk Channel

Black Water Bank

Wexford

North Shear

Traffic Separation Zone

Rosslare

Dunmore East

Carnsore Pt.

Tuskar Rk.

CHAPTER I

Carnsore Point to Dublin Bay

INTRODUCTION

Charts (*see Appendix 1*). The two necessary charts are 1787 and 1468 and only these are normally used. The smaller scale charts 1410 and 1411 would be adequate for passage making; they include the W coast of Wales and the Isle of Man and 1411 includes as far N as Larne. A traffic separation zone is in operation off Tuskar Rock, see chart 1787 and Important Information on page xi.

General. This part of the coast is fronted by a series of banks at varying distances from the shore. There are no very attractive anchorages. Rosslare provides shelter in S winds. Arklow and Wicklow are safe harbours and useful stopping places. Dun Laoghaire is a major yachting centre.

Tides. The flood tide runs into and up St George's Channel while the tide is rising at Dover and the ebb runs out S for the other 6 hours approximately. The stream turns more or less simultaneously everywhere outside the banks but the time of HW which is roughly −0500 Dover at Carnsore Point becomes progressively later between this and Dublin Bay where it is +0020 Dover. Inshore the stream turns earlier than in the open sea. It flows across the sandbanks, the flood setting onto their inner side and the ebb onto their outer side. A description of local tidal streams is given where necessary.

Approach from W. The areas W of Carnsore Point is described in the club's *Sailing Directions for the South and West Coasts*. In ordinary weather yachts usually take the short route through Saltee Sound, close round Carnsore Point, thence up to Greenore Point and either in to Rosslare or N inside the banks. However if there were any possibility of fog, yachts would be well advised to keep outside the Coningbeg LV and the Tuskar Rock.

Approach from S. For yachts coming from Land's End the SE corner of Ireland is always a potentially dangerous landfall owing to the combination of offlying rocks and cross tides. It is difficult to estimate the tidal set off the Bristol Channel and as Ireland is approached the streams become stronger. In poor visibility it would be dangerous to come in W of the Tuskar. If the bearings of its radio beacon can be taken the landfall is simplified. While the Tuskar is not an ideal landfall it is much better than the Smalls and Welsh coast. Yachts bound from Land's End to Dublin whose direct course passes close to the Smalls should nevertheless aim to pass close to the Tuskar. Yachtsmen not pressed for time might prefer to sail from the Scillies to Dunmore East which has the advantage of avoiding the shipping.

If bound for Rosslare from the S a yacht need not leave the Tuskar to port; instead leave South Rock buoy (*below*) fairly close to starboard and proceed 330° towards South Long buoy (*see page* 7) at the entrance to South Shear. Take care that strong ebb tide flowing SSW does not set you near The Bailies.

Traffic separation lanes are shown on chart 1787. The inshore lane is for SW-going ships and passes 2 miles SE of the Tuskar. Yachts bound round the Tuskar should therefore keep within 2 miles of it where nothing larger than coasters should be encountered. A yacht which must cross the lanes should do so as quickly as possible at a broad angle.

DIRECTIONS

Tuskar to Dublin Bay. The normal route is outside the Blackwater bank, inside the South Arklow lanby and thence past Wicklow Head. In foggy conditions it would be safer to keep well outside the banks; if the Codling lanby were not sighted the Kish radiobeacon would in due course provide a safe point of approach to Dublin Bay. The danger in being too close outside the banks is that the ebb sets obliquely across them from seaward. Conversely if sailing inside the banks the flood setting onto their inner side must be avoided. **Bound S from Dublin Bay** a yacht should first make for Wicklow Head. After passing W of Arklow Bank, Arklow lighthouse buoy may be used to depart for the English Channel, a course 180° from it leading between Cape Cornwall Bank and Seven Stones. Alternatively after passing Horseshoe buoy (off Wicklow Head) a course 190° from it leads to the Tuskar, the usual departure point. If bound for the S of Ireland an inshore route may be preferred passing outside Glassgorman banks, through the Ruck channel towards Rosslare and finally close round Greenore and Carnsore points; this passage should not be attempted at night.

Carnsore Point, the SE extremity of Ireland, is a clay cliff 16 m high with rocky shelves below it and a depth of 18 m 3 cables off. In clear weather its position may be judged by Forth Mountain, just SW of Wexford, which is 225 m high and often visible from 20 miles offshore. In rough weather with wind against tide there is quite a dangerous race off the point around the times of local HW and LW.

Tuskar Rock, 6 miles ENE of Carnsore Point, is 5 m high with a tall lighthouse and a radio mast. It is foul for one cable on its N and W sides but steep-to on its E side. At 2 cables SW of it there is a rock awash. About 6 cables SSW of it is South Rock, 2·4 m deep, 7½ cables S of which is a S Cardinal buoy showing Q (6) + LFl 15 s. Gipsy Rock 2 m deep lies 2 cables NNW of the Tuskar. **Tuskar lighthouse** is white, Q (2) 7·5 s 33 m 28 M Horn (4) 45 s RC Racon. **Tidal stream.** Outside the rock this runs about NE from −0530 Dover till HW Dover and then SW for 6 hours at 2½ knots. Yachts should give the Tuskar a good berth, particularly in light weather, for as well as the tide setting onto the rock there is probably an eddy running back towards it on the other side.

Rocks.—Fundale Rock is the end of a reef running SE from Crossfintan Point. It is ½ mile offshore and 1 mile NE of Carnsore Point. It dries at half tide and till recently was marked by a perch which has broken down. At present there is an unlit red buoy 3 cables SE of where the perch was, not much more than 2 cables from the rock, so it is safest to pass outside it. Should the buoy have gone Black Rock open of Carnsore Point leads SE of the rock. **Collough Rock,** ½ cable wide and awash at its N edge is not marked and lies about 1¾ miles NE of Carnsore Point and ½ mile E of Crossfintan Point. Black Rock just open of Carnsore Point leads SE of it. Ballytrent House in line with Whilkeen rock and bearing 340° leads close NE of it. **Whilkeen Rock** lies 8 cables N by W of Collough Rock. It is at the outer end of a reef extending 4 cables out from the shore. It often cannot be spotted near HW and is awash at HWS. Ballytrent House bearing 330° leads close NE of it and Carna pier bearing 240° leads close SE of it. **The Bailies** is an irregular bank of rocks and coarse ground 9 or 10 m deep in places. It is situated halfway between the Tuskar and the coast W of it. The tidal streams crossing it cause heavy overfalls which are frequently dangerous although on approach it may not appear so. The area should be avoided, which fortunately is not difficult as the channels E and W of it are both over a mile wide.

St Margaret's Bay, between Whilkeen Rock and Carna pier ½ a mile SW of it, provides shelter in winds between SW and NNW. Approaching from Carnsore Point pass close to Fundale buoy and from it steer N, which leads between the offshore rocks and Collough Rock. When Carna pier bears WNW turn in steering NW. Coming from N having cleared Whilkeen Rock by 2 cables steer towards the pier. Anchor 2 or 3 cables NE of the pier in 3 or 4 m, sand. It is a useful and comfortable anchorage in strong NW wind to which Rosslare is dangerously exposed. The pier dries and yachts should not consider mooring alongside. Fl R3 s light on the pierhead. There is a small shop, also a restaurant.

Greenore Point, the SE end of Rosslare Bay, is 18 m high with clay cliffs. It is surrounded by dangers. Carrick Rock extends 3½ cables ENE of the point and is marked by a red mast. There is a dangerous unmarked wreck, the remains of a steamer, 6½ cables E of the point where the depth is only about 3 m. **Splaugh Rock** covers a large area 6 to 7½ cables SE of Greenore Point. Part of it would be dry at LAT and all of it is less than 2 m deep. The red buoy marking it, Fl R 6 s, is 8 cables ENE of it. **Calmines** (locally called The Cawmeens) is a shoal patch which dries along part of its outer edge about 4 cables offshore and which extends ½ mile NW of Carrick Rock. A red buoy, Fl R 2 s, marks its NE side is 1·6 M and 106° from Rosslare Lt. The red sector of Rosslare light covers it.

Carnsore Point to Rosslare—Directions (*see plan*). This passage should not be attempted at night. Keep a sharp look-out for lobster pots. In rough onshore weather it is better to sail outside Collough Rock (*see above*) and outside or a cable W of Splaugh buoy, but avoid The Bailies by keeping Splaugh buoy bearing NE when within 2 miles of it; going S this means heading for Carnsore Point till Ballytrent House is abeam and then turning S till Black Rock appears outside Carnsore Point. The normal and shortest route is from 1½ cables off Carnsore Point to Fundale buoy, then N to pass between Collough Rock and Crossfintan Point, and when the latter comes abeam steer towards Greenore Point, about 016°; this should lead outside Whilkeen Rock, but if it cannot be seen before Carna pier bears 240° head out a bit. When Ballytrent House comes abeam alter course to 030° to leave Carrick mast about 1½ cables to port, then steer for Calmines buoy and after leaving it to port head for Rosslare pier and do not go S of the

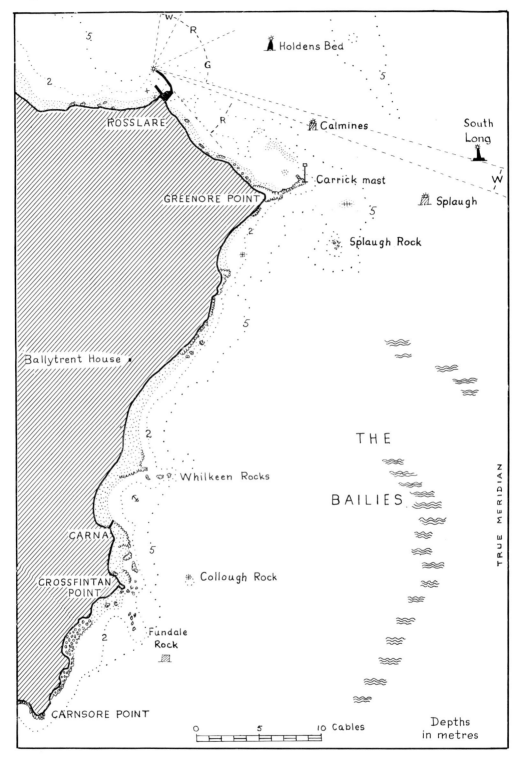

W
R
G
R

⚓ Holdens Bed

5

5

2

ROSSLARE

🏛 Calmines

South Long

GREENORE POINT

⌐ Carrick mast

🏛 Splaugh

2

5

🌀 Splaugh Rock

5

Ballytrent House .

THE

2

BAILIES

TRUE MERIDIAN

🌀 Whilkeen Rocks

CARNA

5

🌀 Collough Rock

CROSSFINTAN
POINT

2

Fundale
Rock
🏛

CARNSORE POINT

0   5   10 Cables

Depths
in metres

straight course to the pier. **Bound S** from Rosslare pier, after rounding Carrick mast steer SW till ½ mile off the shore, the continue at this distance off and when past Ballytrent House if Whilkeen Rock cannot be seen take bearings to clear it (*see above*). When past it steer for the furthest land and when E of Carna pier get Fundale buoy bearing S and steer for it. **If beating** it is simplest to pass outside Collough Rock but do not tack out too far as it is best to keep well away from The Bailies. Careful pilotage is essential beating past Splaugh Rock. Splaugh buoy bearing 050° leads a cable SE of it. Rosslare pier lighthouse in line with Carrick mast leads 1¾ cables NE of it but only about 60 m SW of the dangerous wreck so keep the lighthouse slightly open left of the mast. To pass NE of the wreck keep Calmines buoy bearing 325° or less, or Carrick mast 280° or less. In winds about N or S it is simpler to beat inside Splaugh Rock and the wreck. Rosslare pier visible outside Greenore Point leads only ½ cable SW of the rock so keep it closed. On the other tack keep between 1 and 3 cables away from Carrick mast; avoid the rock 2 cables offshore ½ mile SSW of Greenore Point; closer to the point it is safe to tack 1½ cables offshore.

South Shear, the channel between Holden's Bed (*see below*) on the N and Greenore Point foreshore and rocks, is ½ mile wide and leads into South Bay and Rosslare harbour. It is entered between Splaugh buoy and South Long buoy and from nearer the latter it is a direct course in to Rosslare leaving Calmines buoy close to port and Holden's Bed buoy some distance to starboard. At night the white sector of Rosslare light leads in. Coming in from the Tuskar allowance must be made for the strong cross tide (*see below*) so in poor visibility it is unwise to attempt entry unless you have facilities for establishing the course made good.

Tidal streams. Inshore of the Tuskar the flood usually starts at +0500 Dover and runs NNE at up to 2½ kn at springs; the ebb starts at −0200 Dover and runs SSW at up to 3¼ kn at springs; unfortunately in this area the time of change, direction and rate is apt to vary a lot. In the South Shear the ingoing stream averages 1 kn running from −0600 Dover for 3 hours, the outgoing stream averaging 2 kn for 9 hours from −0300 Dover. Inshore of Long Bank the N stream ceases at −0200 Dover and the S stream ceases at −0400 Dover. In Rosslare Bay the streams are weak making generally N from −0500 Dover to −0100 Dover.

Banks and buoys. The following banks are between Greenore Point and Cahore Point. They are not very shallow everywhere but being mostly of sand their positions and their depths tend to alter. It is therefore important to keep clear of them.

Holden's Bed, NE of the South Shear channel, has a least depth of 0·6 m. Close N of it **Long Bank** starts; it also has a 0·6 m patch near its S end and it extends N for 4 miles. The following buoys mark these banks. **South Long,** S Cardinal, V Q (6) + LFl 10 s Horn (2) 10 s is off the SE end of Holden's Bed. S. Holden Buoy Fl (2) G 2 s is due S of the Bed. W Holdens Fl (3) G 10 s lies SW of Holden's Bed. **West Long** QG lies NW of the shallow parts of Long Bank. **North Long,** N Cardinal, Q, Horn (3) 30 s, lies off the N point of Long Bank. Barham Shoals, 8 m deep, extend N of North Long buoy.

Lucifer Bank, least depth 2·7 m, lies 1½ miles E of Long Bank. **Lucifer buoy,** E

Cardinal, V Q (3) 5 s, is moored well E of the S end of the bank which is called New Ground.

Blackwater Bank N of Lucifer Bank is 8 miles long. Its S part has a least depth of 2 m and its N part, called Moneyweights Bank, dries for about half a mile. The following buoys mark it. **South Blackwater,** S Cardinal, Q (6) + LFl 15 s, Horn (2) 30 s, is between it and Lucifer Bank. **SE Blackwater,** red, Fl R 10 s, is off the E side of its S part. **East Blackwater,** E Cardinal, Q (3) 10 s, Horn (3) 20 s, is off the E side of its N part. **West Blackwater,** green, unlit, is off the W side of its S part. **No 1 Rusk,** green, unlit, is off the W side of its N part. **North Blackwater,** N Cardinal, Q is off its N end.

Rusk Bank has a least depth of 2·4 m. Its S part is separated from Moneyweights Bank by the ½ mile wide Rusk Channel. Its N part extends a mile towards Cahore Point. It is guarded by three unlit red buoys, No 2 and No 4 Rusk close to its E side and No 6 Rusk near its N tip. **The Ram,** between Rusk Bank and Cahore Point, has a least depth of 1·4 m, less water has been reported on a number of occasions in the last few years.

Rosslare Harbour (*see plan*). HW −0500 Dover. Rise: 2·0–1·5–0·9–0·4 m. Rosslare Radio can be called on VHF 16 & 23. Rosslare Harbour on VHF 16, 14, 12, 6. This has become a very busy container, ferry and passenger ship harbour. Yachts may lie alongside for fuel, water and provisions with the H.M. permission. However, it is uncomfortable berth in SW winds which is often when yachts going S require shelter. The new inner pier shown on the plan is now finished. Boats are not allowd to anchor within 100 m SW of it or in the approaches. The area SW of the outer pier and marked

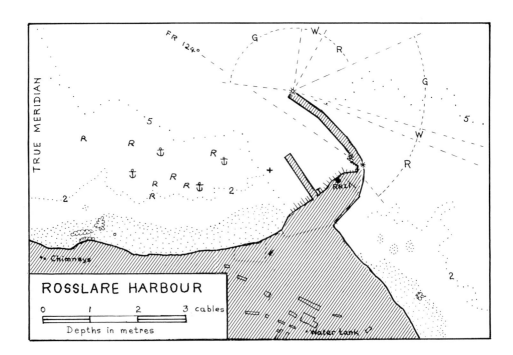

ROSSLARE HARBOUR

0   1   2   3 cables

Depths in metres

with anchors on the plan may be fully occupied by local boasts, in which case the only likely anchorage for visiting yachts is further W, beyond an area with rocky bottom; anchor there in 2 to 5 m with the head of the outer pier bearing between 060° and 070°, see anchors on plan. This should be safe and comfortable in winds between WSW and SE. It will become uncomfortable in moderate winds from WNW probably to ENE and dangerous if winds freshen between W and NE; if this happens leave without delay, at night putting to sea through the South Shear. It is clear that, as in the past, this is an anchorage most valuable for yachts bound S and held up by head winds.

Facilities. Water on quay. Fuel and gas from local garage. There is a good supermarket in village. There is a wide selection of hotels (4) for all tastes. Tourist office in terminal building where taxis can be hired and public transport is available. There is a slip for landing. If not wishing to go ashore an alternative anchorage, more sheltered in W wind, would be 3 cables offshore about a mile due W of the outer pierhead in about 2·5 m. **Light:** from a tower on the end of the pier, elev 15 m, Fl WRG 5 s, 10 M. It shows (*see plan*): Red over foul ground from Greenore Point. White sector along the South Shear, 286°–291°. Green over S part of Holden's Bed. Red over the N part where Holden's Bed is shallowest. White over the North Shear, 188°–208°. Green over South Bay. There are FR lights in line 124° for leading the ferries alongside the outer pier. Dredging will take place on W side of New Pier during 1991.

Wexford Harbour (*see plan*). On the bar HWS −0315 Dover and HWN +0540 Dover; at the quay an hour later. Rise: 1·7–1·4–0·5–0·2 m. There is a safe sheltered anchorage off Wexford town quays. The port is no longer used commercially but only by local fishing boats. The entrance is marked by a bar buoy and has a reported minimum depth of 1 m at LAT. Approximately 20 orange buoys are laid by members of the Wexford Harbour Boat Club. Steering 225° from the North Long Buoy will bring a yacht to the entrance. In strong wind between S and E the sea breaks on the bar and it is dangerous to go anywhere near it. Slaney wreck, 1¼ miles SE of Raven Point is no longer a serious danger; it does not dry and is not marked and recently the approach to

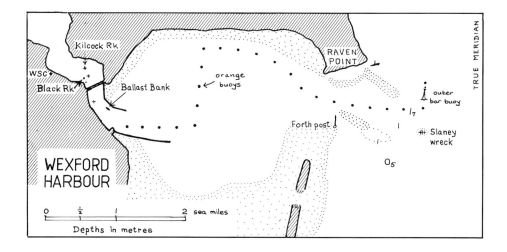

the bar is not very far N of it. **Directions.** Advice regarding the state of the channel and possibly a pilot to guide you in may be obtained from any one of the following: Wexford Harbour Boat Club (053-22039) also on VHF 16; J. Tyrrell (053-22936); R. Stone (053-22060 W or 053-22358 H); John Kewane who lays the buoys; J. Sherwood (053-22875 or 053-22713).

Anchorage. Having entered between the training walls, a yacht should leave the island (ballast bank) to starboard. It is convenient to berth alongside the wooden quays or beside the mussel boats berthed there. Alternatively, a yacht may anchor on the E side between the ballast bank and the bridge. On the W side it is shoal for about 1½ cables below the bridge, and there is a covered rock there. There are two visitor courtesy moorings directly north of the ballast bank.

Motor yachts may pass below the central arch of the bridge clearance 5·7 m and beyond it should leave the 1 m high Black Rock ½ cable to port till it bears S, so as to avoid the unmarked and submerged Kilcock Rock, which lies a cable N of Black Rock.

There is convenient anchorage in 3 m off the Wexford Harbour Boat Club clubhouse and slip on the S shore just W of the abutment of a previous bridge. The river Slaney is navigable as far as Enniscorthy.

Facilities. Petrol, diesel oil along the quays and fresh water. Good shops (6 day week), hotels, banks, etc. close to quay. Swimming pool, caravan park at Ferrybank (end of bridge) also hotel, garage, hospital, launderette. Showers at club where visitors are welcome. Sail repairs—Carmel Kelly 053-24887. Engine repairs—Wm. Furlong 053-35179. Trains to Dublin and Cork. Local buses.

A 200 berth marina for Wexford Harbour is at planning stage.

National Heritage Park 3 km and Wildlife Bird Sanctuary 3 km.

Rosslare Bay to Cahore Point. The passage inside the banks should not be used at night as the buoys in Rusk channel are not lit. S of this channel and N of the entrance to Wexford there is plenty of space and the coast is a sandy beach free of dangers; for six miles N of Blackwater Head it is backed by a clay cliff up to 50 m high. Do not forget that the tide flows obliquely across the banks, the flood setting on their inner sides and the ebb on the outer sides. **Directions.** Pass not more than a mile W of West Long and North Long buoys, then leave West Blackwater buoy to starboard and pass between No 1 and No 2 Rusk buoys into the Rusk channel. No 4 Rusk buoy should be left close to port as the E side of the channel is reported to be shoaling. Pass out between No 6 Rusk and North Blackwater buoys. **Tidal streams.** Between Wexford and Cahore Point the NNE stream starts at +0430 Dover and the SSW stream at −0200 Dover, maximum speed about 2 kn.

The Sluice. If you prefer to sail along the coast keep reasonably close inshore when inside the Rusk Bank. Watch out for No 6 Rusk buoy and when it bears 050° turn out and keep it bearing between 050° and 060° which leads between the shallow N end of Rusk Bank and the 1·4 m deep Ram. A direct course from No 6 Rusk buoy to Cahore Point leads just N of the Ram. Small yachts using echosounders sometimes sail close along the shore inside the Ram where the depth is about 2 m but this cannot be

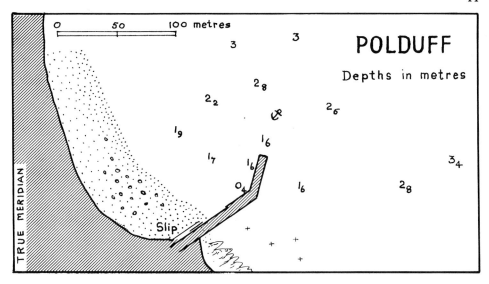

recommended. Less water has been reported by a number of members in this area, so great care should be taken.

Polduff (*see plan*). HW −0330 Dover. Rise (HW): 1·2–0·8 m. This small pier ½ mile NW of Cahore Point provides no shelter in onshore weather. In settled offshore conditions it is a reasonably comfortable anchorage. It is also handy in SW wind for yachts heading S and awaiting a fair tide. The approach from off Cahore Point is clear but in the bay between it and the pier there are rocks about 1 m deep. Coming from the N keep the pierhead bearing not less than 210° to avoid a sand-spit off Glascarrig Point ½ mile N of the pier; it is about 0·8 m deep with a rock at its outer end. Anchor in suitable depth N or NE of the pierhead. Small yachts may berth at the pier if it is calm enough, the depth alongside the outer 20 m being 1·4 m. A slight ebb runs SW along the face of the pier. **Facilities.** Slip for hauling out dinghy. Pub with phone near pier. Good small shop ¼ mile away, turn left at T. Petrol 1 mile away.

In SW gales ships anchor N of Roney Point which is 2 miles N of Polduff. A yacht might like to anchor closer inshore NW of Roney Rock in 3·5 m.

Courtown Harbour. (*see plan*). HW −0300 Dover. Rise (HW): 1·1–0·6 m. This little harbour 4½ miles N of Polduff provides perfect shelter for small shallow-draught boats but the entrance is sometimes blocked by a bank of shingle just inside the pierheads. This is dredged regularly during the season as this harbour is becoming more popular, particularly with shallow draft boats. Mooring fore and aft in harbour in approximately 1·6 m LAT. Do not approach in stormy Easterlies. Courtown Sailing Club is based in the Bayview Hotel (055-25307) and keeps a watch on VHF CH 8 during weekends and days of major activity. Showers adjacent to tennis courts. Outside the harbour there is often good shelter in winds between SW and NW and a yacht can anchor about 2 cables off the piers in 6 or 7 m, good holding in sand. A summer holiday resort with grocers, pubs, RNLI Inshore Lifeboat—summer months only.

COURTOWN HARBOUR

0   50   100   150   200 metres

Depths in metres

S H A L L O W

TRUE MERIDIAN

Glassgorman Banks lie SE of Kilmichael Point. The shallowest patch, 1·8 m, is at the N end of the outer bank 1½ miles E of Kilmichael Point. There is a 3 m patch in the middle of each bank, otherwise the depths are not less than 4 m. The No 1 buoy, red, Fl (2) R 6 s, lies E of the S end 4 miles E by N of Courtown. The No 2 buoy, red, Fl (4) R 10 s, is ½ mile NE of the N end and 2¾ miles SE of Arklow Head. A yacht bound from Cahore Point to Arklow may, in daylight of course, sail inside the banks heading towards Kilmichael Point and when Tara hill bears W keeping ½ mile off the shore. If passing close outside the banks make sure the ebb tide does not carry the yacht inside a line joining the two buoys.

Arklow Bank is a dangerous narrow ridge mostly shallow and awash in places. It is 12 miles long, its S end 5 miles E of Glassgorman Bank and its N end 4 miles E of the N point of Brittas Bay. Yachts should keep away from it, especially in calm weather and in fog or darkness. As on all the banks off this coast the flood turns towards it near its inner side and flows NE across it, the ebb crossing it SW. It is marked by the following buoys (note that there are none on the W side):

South Arklow Lanby, a red pillar 12 m high, Fl (2) 12 s, 16 M. Horn: Mo A 30 s,
    Racon Mo "O". It is 1½ miles SSE of the S of the bank.
South Arklow, S Cardinal, V Q (6) + LFl 10 s, is at the S end.
No 1 Arklow, red, Fl (3) R 10 s, is a mile E of the bank and 4 miles NNE of the
    S Cardinal.
No 2 Arklow, red, Fl R 6 s, is a mile E of the bank and 6 miles N of No 1.
North Arklow, N Cardinal, Q, Horn (2) 30 s, is off the N end.

Arklow Head quarry a mile S of Arklow harbour has a jetty with a 3 m high stone mole extending seaward 2 c S of it. Yachts should not go near this. **Light** Oc R 10 s, 9 M, is shown from the jetty and a QY on mole.

Arklow Harbour (*see plan*). HW −0200 Dover. Rise (HW): 1·1–1·0 m. This is a river port with busy commercial quays and a sheltered dock used by fishing boats and yachts. It is a safe place to leave a yacht.

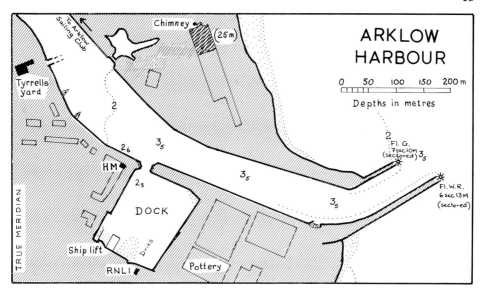

Directions. It may be identified by a 25 m high factory with a 44 m high chimney which stands on the shore close N of the piers. The piers are apt to blanket the wind and yachts must enter under power except in modest winds between N and E. The entrance is unsafe if the wind has been blowing F6 from N through E to SW for 5 or 6 hours, or sooner if the wind is stronger. In F5 N wind there can be a nasty sea but in summer it is usually possible to enter with care and full control. Enter midway between the piers. Careful allowance must be made for the ebb tide which sets SE across the entrance. Proceed in near mid-channel till the 14 m wide dock entrance opens to port, turn in and steer for the middle part of the SE side of the dock berthing alongside it or another vessel. River banks are lit by quartz halogen lights.

Harbour. The bar, the channel to 12 m away from the piers, and the quays on the N side are kept dredged to not less than 3·5 m. There is 2·6 m alongside the old low quay beyond the dock entrance. Do not go beyond this as the next piece of new quay dries alongside and the river beyond it is shallow with obstructions. The entrance and much of the dock is 2·8 m deep, the bottom is very soft mud. At LWS it dries on both sides of the ship lift and in the E corner. Care should be taken in leaving a boat in the dock as it is used by large fishing vessels, consult the H.M.—John Tyrrell (0402-31274) VHF 16. **Lights.** S pierhead: Fl WR 6 s, W from 223° to 350°, R elsewhere, 13 M. N pierhead: Fl G 7 s 10 M. **Facilities.** Water hydrant near NW side of dock. On the SE side water cans may be filled, with permission, in the pottery. Nearest petrol ½ mile at N end of road bridge. Diesel delivered aboard. All yacht facilities except sail repairs by Tyrrells whose yard is marked on the plan. Their syncrolift in the dock makes Arklow the best place on the E and N coast for lifting a yacht temporarily out of the water. Arklow Sailing Club, a single storey building is situated up stream next to the office of Arklow Shipping on the NE side of the river. There is a landing quay that itself has a rocky bottom at only 1 m LWS. A new jetty is under construction. With permission from the A.S.C., the 3 or 4 moorings can be used on a 24 hour basis by visiting yachts. Showers and WC available at the clubhouse when open—most evenings, longer on Wednesdays and at weekends. There is a hardware store some 50 yards up stream from the dock entrance which stocks much useful chandlery. Harbour Master—John Tyrrell (31274); ASC Hon. Sec. Willie Brown (32701). All supplies in the town. EC Wed. Tourist information from Bord Failte in the town.

Arklow to Wicklow Head. The first 5 miles NE of Arklow is a sandy beach terminating at Mizen Head, a rocky point 10 m high with a rock about 2 m high just off it. Beyond this is Brittas Bay, 2¼ miles long, N of which is ⅓ mile of rocky cliff with caravans parked above it. As far as this a yacht may safely approach within 3 or 4 cables of the shore but off the next 1¼ mile long un-named bay, the S end of which is called Jack's Hole, there is a dangerous unmarked rocky shoal called Wolf Rock. It lies ½ mile off the shore of the N half of the bay and covers an area extending from 2½ to 4½ cables S of Ardmore Point. Part of it dries about 1 m which means it is awash at about ¾ flood. The normal course from Mizen Head to Horseshoe buoy, 025°, leads clear of Wolf Rock but if for instance a yacht is beating it is vital not to tack in towards the N part of this bay. Towards the S end of the bay there is a row of white chalets and a hotel. Ardmore Point 15 m high with steep grassy sides has no buildings on it. At night keep Wicklow Head light bearing not more than 010°. **Horseshoe Shoal,** a bank of stones 0·5 m deep in places, lies S of Wicklow Head and yachts should pass to seaward of its buoy, red, Fl R 3 s, bell, which lies 1¼ miles SSE of the head. The unmarked passage inside the bank cannot be recommended. **Anchorages.** In offshore winds temporary anchorage out of the tide (especially the flood) may be had: (1) 2 to 3 cables NNW of Mizen Head in 1·5 to 3·5 m. (2) In Jack's Hole not more than 1 cable N of the point in 1·5 m or a shade further out if greater depth required.

Wicklow Head is 71 m high and has two disused lighthouses on its summit. **Light:** Fl (3) 15 s, elev 37 m, 15 M, is shown from a white tower on the outer slope of the head. The bottom is uneven with 7 to 9 m in places up to 1½ miles off the head; the spring tide there reaches 4 kn so in fresh winds it can be extremely rough. Along the coast between Wicklow Head and Wicklow harbour the tide always runs SE, a weak eddy during the flood and the ebb reaching 3 kn. There is now a sewage outfall buoy, Fl (4) Y 10 s approximately 6 c 038° from the Wicklow Harbour entrance.

Wicklow Harbour (*see plan*). HW −0010 Dover. Rise (HW): 2·7–2·3 m. This is an artificial harbour at a river mouth 1½ miles NW of Wicklow Head. It provides safe shelter alongside in the river and is always accessible. The E pier quay and the packet quay are used by large coasters. Beware of buoy bearing 221° 7·15 c which marks a sewer outfall. (*see photo*)

The outer harbour is open to the NE so a yacht anchored there may roll, but in offshore winds it is comfortable. Anchor halfway between the ends of the W pier and the packet quay outside the yacht club moorings, but clear of turning circle, one of which may be made available; nearer the packet quay it starts getting shallow. A small yacht might anchor between the moorings and the W pier. It is often convenient to berth alongside the E pier. Dredging takes place at regular 6 year intervals.

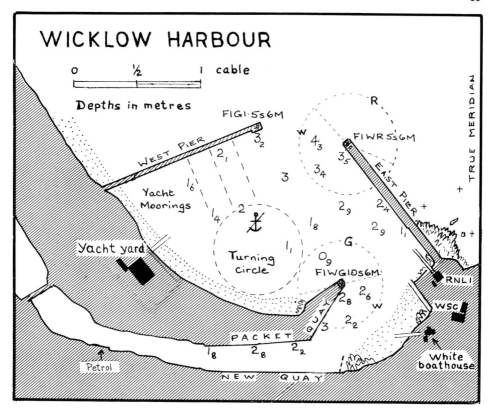

Inner harbour. To enter steer from between the outer piers towards the white boathouse (*see plan*) and when the face of the packet quay opens turn sharp to starboard. To avoid the shallows on the SE side do not allow the front of the RNLI boathouse to close. The S side of the river is dredged and the quays rebuilt. This side is intended to be used by fishing boats and yachts. If it is not available a yacht might go alongside the packet quay but should not be left there unattended without obtaining permission at the HM office (0404-67455/69466) which is in the middle of that pier. Yachts were often left alongside the inner end of the packet quay in the recent past.

Lights. W pierhead, on a metal column, Fl G 1½ s 6 M. E pierhead, from a white lighthouse, Fl WR, 5 s 6 M R from 136° through S to 293°, W elsewhere. Packet quay, on a metal column, Fl WG 10 s, 6 M G from 076° through E to 256°, W elsewhere.
Facilities. Repairs to hulls and engines, also limited chandlery, at Wicklow Marine Services Ltd. S quay (0404-68408), where water and diesel are also available (in your cans). Petrol on S quay (*see plan*) where it can be pumped aboard a yacht. Water tap at WSC and N and S quays. Normal requirements in Wicklow town, EC Thur.
Sailmaker. Wicklow Marine Services (0404-68408). Tourist Information Office. Showers at Sailing Club. Launderette in town. Train to Dublin. Airport 40 M. Small harbour dues.

Wicklow to Dublin Bay—Offshore banks and buoys. There is an almost continuous line of banks between 5 and 6 miles off this coast. The depths are mostly 3 to 5 m but 2 m or less in a few places. In calm weather a yacht may cross the deeper parts of the banks but if the sea is rough they can be very dangerous and must be carefully avoided. The flood sets NE across and between them and the ebb SW.

India Bank 5 miles NE of Wicklow Head has a least depth of 3·5 m. Extending N of it is **South Ridge** with 5 m. South India buoy, S Cardinal, Q (6) + LFl 15 s, lies off the S end. North India buoy, N Cardinal, V Q, lies off the N end of South Ridge.

Codling Bank is of crescent shape and stretches from 3 miles NNE to 5 miles N of South Ridge. Its rocky bottom is covered with narrow ridges of gravel and large boulders. There is a ridge 4 m deep on its N edge and not far from the E end of this a ridge with a least depth of 2·6 m runs SE. It is subject to heavy overfalls and yachts should keep clear of it. **Bray and Kish Banks** extend 9½ miles N from a ¾ mile gap N of Codling Bank. Bray Bank's least depth is 4 m. On the N part of Kish Bank there is as little as 1·6 m. **Buoys and lights.** Codling lanby, a red pillar 12 m high, Fl 4 s, 16 M, Horn 20 s, Racon MoG lies 6½ miles ESE of the bank. South Codling, S Cardinal, V Q (6) + LFl 10 s, lies off the SE end of the bank. West Codling, green, Fl G 10 s, lies off the SW corner of the bank. East Codling, red, Fl (4) R 10 s, lies off the NE of the bank. East Kish, red, Fl (2) R 10 s, lies ½ mile E of the bank where the N half starts getting shallow. North Kish, N Cardinal, V Q, lies close off the N end of the bank. **Kish Bank Lighthouse,** 31 m high, is a white tower with a red band and a helicopter platform on top. Light, Fl (2) 30 s, 14 M, Horn (2) 30 s, Radiobeacon (*Appendix 5*); it is ½ mile NE of the N end of the bank. **Bennett Bank** 3 miles N of Kish Bank does not concern yachts being 10 m deep; its buoy is S Cardinal, Q (6) + LFl 15 s, Horn (3) 30 s.

Coast from Wicklow to Dublin Bay. Except for a short rocky stretch at Greystones there is a beach all the way from Wicklow harbour to Bray Head. Much of it is steep-to but it is simplest to advise yachts not to go closer than a cable except when rounding Six Mile Point which requires a berth of 2 cables. There are two small shoals which yachts usually ignore. Moulditch Bank (3·8 m) is a mile SE by E of Greystones with a red buoy, Fl R 10 s. Breaches Shoal (5 m) is 3 miles SSE of the Moulditch and has a red buoy Fl (2) R 6 s. In rough onshore conditions it is better to sail E of these buoys. Cable Rock which dries 2 m lies ½ cable off the S end of Bray Head. Periwinkle and Crab Rocks are drying reefs which extend almost a cable off the NE part of the head. Between Bray Head and Killiney there are extensive sandy beaches with several rocks some of which dry so this coast must be given a berth of at least 3 cables till abreast of the obelisk on Killiney Hill (152 m) which is ¾ mile WSW of Sorrento Point, the entrance to Dalkey Sound. A can light buoy Fl Y 3 s marking the end of an outfall is in position 53°14·88N 6°05·10W.

Greystones Harbour 2 miles S of Bray Head is small and shallow with a ruined breakwater and in summer it is full of small boats. In settled conditions a yacht can anchor temporarily in 3·5 m N of the mouth of the harbour which is convenient for dinghy landing. Good shops, banks, etc. ½ mile away. Petrol ¼ mile inland. Water tap in the heads on the pier.

Bray Harbour a mile N of Bray Head dries out. The N pier with 3 m alongside at HWS has decayed wooden wharfs used by small local craft. There is a sailing club with dinghies and catamarans. Keelboats should definitely not enter. If a motorboat wishes to do so, which is not recommended, the N pierhead should be approached bearing 220° and rounded very close because part of the head of the S pier has collapsed and only shows at LW. A can light buoy Fl (4) Y 10, marking an outfall is in position 1·55 M 233° Bray North Pier.

Dalkey Island the S end of Dublin Bay is 24 m high with a Martello Tower. Three cables outside it is the Muglins, a rock on which a white conical beacon with a red band exhibits **Muglins Light**, Fl 5 s; The Muglins is clean all round except for one below-water rock inside it and Shanganagh outfill buoy, Muglin Lt bearing 012° 1·7 M (*see below*).

Dalkey Sound (*see plan*) runs inside Dalkey Island and the line of rocks stretching 3½ cables NNW of it. There is a clear passage through the sound keeping within a cable of the steep-to shore and it is the normal entrance to Dublin Bay for yachts coming up the coast. The tide runs strongly through the sound; it turns about 2 hrs before HW and LW at springs, later at neaps. If the tide is foul it is better to use Muglins Sound unless motoring or running before a fresh breeze through the sound. Winds between S and NW are usually calm or fluky in places. The flood tide through the sound is an inshore branch of the tide sweeping round Killiney Bay but a yacht approaching from the S first meets the main flood running right athwart her course out of the bay and S of Dalkey

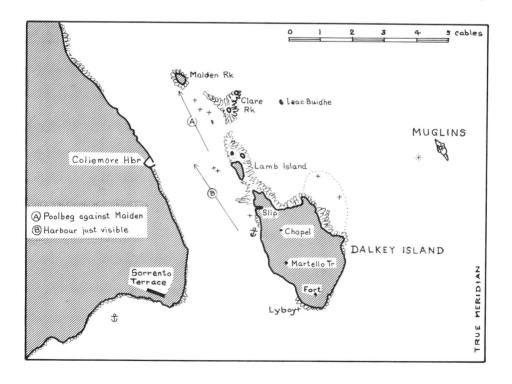

Island towards the Muglins. In light conditions if this has not been adequately anticipated one can of course go through the Muglins Sound instead.

Dangers, all on the island side. A reef extends along the shore from opposite the fort to half-way towards the Martello Tower; its outer point is Lyboy Rock, 0·4 m deep and 50 m from the shore. Close S of the landing steps there is a small rock which dries at LAT. N of the steps a narrow reef runs out ending with a 0·6 m deep rock 70 m offshore. There is another rock with 0·6 m about 90 m W of Lamb Islet. A rock which dries at half tide lies 80 m SW of Clare Rock with other drying rocks inside it. Between it and Maiden Rock there are rocks with 0·5 m depth.

Beating through the sound you may tack quite close to the shore but should avoid the above rocks as follows. Keep 80 m off Dalkey Island between its S end and the Martello Tower. Between abreast of the chapel and a line from Coliemore harbour to The Muglins tack immediately the top of Dun Laoghaire pier shows outside the coast (323°). NW of this keep the red Poolbeg lighthouse (Liffey entrance) to the left of Maiden Rock (bearing not less than 331°). Give the SW of Maiden Rock a berth of 30 m; its NW end needs a berth of 45 m. Near HW a yacht which can ignore the non-drying rocks between Lamb Islet and Maiden Rock should keep the Martello Tower open to the right of Lamb Islet to avoid the half-tide rock off Clare Rock.

Muglins Sound is an alternative approach to Dublin Bay. There are some rocks which must be avoided but the channel between them has a least width of 1½ cables (*see plan*). About 120 m NNE of the NNE point of Dalkey Island there is a rock with 0·4 m over it; SE of this and N of the E point of the island there is a rock with 1·6 m. Almost a cable E of Clare Rock is Leac Buidhe rock which just dries; it lies where the E end of Sorrento Terrace shows over the grassy top of Lamb Islet. On the S wall of the Liffey there is a pair of very high chimneys; the left-hand chimney in line with the outer edge of Dun Laoghaire pier leads clear of all the rocks on this side. The same chimney in line with Dun Laoghaire E pier lighthouse leads clear of the rocks off Dalkey Island but would lead *over* Leac Buidhe. About 90 m W of the Muglins where the beacon is in line with the NW end of the landing quay there is a rock with 1 m over it; below half tide most yachts should keep clear of it. The tide runs N or S between the E side of Dalkey Island and the Muglins.

Buford Bank lies a mile outside Dublin Bay. It is narrow and runs N and S with a buoy off each end which lie 2½ miles apart. S Cardinal, V Q (6) + LFl 10 s, Horn 20 s. N Cardinal, Q Horn (2) 20 s. The least depth on the bank is 4·6 m so yachts need only avoid it in rough weather.

Dublin Bay is W of a line from the Muglins to The Baily, the SE point of the Hill of Howth. Shipping has right of way over yachts within the bay. VHF Coastal Station Call 16 Work 67, 65, 83. **Baily lighthouse,** a conspicuous 13 m high tower, shows Fl 20 s, 27 M, Diaphone 60 s. There are no offshore dangers in the bay. The S shore is steep-to for about a mile from Sorrento Point, the entrance to Dalkey Sound, to a Martello Tower. Between this tower and Sandycove Point ½ mile further in keep a cable offshore. In Scotsman's Bay between this point and the E pier of Dun Laoghaire harbour keep 2 cables offshore. Beyond the harbour keep its E pier open of its W pier and do not let the red Poolbeg lighthouse at the Liffey entrance bear more than 005°. On the N side of the bay keep the Poolbeg bearing more than 235° and on the Howth shore keep outside the bay between Drumleck Point with a beacon on it and Lions Head, 4 cables NNW of The Baily. Yachts may pass any side of the buoys within the bay except that in onshore near gale conditions Rosbeg Bank, least depth 4·6 m, should be avoided by keeping E of a line between The Baily and Rosbeg East E Cardinal buoy about 7 c SSE of The Baily and Rosbeg S. Cardinal Q (6) + LFl 15 s, bearing 204° 1·86 M Baily. There are a number of unlit racing buoys SW of a line from the Muglins to Poolbeg lighthouse.

Tidal streams. The flood, entering on both sides of Dalkey Island, sweeps round the shores of Dublin Bay and rejoins the main stream outside Rosbeg Bank. Along the S shore the tide turns about −0310 local HW and LW. Off the N shore the tide runs to seaward for 9 hours from local HW + 0315 to −0015 next HW and then runs in from The Baily for about 3½ hours. There is not much stream in the middle of the bay but just outside the bay the tide flows at up to 3¼ kn at springs, the N-going flood starting at LW and the S-going ebb at HW Dublin Bar.

Bullock Harbour a mile SE of Dun Laoghaire is of little interest to yachts as it dries out and is packed with small boats. There is a patent slip and a large yacht chandlery. Should a yacht need to be taken in, do so near HW and, to avoid those rocks in the approach which dry at neaps, enter keeping a black and white post with a black board on top in line with the left edge of the lower notice "Danger Slow" (both on the shore side of the entrance); when 10 m from the entrance turn sharp to starboard to open it before turning in. At HWS there is 2·7 m in the N corner and at the crane and 2 m further along the quay.

Anchorages. Dun Laoghaire is the only proper harbour in Dublin Bay and is a major yachting centre. However in certain conditions some people might like to try moving to one of the following places. **Off Bellingham** a tiny harbour with a red boathouse behind it 4 cables NW of Drumleck Point the S tip of Howth. Anchor not less than a cable off the harbour in 3 to 5 m, well sheltered in winds from NW to ENE, slightly tide-rode. **In Scotch Bay** just a cable SE of the bandstand on Dun Laoghaire E pier (*see plan*). Depth about 6 m, well sheltered in winds from SSE to WNW. **In Dalkey Sound** (*see above*) fairly close to Dalkey Island near the white water-fountain SE of the landing place. Depth about 4 m, well sheltered in all except S winds, much quieter than Dun Laoghaire in NE swell; tide-rode.

Dun Laoghaire Harbour (*see plan*). HW + 0030 Dover. Rise: 4·1–3·4–1·5–0·6 m. Port operations VHF Call 16 Work 14 (also telephone 01-801130). This large harbour is alongside the town on the S side of Dublin Bay. It has suitable depths for sailing yachts except in the old harbour and the S half of the inner harbour. Much of the main harbour and all of the old and inner harbours are occupied by yacht moorings.

Four yacht clubs have premises alongside the harbour. There is now a floating pontoon at the National Yacht Club (*see plan*) for four visiting yachts to lie alongside for fuel, water and stores. It is 60 ft long has 0.3 m at LWS at the end and 0.9 m at LWS at

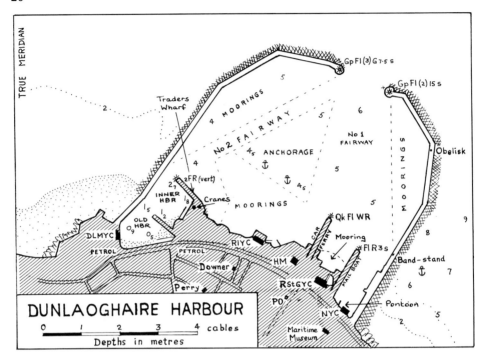

DUNLAOGHAIRE HARBOUR

0   1   2   3   4 cables

Depths in metres

W end. The spring tidal range is about 3.3 m. Contact Boatman on VHF—M to get clearance. Showers, meals, bar, diesel. Royal Irish YC; R St. George YC (01-801811) VHF 37 and National YC have all permanent secretaries who should be contacted on arrival if you wish to use their facilities, which include bars, meals, showers, etc. Visitors are expected to conform to a reasonable standard of dress when using the club premises. Enquire about visitors' moorings. Ferry service during normal day time and evening racing. (*see photo*)

Caution. When passing through the harbour entrance keep a bit away from the pierheads; there are drying boulders 8 m off the E side and many fishing lines are often being cast off the W pier. Avoid entering or leaving at the same time as the Sealink car ferries because when they are under way it is obligatory to keep clear of the fairway and the harbour mouth. The ferries berth at the piers in the S corner and fishing boats use the inner harbour; anchorage is prohibited in the fairways to both. The International Code Hoist MB3 (Keep fairway clear) is displayed by day from the red turret on the car ferry pier when ferry traffic is imminent. It is supplemented by a VQY light day and night from the same position.

The anchorage area is shown on the plan. The anchorage area shown on the plan is covered by a sectored light Q Fl W R from the head of the Car Ferry Pier. It is best to anchor just outside the yacht moorings; at night if the ferry pier light turns red you are too far in. Visiting yachts are often allocated moorings by the club boatmen. In the unlikely event, in summer, of a NE gale the anchorage becomes untenable. Winds between N and E can make it uncomfortable on board and in fine anti-cyclonic weather there is often an unpleasant roll; the R St George YC moorings off the E pier are the least affected in these conditions; this club also has a couple of moorings E of the root of the W ferry pier, the best place for a visitor if one of them is free. Yachts sometimes berth at the shoreward face of Traders Wharf but a big swell in the harbour gets in there too and in such conditions someone should remain on board. The seaward side of Traders Wharf is foul.

Facilities. If a Customs Officer does not come on board, clearance may be obtained by visiting the office at the Car Ferry Examination Hall (which is below the HM Office) or visitors should report the arrival of their yacht at the HM office. Yachtsmen are often offered temporary honorary membership by the local yacht clubs and may then use their slips for landing and hauling out dinghies. Club boatmen can give advice about visitors' requirements. Royal St. George YC; Royal Irish YC; and National YC all have electrically operated cranes to lift 5 tonnes and a drying out dock. Visitors' moorings are also available. Water and diesel can be supplied by pipe alongside the R Irish YC. There is a water hydrant and two hand cranes (SWL 2 & 5 tonnes) near Traders Wharf and there is also a patent slip (used mostly for yachts) and boat yard; in the old harbour yachts can be dried out alongside at LW; apply to the HM for the use of these facilities. There are shipwrights, yacht chandlers and a sailmaker not far from the harbour. All stores are available in the town. Very good rail connections to centre of Dublin every 15 mins. No harbour dues, however, a small charge for the use of cranes and slips. EC Wednesday.

Lights. E pierhead, 12 m tower, Fl (2) 15 s, 11 M. Diaphone 30 s, or bell 6 s. W pierhead, 9 m tower, Fl (3) G 7½ s, vis 188°–062° (234°). Mail pier Fl R 3 s. Ferry pier Q W R (*see plan*). Traders Wharf 2 FR (vert). Port operations—VHF. Call 12, 16, Work 09, 12, 13, 14.

Dublin (*see plan*). HW + 0035 Dover. Rise: 4·1–3·4–1·5–0·5 m. The busy commercial port in the river Liffey has little to attract yachts and no special provision for them. It provides better shelter than Dun Laoghaire in strong NE wind. It has nowhere available for anchoring and yachts are usually berthed near the inner end of the S quays which is 3¼ miles from the entrance. It is unwise to leave a yacht unattended there owing to theft and vandalism. The new lifting bridge across the river is now in operation. There is 30 m between the bridge dolphins. The height of the lifting span is 6·35 m above LAT. It requires 60 mins notice to be raised; it is without charge, call on VHF. Yachts should give longer notice as the moorings between this bridge and Butt bridge are not much used. There are the usual Port Traffic Signals—3 lights in vertical line—red "stop" and green "go" other combinations with a white light are as published in ANM 568 1983. Yachts should only transit bridge under power. If in doubt berth at North Wall Extension and contact berthing master before proceeding.

Directions. The entrance is between Poolbeg and Bull lighthouses in the middle of Dublin Bay. Yachts should show that they are taking care to keep out of the way of ships. They may pass either side of the buoys outside but after entering should remain within the dredged channel which is marked by red buoys on the S side and by green buoys and beacons on the N side. There is no difficulty in sailing as far as the river Dodder except to keep clear of the traffic if beating; further in N and S winds are fluky

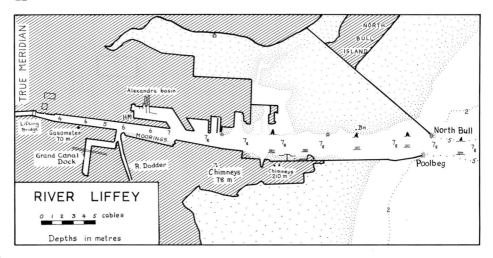

RIVER LIFFEY

0 1 2 3 4 5 cables

Depths in metres

and it is better to motor if possible. If you do not have radio to ask the Harbour Office where to berth choose a vacant place on the S quay and await instructions from a harbour constable.

Lights at the entrance. **Poolbeg,** a red tower 20 m high with a white building behind it, Oc (2) R 20 s, 12 M. Horn (2) 60 s. **N Bull Lighthouse** Fl (3) G 10 s 15 m 15 M Bell (4) 30 s. The S side of the channel to Dublin is marked by red lights and the N side by green lights, see chart 1447.

Facilities. The city has three yacht chandlers, (*see Appendix 13*), stores and service of all kinds are available. There is no yacht yard but there are shipwrights in a yard in the NW corner of Alexandra Basin.

The Grand Canal is entered through the dock shown on the plan (for two hours either side of high water) and enables boats drawing 1 m to reach the Shannon. It is no longer used commercially. It is advisable to contact the office of Public Works, Waterways Division, 51 St Stephen's Green, Dublin 2. Tel. 01-613111 if planning to make a passage through the canal or information may be had from the Inland Waterways Association of Ireland, Ruth Heard, Stone Cottage, Claremont Road, Killiney, Co. Dublin, Tel. 01-852258.

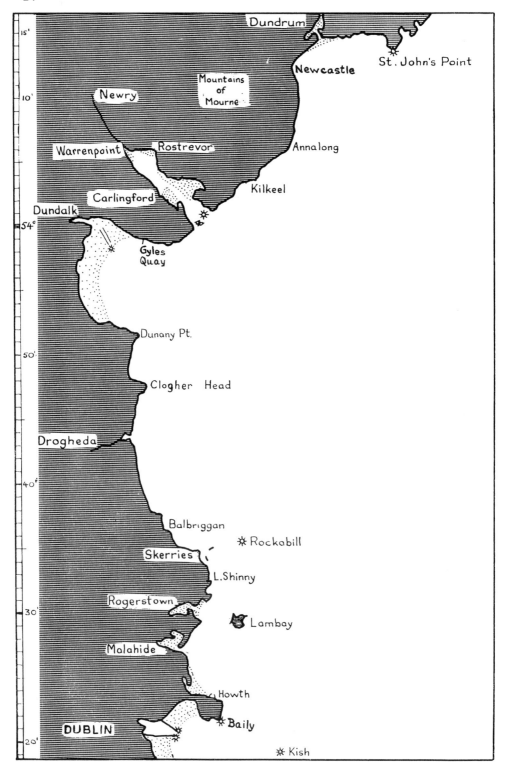

15'

Dundrum

St. John's Point

Newcastle

Mountains
of
Mourne

Newry

Annalong

10'

Warrenpoint   Rostrevor

Kilkeel

Carlingford

Dundalk

54°

Gyles
Quay

50'

Dunany Pt.

Clogher   Head

Drogheda

40'

Balbriggan

✱ Rockabill

Skerries

L. Shinny

Rogerstown

30'

Lambay

Malahide

Howth

✱ Baily

DUBLIN

20'

✱ Kish

CHAPTER II

Hill of Howth to St John's Point

Charts. This coast is covered by chart 44. Chart 2800, Carlingford Lough, is the only larger scale one likely to be required by visitors. (*See Appendix 1*).

General. Yachts making a direct passage betwen Dun Laoghaire and the North of Ireland will bypass the coast described in this Chapter and need only note that the course from the Baily to St John's Point is 015°, 54 miles. Those wishing to shorten the passage can anchor at Skerries or Port Oriel in SE to W winds and at Lambay in wind between N and NE and between E and WSW. The only really attractive inlet on this coast is Carlingford Lough.

Tides. HW everywhere along this coast occurs close to HW Dover. Between Dublin Bay and Anglesea the main flood runs N while the tide is rising at Dover; out towards the Isle of Man it turns E to fill Liverpool Bay. The ebb runs in the opposite direction for the other 6 hours. Along the coast the tides run fairly strongly S of Rockabill but become weaker further N, and particularly so offshore; the streams are negligible S of St John's Point, SE of which the floods from N and S meet. It is best, sailing N or S, to aim to pass St John's Point at HW, though this usually involves some adverse tide at Rockabill unless you stop somewhere in between. After leaving Liffey River the area to the N is very shallow, so medium draft yachts and above should make for the Baily Lt. Inside the North Bull Lt. is an anchorage for shallow draft craft off the Clontarf YC, with bar and shower facilities, close fuel, a regular boatman is available, and watch is kept on VHF—M c/s "Tarf base".

Coast. The E side of Hill of Howth is steep-to except close in 2 to 6 cables N of the Baily, and at Casana Rock which is 4 cables S of the Nose and must be given a berth of 50 m. Just NW of the Nose there is a rock which dries about 50 m outside Puck's Rocks; a berth of a cable clear it. There are loose boulders off the E pier of Howth harbour.

Ireland's Eye (*see plan*), a mile N of Howth, is a rocky island 97 m high. **Dangers.** There are two reefs running out from Thulla, the islet at its SE end. Do not pass between the islet and the buoys marking them, Rowan Rocks E Cardinal buoy, Q (3) 10 s, marking N Rowan rock and a green buoy, Q G, marking S Rowan rock. The NE corner of the island is a prominent high pillar-shaped rock called The Stack; keep outside a line from the E Cardinal buoy to The Stack to avoid a drying rock a cable NE of Thulla. There are drying rocks in the bay SSW of The Stack. At the NW corner of Ireland's Eye there is an islet, The Steer, close N of the Martello tower. The N coast of the island is steep-to except for a rock which dries 2 m about 100 m NE of The Steer.

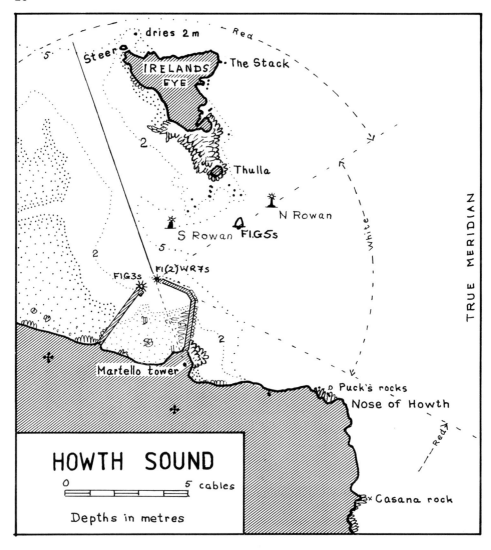

There is also a sunken rock close W of The Steer. On the W side of the island the water is shoal with a sandy bottom and a few projecting ledges.

Howth Sound (*see plan*). Approaching from seaward Rowan Rocks buoy must be left to starboard and Nose of Howth given a berth of a cable; between The Nose and the harbour watch out for lobster pot buoys. After leaving S Rowan green buoy to starboard turn NW and when the Martello tower above the root of the E pier comes in line with the outer end of that pier (160°) keep on this transit to pass through the sound till abeam of the NW end of Ireland's Eye.

Howth Harbour HW +0025 Dover. Rise 4·1–3·4–1·2–0·5 m. This has always been an active fishing port and yaching centre. A new marina has been opened and is shown

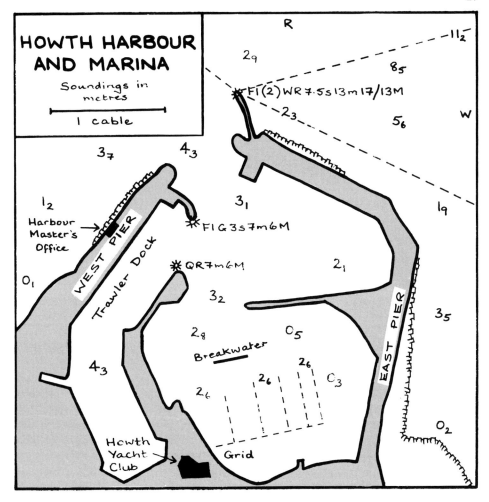

on the sketch plan. **Directions:** Approaching from the E give the pier a berth of 50 m, do not turn until the harbour is well open, entering nearer to W pier head. Contact the Marina Office or Howth YC on VHF Ch 16 or 37 who will allocate a berth. Channel and Marina dredged to 3 m MLWS. Howth YC, HM, and Marina Office as shown on plan. There are floating pipes on each side of the marina entrance. **Facilities:** Visitors' mooring and/or alongside berths are available in the harbour and marina. Showers, meals and bar in Howth Yacht Club which has a full-time secretary who will advise VHF Ch 37 24 hours c/s "Howth Marina". Fuel and water in marina. All repairs, victualling in town, launderettes. Train service to Dublin every 15 mins., taxis, Dublin Airport 20 mins. Pubs and restaurants to suit all pockets. Marina charge 30p per ft. (1990). EC Sat. **Lights:** E pier Light Tower Fl (2) WR 7·5 s. White 256°–295° (39°). Red 295°–256° (321°). Trawler breakwater W pier Fl G 3 s. Trawler breakwater head QR. Marina Entrance 2 F R vertical. (*see photo*)

Inshore Tidal Streams (times refer to local HW and LW). At the Baily the stream coming out of Dublin Bay causes overfalls, quite nasty at times, where it meets the main stream. Close inshore on the E side of Howth Hill the stream turns N −0130 LW and S −0115 HW and runs at 2 kn. This stream divides at Ireland's Eye, one part running N and on through Lambay Sound and the other part passing up Howth Sound where the flood begins −0130 LW and the ebb −0130 HW, running at 2 kn. This latter flood stream slackens in pace beyond Ireland's Eye and after filling Baldoyle, Malahide and Rogerstown inlets joins the stream passing through Lambay Sound where it attains a rate of 2½ kn.

Light. Dublin Airport Control tower at 53°26′N, 6°15′W, some 4 miles N of Dublin and the same distance inland, shows Aero Al WG 7½ s, elev 95 m.

Malahide (*see plan*). HW + 0020 Dover. Rise: 4·2–3·5–1·5–0·5 m. This estuary 4 miles N of Howth is a safe and quiet anchorage for yachts drawing up to 2 m. The bar outside the entrance is 0·3 m deep and there are sandbanks on either side of it. During the summer the S bank is marked by a red buoy and the N bank by a green buoy; they are moored near the edge of the narrow channel rather than on the banks and may therefore be passed very close. Another black buoy marks the middle of the channel 4 cables further in. These buoys may be considered reliable. They are maintained by the Malahide Yacht Club and their positions are altered after any major change around the bar or in the channel. The entrance is not lighted and should not be approached after dark or in thick weather. In daylight strangers can enter easily at half flood. The flood stream runs up to 3 kn at springs and the ebb may run 3½ kn.

Directions. Approaching from the S, in order to clear the S bank aim to be at least ¾ mile to seaward of the square tower (which has buildings around it) when it bears 240°.

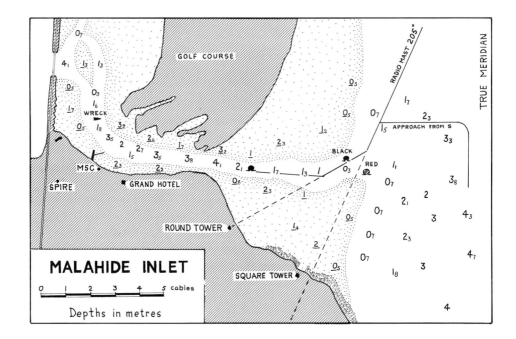

Then steer N until the church spire is open just over one breadth of the prominent Grand Hotel to the N of the hotel, then steer W until the radio mast on top of the hill to the S bears 205°. Go in on this bearing till the round tower (now part of a house) comes in line with the black buoy. Then steer towards the round tower, leaving the green buoy close to starboard, till the spire comes in line with the N side of the Grand Hotel. As soon as this line is reached turn to starboard and make a direct course towards the inner black buoy. After passing close on either side of this buoy bear very gradually to starboard. **Approaching from the N** get the radio mast bearing 205° when at least a mile or so away from the S shore. Go in on this bearing and continue as described above. The bar has 2·4 m two hours each side of HW.

Although the channel at the entrance and inside is very narrow, the banks on either hand are clearly defined at half-tide as they are fairly steep-to. There is a slipway and concrete landing stage which is accessible at most states of the tide. The deepest channel is close to the N of the line of moored yachts all the way up to the shipyard. The river is extremely full of moorings and yachts are advised not to anchor further in than 3 or 4 cables to seaward of the Grand Hotel; even there it is advisable to rig a tripping line. **Facilities.** Visiting yachtsmen are welcome to use the facilities of MYC which is open at weekends and most evenings during summer. Otherwise every facility is available in the village centre within a few hundred yards of the slip: Good shops, several hotels, pubs, a wide range of good eating houses; dry cleaning and launderette; petrol and diesel from a garage; gas from a hardware; doctors and dentists; frequent bus and train service to Dublin. The Malahide shipyard is now defunct. A comprehensive repair service is available (Tel. 450751) as well as outboard engine repairs. Moorings may be available on application to MYC boatman who is on duty at weekends and any evening when tides permit racing: there is also a local boatman who runs a ferry service, may have moorings available and would look after boats left at anchorage or in emergency (Mr Wm. Hatch). It is proposed to construct a marina at the site of the old shipyard.

Lambay Island (*see plan*), 6 miles N of Howth and 2 miles offshore, is private property and a bird sanctuary; people should therefore not enter the harbour or land anywhere on the island without permission from the owner, Lord Revelstoke. The harbour dries. There are no offshore dangers except for three rocks on the W side. **Burrin Rocks** are 2 cables W of the W point of the island with a reef in between. They are dry at LW and are marked by a starboard hand minor beacon. A ledge extending W of the rocks is marked by the tide flowing across it but it has adequate depth for yachts if the perch is given a berth of 30 m; do not go between the perch and the point. **Tailor's Rocks** extend 1½ cables NNW of Scotch Point, the NW corner of the island. They are marked by a green conical unlighted buoy painted with the letters "TR" moored 120 m due N; they dry and should be given a berth of at least a cable. There is an **unmarked rock** with 1·2 m over it a cable N of the harbour and a cable off the shore; so it is best to keep at least 1½ cables off the shore between the harbour and Scotch Point and a cable W of the Tailor buoy. About 60 m S of the outer part of the harbour there is a small rock which dries 0·8 m.

Anchorages, all on sand in about 3 or 4 m. **Saltpan Bay** (Swallow Cove on old charts) gives excellent shelter in S winds when it is often quite free from swell and relatively calm; it can in fact be used in winds between SE and W. It is a very useful

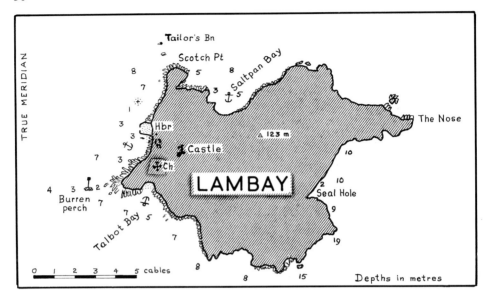

stopping-place for a yacht beating S. **Talbot's Bay** gives shelter from N and NE wind but there is often an uncomfortable swell there. **On the W side** of the island anchor SW of the harbour where there is good shelter between E and S winds; it is open to a fetch of 2 or 3 miles from the W quarter and is of course exposed to winds from the N quarter.

Rogerstown Inlet (*see plan*). This sheltered creek in the bay facing Lambay Island is entered across a bar of sand and gravel which almost dries and tends to vary in position. It should therefore be entered only in modest weather and at least an hour before HW as there is the possibility of accidental grounding. Mosts of the local boats are shallow draught and moored W of the pier and there is some space E of it for yachts drawing not more than 1·7 m to anchor. The S end of Rogerstown Bay is Portrane Point where there is a Martello tower, a round tower, a new water tower and a clock tower. Cable Rock off this point covers at HW.

Directions. Approaching the entrance keep the whole of Howth Head well open of Portrane Point. Enter steering 313° towards the most E house on the N shore of the channel; this house has trees close around it. When the round tower bears 194° (see transit) alter course to 330° till the round tower bears 188° (see transit) when the glass-house should be just clear of the end of the pier (about 292°). Then alter course to 275° till abeam of the house with trees when alter course again and steer towards the end of the pier which should be in line with the gable of the cottage to the right of the glass-house (there is an inconspicuous cottage in between them). Anchor downstream of the pier and of any yacht moored there, 2 m, sand and mud. The channel is narrow and the ebb can reach 4 kn at springs so it might be wise to moor. It is best to land on the sand E of the pier. The YC slip N of the pier is inaccessible at LW. The pier dries and the end of its W side is occupied by the Lambay ferry. Water at inner end of pier. Nearest facilities 1½ miles away at Rush.

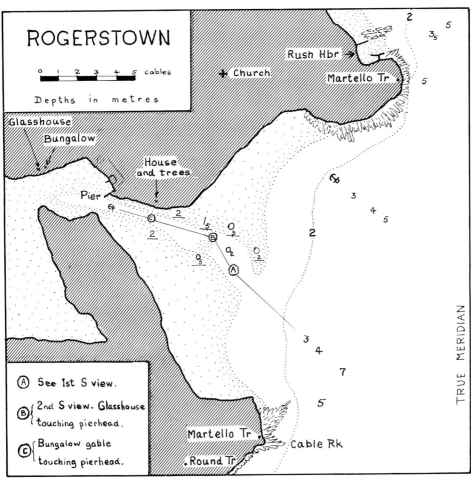

ROGERSTOWN

0 1 2 3 4 5 cables

Depths in metres

Glasshouse
Bungalow
House and trees
Pier
Rush Hbr
Church
Martello Tr
Glasshouse
TRUE MERIDIAN
Martello Tr
Cable Rk
Round Tr

(A) See 1st S view.

(B) { 2nd S view. Glasshouse
{ touching pierhead.

(C) { Bungalow gable
{ touching pierhead.

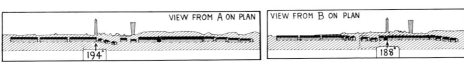

VIEW FROM A ON PLAN   VIEW FROM B ON PLAN

194°   188°

Coastal anchorages. On the N side of Rogerstown Bay it is usually quite comfortable to anchor in NW wind, but not suitable for landing. Off **Rush Harbour** is is possible to anchor temporarily in offshore wind and quiet conditions and convenient for landing by dinghy. However the nearest shops and garages are ½ mile away. The harbour dries at ½ tide so could only be used by small shallow draught yachts.

Lough Shinny (*see plan*) is a cove about 1½ miles N of Rush Point. Near its S point there is a Martello tower and on the N side a pier of SE of which is a perch. Much of the cove is shallow but there is a limited area over 2 m deep in the centre where there is good shelter in winds between SW and NW. In SW to S wind it may be comfortable but in NW to N wind a yacht is usually rolling. To avoid the reefs on both sides of the entrance

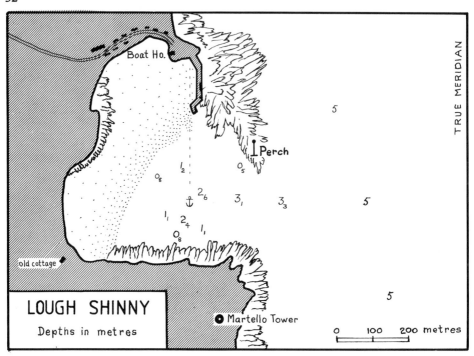

LOUGH SHINNY

Depths in metres

Boat Ho.

Perch

old cottage

Martello Tower

0   100   200 metres

TRUE MERIDIAN

steer W halfway between the perch and the S point; anchor as soon as the pierhead bears N, when the inner end of the quay will appear beyond it. The pier dries at LW, otherwise landing is convenient but there is only a very small shop, with phone, and water might be obtained from a house, otherwise no facilities.

Skerries Islands (*see plan*). Red Island is joined to the mainland. Shenicks and Colt Islands are almost joined to the beach at LW. St Patrick's Island is very foul but there is a good passage inside it with a least depth of 3 m. Passing between Colt and St Patrick's Islands keep the Martello tower on Shenick's in line with the top of Pope's Hall Hill bearing 188°. To pass between St Patrick's and Shenick's keep the middle of Colt Island bearing 325°.

Skerries Bay has good holding and is well sheltered in winds between W and E by S. It is completely exposed to the N quarter and strong wind between NE and ESE makes it pretty rough. Yachts are moored there in summer. The pier dries except for the outer 60 m which has less than 1 m. The whole of it is used by fishing boats so it is inadvisable for yachts to berth alongside. **Light**, on the pierhead, shows Oc R 6 s between 103° and 154°. **Directions.** Approaching from the E take care to avoid the reefs. Keep well clear of the Skerries and Red Island and pass N of Cross Rock red buoy, Fl R 10 s. Do not turn into the bay till the pierhead bears less than 154°. Anchor outside the moored yachts in 3 or 4 m. Alternatively, if space is free, anchor E of the moorings and about a cable away from the pier which should be bearing 090° or more. Land at the pier or on the slip just N of it. There is a Sailing Club and most facilities in Skerries. EC Thur. (*see photo*)

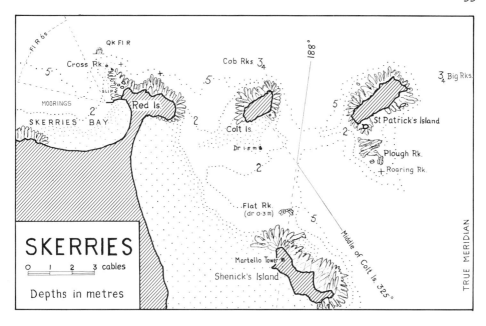

Rockabill lies about 2½ miles E by N of St Patrick's Island. It consists of two 9 m high rocks, close together and steep-to. **Light,** from a white tower with black band 32 m high, Fl WR 12 s, W from 178° through W to 329°, R elsewhere; 16 M. Horn (4) 60 s. **Tidal streams** between Rockabill and Skerries run NNW and SSE, 6 hours each way starting at LW and HW Dover, but inshore the ebb starts at −0030 Dover and runs for 7 hours; speed at springs 1½ kn, faster between the islands. (*see photo*)

Balbriggan (*see plan*). HW + 0015 Dover. Rise (HW): 4·4–3·6 m. This small artificial harbour is 3 miles NW of Skerries. It dries out completely and is well sheltered. It is used by local yachts as well as by many trawlers and is attractive for visitors who are happy to dry out alongside. The sand tends to drift up steeply along the quays but at present it is occasionally shovelled away to make level berths. **Light,** shown from a white tower on the N corner of the pier, Fl (3) WRG 20 s, 10 M W from 193° to 288°, R over the Skerries, G over Cardy Rocks. (*see photo*)

Directions. You cannot anchor near the harbour at LW as it is shallow for 4 cables offshore. The depth at HWS alongside the quays is about 3·5 m so a yacht drawing 1·5 m could normally enter 2 hours before HW. Approach steering between W and SW towards the middle of the beach just N of the harbour and when the inner pier opens up bear round for the entrance. Go in nearer the N pierhead and steer SE till on line between an old capstan on the pier near the lighthouse and the entrance to the inner harbour, then go through the outer harbour keeping on this line. From the inner harbour entrance steer to pass half-way between the N corner of the pub and the NW quay, then bear round towards the SE quay and go alongside there. **Facilities.** The main street with shops etc is quite close, EC Thur. Beside the slip there is a building with restaurant, bars, saunas, and a swimming pool. Water, diesel and gas available.

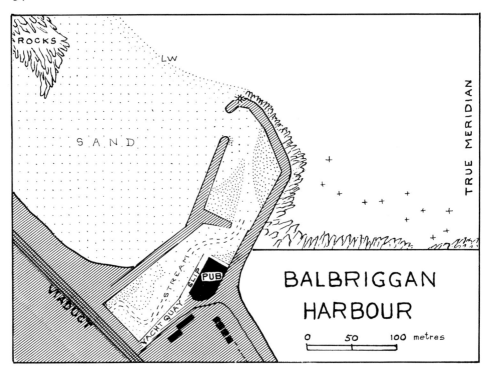

BALBRIGGAN
HARBOUR

0   50   100 metres

Engine repairs: J. Jennedy at Balrotheny (411496) or M. Redden at Skerries (491462). Restaurants and takeaways in town. Good eating in Skerries 4 M.

Balbriggan to River Boyne. The coast between Balbriggan and River Boyne is low-lying and unwelcoming to the yachtsman. In particular keep well clear of Cardy Rocks about 1 mile N of Balbriggan which extend eastwards, dry at ½ tide and are marked by a red perch. Gormanstown Aerodrome borders the coast about one mile N of the Cardies. It can be recognised by a conspicuous radio mast (height 150 ft) lit during darkness by three vertical red lights and some lower level red lights, visible at sea for a considerable distance. **Irish Army Exercises:** Between March and October firing exercises may be carried out from Gormanstown at intermittent times. Red flags are flown outside the coastal railway line when the exercises occur. Careful watch is maintained by army authorities for sea traffic. Range 10 miles centred on 53°38′41″N and 06°13′41″W. Radial boundaries bearing 015° and 122° from firing point. Further information obtainable from E coast Garda barracks or by phoning (01) 412102. Platen cement works chimney (153 ft) situated about 5 miles from coast and 2 miles SW of Drogheda, has an aero beacon Q Fl R and 2 FR 11 M. This beacon is in line of River Boyne leading lights (248°).

River Boyne (*see plan*). HW at the mouth +0015 Dover. Rise (HW): 4·5–3·7 m. The Boyne enters the sea about 9 miles N of Skerries and at suitable rise of tide gives access to the commercial port of Drogheda 4 miles inland. The navigable channel is between 50 and 75 m wide upstream of the part shown on the plan and it is approximately in the middle between the training walls which confine the river all the way to Drogheda. There is nowhere suitable for anchoring nor is there any special berth for yachts in Drogheda but they are not unwelcome there and it is a well sheltered place to spend a night. New chart No 1431 is essential to help identify the lights if entry in the dark.

Lights and Daymarks. Leading lights in large white lanterns Oc W 12 s, 9 M, are in line 248°. Front light is much brighter and visible over a wide area than rear light. **North Light,** a similar white lantern, Fl R 4 s, 8 M between 282° and 288°. **Bar Light,** a 6 m high steel pillar outside the entrance Fl (3) R 5 s 3 M. **Aleria Beacon** on the end of the N training wall, Fl G 4½ s. **Lyons Light,** a perch on the end of the S training wall, Fl R 2 s. **South Bull,** a perch half-way along the S training wall, Fl R. All lights and marks are fixed beacons showing Fl R on S bank and Fl G on N bank up to Drogheda. **Warning Lights,** three R vertical lights near North Light, mean that the bar is dangerous (no sign by day). The **Beacons** are large, built of stone, tapering slightly to a rounded top. **Maiden Tower** is an old narrow square stone tower 21 m high. All lights and marks are fixed beacons showing Fl R on S bank and Fl G on N bank up to Drogheda.

Directions. The bar off the entrance is about 0·8 m deep. When calculating what time it will be safe to enter make allowance for the sea on the bar and for a reduction of 0·6 m or even more caused by fresh N winds. In quiet conditions a yacht drawing 1·5 m might enter at LWN or 2 hours after LWS. If approaching as soon after LW as suitable it is best to keep the leading lights (lanterns) in line; even if the tide is well up do not go N of the leading line and leave the Bar Light to port. Having entered midway between the training walls carry on parallel to the N side giving the beacons and perches there a berth of not less than 50 m. It is possible to sail up-river to Drogheda in wind between S and NE, otherwise an engine is needed for at least part of the way. When approaching from the S avoid a rock a cable or more E of Lyons light, covers at HW.

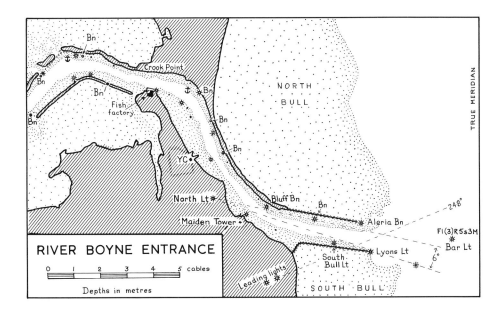

Anchoring. Not advisable in river. Commercial shipping moves into and out of the river 3 hours before high water and up to 2 hours after high water. When really necessary, however, anchoring is possible for short periods, i.e., from 2 hours after high water up to 3 hours before the next high water. The only possible anchorages are shown on the plan close in to the N bank about 3 cables E of the old fish factory (situated on the S bank) and again further up the river at the bend about 2½ cables W of Crook Point beacon (The Hole). A concrete pumphouse will be seen between Crook Point and The Hole. Moor with 2 anchors. Use a riding light at night. Apart from commercial shipping there is risk of trawler damage and of interfering with salmon fishers.

Drogheda. Railway viaduct 27 metres clearance above HWS. Berthing above viaduct on N side. Mooring alongside dredger is no longer possible. 198 metres of new quays should be available by July 1990 when moorings could be available outside steamers. New quays will be fenced in and permanently supervised. Quay upriver of this area is protected by gabions not visible at high water and therefore should not be used for yacht moorings. Capt. Hanrahan, HM, will readily advise. Phone: Office Nth. Quay 041-38378. Home 041-38385. No specific yacht facilities. The YC on S bank near river mouth is not now operative. Shopping, water, diesel, convenient to quays. Port Control VHF Ch. 11. Check with security re tides and any shipping movements. Hotels and restaurants available in Drogheda. There are no harbour dues. Rail and bus links to North and South. An area of historical interest is behind the town in the Boyne Valley.

Clogher Head 4½ miles NNE of the Boyne is steep-to on its E side. In NW and N wind the S side is a safe place to anchor and probably comfortable unless there have been recent onshore winds. Anchor SW of the outer bungalow going in about a cable off the rocks till the depth is 3 or 4 m; good holding. The RNLI boatshed is above the beach W of the head.

Port Oriel (*see plan*). HW +0010 Dover. Rise (HW): 4·8–4·3 m. The pier is close inside the NE corner of Clogher Head. Be careful rounding it as a stream sets across the end at 1 kn in an E direction except during the first 2 hrs of the flood. It is a very pleasant offshore anchorage in winds between SE and W but is unsuitable for yachts in winds between NW and NE and there is a possible swell in an E wind. It is a fishing port and the pier and the small dock are used by trawlers. A yacht can berth alongside the pier, probably outside a trawler, but should not be left there unattended. The dock, which dries, is never empty and at weekends is crammed with trawlers. It is therefore not recommended for yachts but if drying out is necessary it might be possible to arrange it with the HM near the middle of the week. The dock can be protected from swell in N and E winds by booms across the entrance but this is rarely done in summer.

It is best to anchor in 2·5 to 3·5 m opposite the slip or between this and about 70 m from the quay. There are four moorings in the area of the anchors shown on plan—one could be vacant for an overnight stay. It is unsuitable to leave a dinghy at the quay steps and unless going ashore for a short time it is better to land on the slip, where the dinghy must be left ashore. **Facilities.** Stores at Clogher, 1 mile. Diesel stocked on the quay. Water tap on wall beside WC at root of pier, also at W end of dock. HM Mr Patrick Hodgins phone 041-22225, VHF call "Kilfinor".

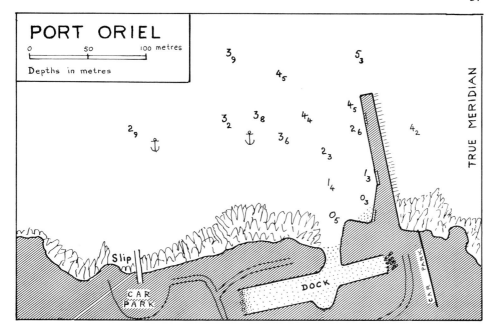

Dundalk Bay is entered between Dunany and Cooley Points both of which are very foul. Dunany red buoy, Fl R 3 s, is 2½ miles NE of the point. Imogene red buoy, Fl (2) R 10 s, is 1¾ miles SE of Cooley Point. Yachts should pass between these buoys if entering the bay. There are no dangers within the bay except that much of it is shoal and the inner half of it dries.

Gyles Quay is situated 2 miles E of Dundalk Pile Light. It is the only place in the bay suitable for a yacht to anchor. The pier is 120 m long running out SW with a spur running WNW at its head. The whole of it dries. There is good shelter anchored off it in N winds and good holding on sand, depth at least 2 m a cable from the pierhead if it is bearing between 335° and 060°, but a cable W of it only 1 m. At half tide there is 2 m alongside the 17 m long quay spur which has a ladder. There is a boat slip with a windlass inside the pier. There is a very small shop and a pub close to the pier; they are only open during holiday months. However, the village is much improved in recent years; there are some B&Bs and Ballymascanlon Hotel is about 3 M away.

Dundalk. (chart 1431) HW +0025 Dover. Rise: 5·5–4·0–1·6–0·4 m. VHF call 16, work 06 or 12. Dundalk quays are on the S side of Castletown River which runs 4 miles to the bay between banks and training walls. It is well marked and lit. The quays are used for the discharge of bulk cargoes and are unsuitable for yachts. They do provide a sheltered if unpleasant berth on soft mud at LW if in desperation. It is not frequently visited by yachts because Carlingford town harbour provides similar shelter in more agreeable surroundings and is not so far from the sea.

Lights. Pile Light on a white house on red piles at the river entrance shows Fl WR 15 s, 10 m, 12/18 M. The W sector 284° to 313° shows the safe approach into Dundalk

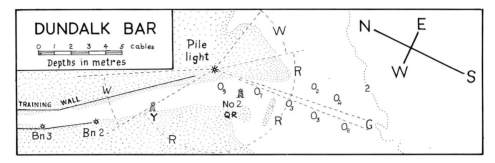

Bay. Below the main light Oc G 5 s 332° marks the close approach to channel. **Beacons** on W or S side have a square topmark even numbers and show Q R; those on the E or N side have a diamond topmark odd numbers and show Q G. (*see plan*).

Caution. The entrance should not be approached in strong winds between SW and NNE and particularly in SE winds as these cause dangerous seas on the extensive bar. The port cannot be recommended for yachts without engines. It is best to enter at half flood or earlier when the training walls are uncovered; the least depth in the channel at −0300 HW is 3·3 m and at −0400 HW is 2·5 m. In the past the position and the depths of the channel have altered so presumably this may happen again. The directions below are based on the new chart 1431 which is recommended to anyone planning a visit.

Directions. Coming from South leave Dunany Point Buoy to port and head NW (bearing 330°). Coming from N leave Imogen Rocks Buoy to starboard and head W until pile light (keep black triangle with vertical yellow stripes in line) shows white sector, the safe approach to Dundalk River mouth. White sector 313°–322°. On closer approach occulting G light as described under "lights" above. When No 2 beacon comes abeam to port turn into channel. Leave Nos 2, 4, 6, 8 and 10 beacons close to port hand. After passing 10 steer mid-channel between 5 (now lit) and 12, leave 7, 9, 9A and 11 close to starboard. Leave 16 and 18 close to port hand. Between 16 and 18 steer mid-channel passing sewerage works to port. Leave 18 fine to port hand then hug the S bank until clear of "Towers" (1 cable W of 18). Then head for mid channel between oil depot on S bank and beacon 15. Berth dries to soft mud. Ask for advice. HM offices on quay and in Quay St. close by. Phone: Office 042-34096. Radio watch available 2 hours before HW and 1 hour after HW. VHF Ch. 16/14. After HW only when commercial shipping entering or leaving. Pilot boatman's phone 042-35644 always available unless on holidays. Crane and all advice from Pat Gaskin, lighthouse man. Phone 042-71465. Quay available for drying out at Ballurgan Point (N bank). Water and diesel available on pier. Shops open Thurs. and Fri. until 9 p.m. Small shops until 11 p.m. All repairs except sails. Dundalk is on the main N–S rail link, with hotels, pubs, buses, taxis. No harbour dues.

Carlingford Lough (*see plans*). HW +0015 Dover. Rise: 4·8–4·3–1·8–0·7 m. This lough is the most picturesque inlet on the E coast and well worth a visit. It is 8 miles long and its upper part lies between the wooded lower slopes of the Mountains of Mourne and the steep barren Carlingford Mountain. This makes its position very conspicuous

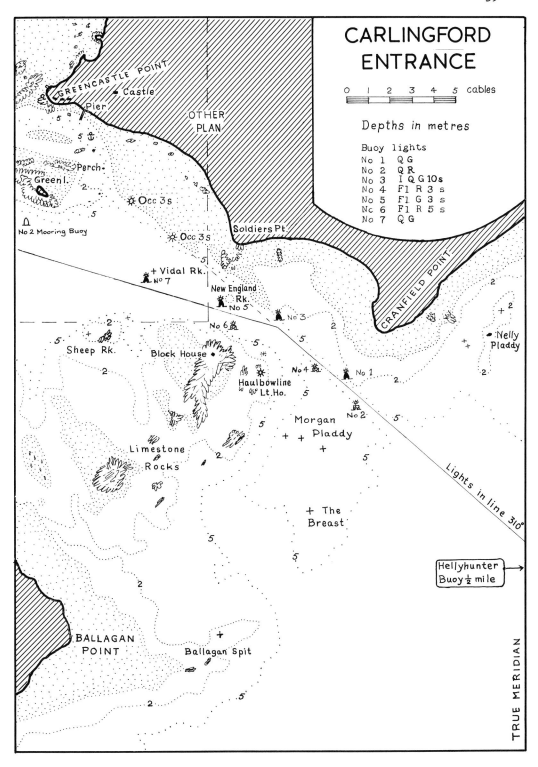

CARLINGFORD
ENTRANCE

0 1 2 3 4 5 cables

Depths in metres

Buoy lights
No 1   Q G
No 2   Q R
No 3   I Q G 10 s
No 4   Fl R 3 s
No 5   Fl G 3 s
Nc 6   Fl R 5 s
No 7   Q G

from seaward. The mouth of the lough is encumbered with rocky shoals, access being through a narrow buoyed channel with 5 m least depth. Inside there is complete shelter from swell but no really snug anchorage. In the upper part there is a very large area suitable for anchoring but nowhere sheltered in NW wind except Warrenpoint. There are three small towns, Carlingford on the Republic shore and Warrrenpoint and Rostrevor on the Northern Ireland side. It is useful to have chart 2800 but by using this book and keeping in the buoyed channel the anchorages may be reached safely. At the top end of Carlingford Lough on the port side is the border between the Republic of Ireland and Northern Ireland. Skippers should contact the Customs Authorities at the next port of call after passing this frontier. Flag Quebec should be flown close up at the yard and courtesy ensigns as appropriate. If the Customs are not available easily report to the nearest Police Station (N.I.) or Garda Station (R. of I.) for clearance to proceed. (*See page 153*).

Dangers in the approach. Ballagan Spit with detached rocks at its outer end extends ¾ mile ESE from Ballagan Point, the SW side of the entrance. The breast and Morgan Pladdy with depths of 1·8 and 1·3 m respectively lie between Ballagan Spit and Cranfield Point. Nelly Pladdy, a dangerous unmarked rock which rarely uncovers, lies about 2½ cables SE of Cranfield Point. Hellyhunter Rock, 1·4 m deep, lies about 1¼ miles SE of Cranfield Point and is marked by a S Cardinal buoy ½ miles S of it.

Lights. Carlingford Safe Water spherical buoy, L Fl 10 s, whistle, is 3 miles SSE of Cranfield Point. **Hellyhunter** S Cardinal buoy (see above) Q (6) + LFl 15 s, Horn (2) 20 s. **Haulbowline Lighthouse** a grey tower 34 m high shows Fl (3) 10 s, 14 M. At 11 m below the main light FR shows from 196° to 208° indicating the turning point in the fairway. Horn 30 s when visibility is bad in the entrance. **Leading lights** on pile structures in line 310° show Oc 3 s, 11 M. (*For buoys see plans*). (*see photo*)

Caution—Entrance. A yacht would not normally attempt to enter against the ebb, though for a large vessel with plenty of power this is possible. With onshore wind and ebb the entrance becomes dangerous and should on no account be approached. With strong onshore winds there is an element of danger even with the flood. In light conditions the wind or the engine must be reliable enough to take the yacht clear of dangers on which the strong tides might set her.

Tidal Streams. The flood starts about −0500 Dover and the ebb +0020 Dover. A mile outside the entrance the streams are not felt. They reach a rate of 3½ kn in the buoyed approach channel, 4½ kn just E of the lighthouse, 1½ kn between the entrance and Greenore, 5 kn off Greenore, 2½ kn between Stalka and Watson Rocks and 1½ kn off Carlingford. They are only just perceptible off Rostrevor. From abreast the lighthouse to No 5 buoy the flood tends to set N. There is a S-going eddy during the flood along the E side of Block House Island. Otherwise the flood follows the channels normally, as does the ebb.

Directions (*see plans*). From the N or from the Carlingford buoy pass S of the Hellyhunter buoy, where the line of the leading light beacons will be picked up. Coming from the S the offshore dangers must be given a safe berth. After passing

41

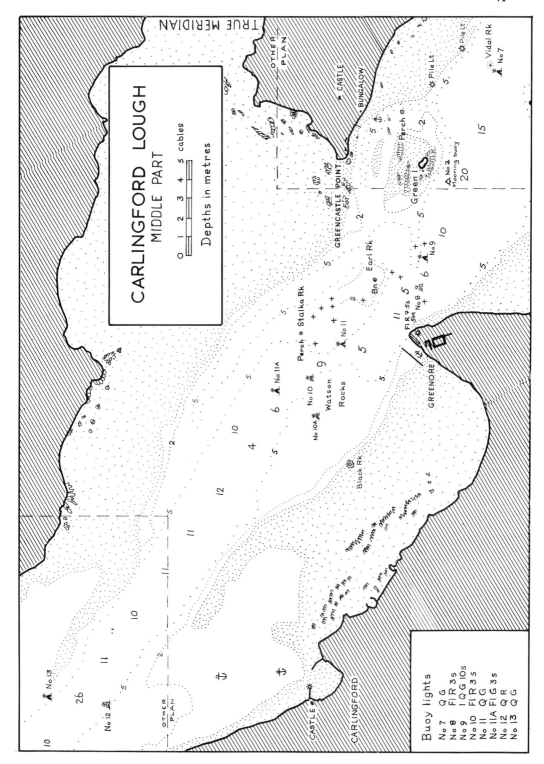

CARLINGFORD LOUGH
MIDDLE PART

0 1 2 3 4 5 cables

Depths in metres

TRUE MERIDIAN

OTHER PLAN

CASTLE
BUNGALOW

Pile Lt

Pile Lt

Vidal Rk

No 7

Perch

Perch

GREENCASTLE POINT

No 2
Mooring buoy
20
15
Green I

Earl Rk
No 9
10

Bn
6
No 8
SM

Perch Stalka Rk

Perch
No 11

No 11A
No 10
No 10A

Watson Rocks
9
5

FI R 4.5s
5

FI R 4.5s

GREENORE

Black Rk

10
4
5
6
5
12
5
11
5
2

5

No 13
26
No 12
5
OTHER PLAN
10
11
2

10

CASTLE

CARLINGFORD

Buoy lights
No 7   Q G
No 8   Fl R 3s
No 9   I Q G 10s
No 10   Fl R 3s
No 11   Q G
No 11A Fl G 3s
No 12   Q R
No 13   Q G

42

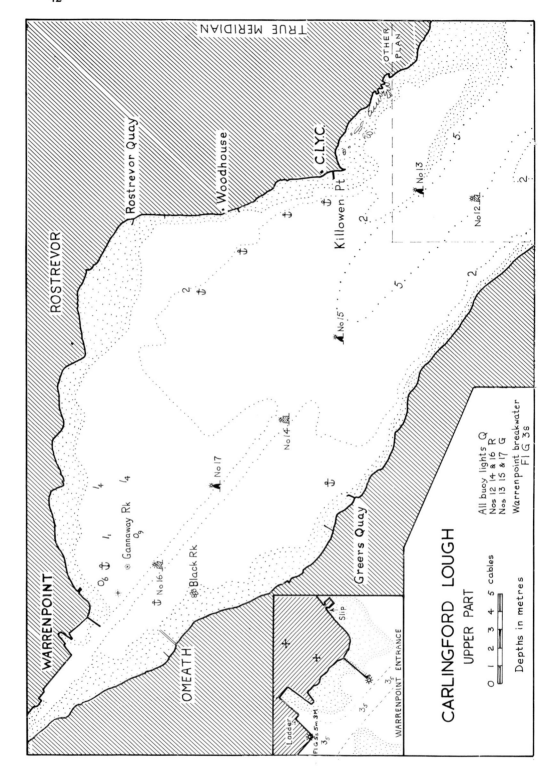

CARLINGFORD LOUGH

UPPER PART

0 1 2 3 4 5 cables

Depths in metres

All buoy lights Q
Nos 12 14 & 16 R
Nos 13 15 & 17 G

Warrenpoint breakwater
F I G 3s

Imogene buoy, Cranfield Point (which has a steep round-topped hill due N of it) should be kept bearing 000° or less; if there is any doubt about identifying this point make first for Hellyhunter buoy which bears about NE from Imogene buoy. Enter the lough between the buoys with the leading lights in line 310° till the lighthouse is past abeam, then alter course to port and head for Greenore Point which has buildings and a plantation of pine. Proceed leaving odd numbered buoys to starboard and even numbered red buoys to port. Without chart 2800 it is best to remain in the buoyed channel as there are some dangerous rocks outside it. With head wind it is better to motor but if necessary it is possible to beat in. This involves short tacks where there are dangers on both sides as between buoys 3, 5 and 6 but do not tack too far outside the buoys in clear areas lest the tide sweep you onto a rock before you get back.

Greencastle on the N shore is the nearest anchorage to the entrance and as sheltered as any other in the lough, but it is the only one whose approaches are not buoyed and they are rather narrow and only practicable by day. It is best to go in near LW when the rocks on the S side can be seen. There are no shore amenities.

From seaward, having passed Vidal Rock buoy, No 7, steer towards the houses on Greencastle Point. When the rear light pile comes abeam about ¾ cable to starboard look out for a very thin perch; at HWS only 1 m of it shows. Keep this perch in line with any part of Greencastle pier, a derelict wooden structure, and as you approach the perch turn to starboard for a moment so as to leave it not less than 10 m to port; then head for the root of the pier and when the moorings are reached it is better not to go SW of them unless the rocks there are visible. **Going out** this way keep the blockhouse just open W of the rear light pile till past the perch which should be immediately kept astern in line with the pier. The rear light pile astern with the pier just open NE of it leads safely NE of Vidal Rock.

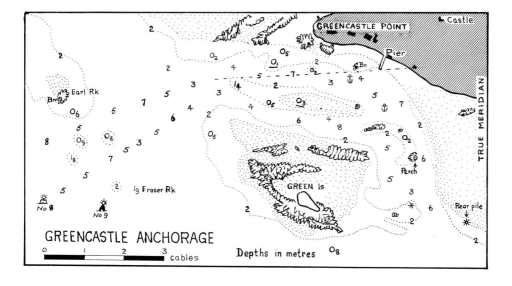

GREENCASTLE ANCHORAGE

Depths in metres

From Greenore, Greencastle may be reached by passing beween Earl Rock and the rocks S and SE of it which have a least depth of 0·8 m. As there is no mark for these latter it is necessary, unless with ample rise of tide, to leave Earl Rock beacon just ½ cable to port. When this beacon comes on the port quarter proceed in keeping the outer end of Greencastle pier in line with the small red bungalow on the shore about a cable E of the pier. Just before Greencastle Point comes abeam bear to starboard towards the moored yachts.

Caution. The large shoal on the S side of the channel SW of the pier very seldom dries and is not marked by a post as shown on the chart; take care not to go too close to it. N of Greencastle Point there is a buoy depot with a quay; yachts should not go near it as the whole approach to it dries out. The small rock which dries ½ cable W of the pierhead is now marked by a thin perch.

Anchorage. Much of the area is now occupied by yachts on moorings. It might be possible to anchor between them and the rocks which dry S of them but this should not be attempted except at LW. A safer place to anchor is W of the NW moorings, not more than ¾ cable from the perch on the rock W of the pier and not N of the red bungalow and pierhead transit; the tide runs more strongly here than S of the pier. Land on the beach near the pier. There are a few fishermen's and holiday houses in this rather out of the way spot. The Carlingford Lough pilot's house is beside the root of the pier.

Greenore Harbour just W of Greenore Point is used by commercial shipping. It consists of a quay protected by a detached breakwater about 100 m NW of it. The quay is not suitable or available for yachts to lie alongside. Anchor just past the end of the old railway station in 3 m, gravel bottom. Further in the bottom shoals rapidly and dries about 50 m within the end of the breakwater. A strong tide runs across the entrance of the harbour and weak variable eddies run through it so that a yacht is inclined to sheer about. Landing is at stairs outside the enclosed goods depot and gives easy access to the street. Limited stores at shop. No fuel. Greenore Light Fl R 7·5 s 10 m 5 M. The harbour VHF is manned during working hours VHF 16 c/s "Greenore Ferries" (042-73170). Electrical repairs at Dundalk (042-73554). Bus to Dundalk. Crane for lifting out can be arranged. No harbour dues.

Carlingford Harbour, easily recognised by the town and the old castle, lies nearly 2 miles beyond Greenore on the SW side of the lough. The harbour dries and is fronted by a large shoal extending to the edge of the buoyed channel. At neaps a yacht drawing 1·4 m could anchor a cable N of the E pierhead and one drawing 1·7 m ½ cable further N; this anchorage is seriously exposed only to the N quarter though subject to violent gusts in strong SW winds. The harbour offers good protection in all winds alongside either pier. The NW pier has 2·7 m at HWN as far as the second steps; the bottom is deep mud and rather unstable so somewhat dangerous for keelboats. The E pier has a better bottom but the disadvantage that it is a lot longer to walk to the town than from the NW pier. The home of Dundalk Sailing Club (042-73238) active during the season at weekends, particularly Sunday. VHF, limited meals, showers and bar. Fuel, water and most services are available in this quaint village. Hotels, pubs and guest houses. Good area for walking ashore. **Light.** A small light on the end of the NW pier Fl 3 s 2 m, 2 M.

Upper Part of the Lough. The SW side is fairly shallow for ½ mile N of Carlingford but from there a berth of 2 cables clears any dangers as far as **Greer's Quay** where the depth 2 cables NE of the quay is just 2 m, so this is a suitable anchorage for most yachts in winds between S and W. The quay dries completely and there are no facilities ashore. Beyond Greer's Quay the head of the lough shoals gradually. At MLWN most yachts can proceed NW, minimum depth 0·6 m, passing between No 16 buoy and Black Rock beacon and anchoring in about 1 m 2 cables N of the beacon and about 3 cables offshore from **Omeath**. The boatslip here is available at all states of tide. **Facilities.** Hotel, grocery and petrol pump are all conveniently close.

The NE side. Carlingford Lough YC, just N of Killowen Point, has a slip where one can always land but at LWS it should be approached with caution. Anchor off the moored yachts; there is 2 m 1½ cables offshore. When the Club is open, visitors are welcomed and may use the showers and the bar. Close by on the main road there is a PO, phone and a small shop. 1 cable N of Yacht Club is a new jetty 190 m long with slip on either side. A perch marks the seaward end. It does however dry out. Opposite **Rostrevor Quay**, a mile further NW, the 2 m line is ½ mile offshore. Apart from the distance it is a convenient place to land except near LW when both the slip and the quay are surrounded by impassable mud; however you can then land on the stony beach about 1½ cables to the SE where steps lead up to the road. There is a garage with diesel and petrol opposite the quay. It is ¾ mile to Rostrevor town, EC Wed. Anywhere between these two places is very pleasant for anchoring but there is nowhere else you can get ashore; suitable depth is further offshore the further NW you anchor, holding is good and there is virtually no tidal stream.

Warrenpoint (*see inset on plan*). GW +0025 Dover. Rise: 5·1–4·3–2·5–0·7 m. This is a fairly new commercial port. It is approached along a straight buoyed channel 80 m wide and dredged to 5·5 m. The breakwater light shows Fl G 3 s and the light on corner of dock Fl G 5 s 5 m 3 M. The area just NW of the breakwater now dries out completely. The commercial quays have vertical timber fenders and the area around them is dredged to 5·5 m. Consult the harbour master about staying there; you may have to move somewhere else. VHF 16 & 12. c/s "Warrenpoint". Harbour Master 73381 during working hours , 73272 outside these hours. Pilot available at Kilkeel (63462). Warrenpoint is the best shopping place in the lough. Hotels and pubs. Buses to Newry. Taxis. **Anchorage.** At neaps a yacht might prefer to lie at anchor E of the breakwater in NW or N wind. Approach outside Gannaway Rock which is marked by a thin perch and anchor about 1½ cables N of it, depth 0·8 m. Landing is possible near HW just SW of the pier, alternatively row around to the breakwater or as the Warrenpoint Boat Club has the use of the floating pontoon behind the harbour breakwater, and mooring facilities between the breakwater, the old Customs House, and the old Warrenpoint/Omeath ferry landing point. They also have toilet and shower facilities in the old Customs House. Lying along the pontoon is safe, with 7 ft. depth at low water (dredged 1988). The first 25 ft. or so is used by the Warrenpoint/Omeath ferry (Red Star Motor Boats) which finish at 5.00 p.m. After that time the whole pontoon is free, i.e. two 30 ft. boats alongside, with the rest rafting up! There is total protection—passing ships cause a bounce! Excellent restaurants and night life for the young crews. Warrenpoint Harbour: Mr Bill Bryan, Chief Executive, Warrenpoint Harbour Authority, The Docks, Warrenpoint. Phone: 06937-73381.

Coast. Between Hellyhunter Rock and Roaring Rock near the S end of Dundrum Bay there are no other isolated dangers. After steering NE for a mile from Hellyhunter buoy the coast should be given a berth of not less than ½ mile. N of Annalong there are many lobster pots.

Kilkeel Harbour (*see plan*). HW −0005 Dover. Rise: 5·3–4·4–1·9–0·7 m. This busy fishing port is 3½ miles NNE of Hellyhunter buoy and is included on chart 2800. It can be a useful place to stop and the inner basin is completely sheltered. It is not the safest harbour for yacht because it becomes very crowded in the evening, but visitors are permitted to berth there. The depth is 1·2 m at LAT throughout the harbour. In a SW gale sand builds up near the entrance and makes a drying shoal just outside; the river, which now flows through the harbour, then gradually forms a shallow channel through the shoal. The permanent drying bank extends up to 2½ cables off the shore E of the harbour and has some stones on it. A shallow shoal extends ½ mile SE of the harbour. (*see photo*)

Directions. From about a mile away approach with the harbour bearing between 341° and 350°; if it cannot be identified steer first for the CG station (red brick with a white flagstaff) which is easier to see. The recommended approach is with the pierhead bearing 341°; when 100 m away from it turn to starboard and steer 010° to 015° till the inner side of the pier is visible, then turn to port and enter. To avoid the edge of the bank on the NE side the E end of the shipyard building should not come in line with the

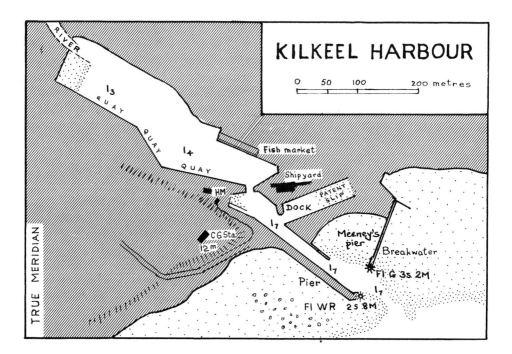

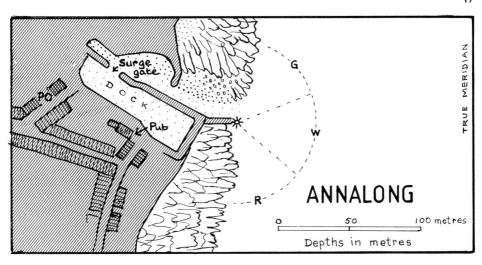

S end of the breakwater. Go straight up the channel to the inner basin, tie alongside and ask the HM where to stay. **Facilities.** Water on the quay. Diesel and gas available. Shipwrights operate N of the dock where there are two patent slips. All stores in Kilkeel town ¾ mile distant. All repairs, except sails. HM on VHF 16/12/14 or phone 62287. Hotels, restaurants and pubs. Laundrette. Area is close to Mourne Mountains for walking. EC Thur. **Light**, on small metal post on the pierhead, Fl WR 2 s 8 m 8 M. New light on Meeney's pier, Fl G 3 s 6 m 2 M.

Annalong Harbour (*see plan*) is 4½ miles NE of Kilkeel and used by local fishing boats. There is excellent shelter in its small tidal basin except in strong onshore wind when it may be subject to swell. If necessary it can then be closed by a surge gate so obviously yachtsmen should not consider entering in such conditions. It would be a very pleasant place for a yacht to visit in settled weather. It has recently been dredged and now only dries around LWS so it should be about 2 m deep 3 hrs before HW and at least 2·5 m deep 2 hrs before HW. The breakwater runs out E with the entrance, difficult to detect until close in, on its N side. A small launching slip has been built about 1 cable N of harbour. Seaward end marked by a perch.

Directions. Having made sure that the tide is really high enough head straight in for the entrance, but not any faster than necessary for control. To avoid the rocky foreshore keep close to the N side of the breakwater and the harbour wall beyond it. It is all right to move away a little before making the sharp turn to port through the 9 m wide entrance to the basin. Seek advice as to where the yacht should be left alongside. **Facilities.** PO, small shops. Good pub. **Light**, on the breakwater head. Oc WRG 5 s, G 204°–249°, W 249°–309°, R 309°–024°, 8 M. To enter at night would of course be more difficult for a stranger, so cannot be recommended.

Dundrum Bay, about 9 miles wide and 4 miles deep, lies between the Mourne Mountains and St John's Point, described later. Its two harbours, accessible only in

48

settled weather and near HW, do not often attract yachts. In W winds is is noted for squalls and in strong onshore winds there is an indraught and a heavy sea into the bay.

Dangers. 1¾ miles N of Mullartown Point, the SW limit of the bay, the unmarked Roaring Rock, which dries at LWS, lies 3 cables offshore. At Newcastle and E of it the shores of the bay are shoal. Cow and Calf Rocks, 3¾ miles W of St John's Point and a mile offshore, stand at the S end of a submerged reef; they just cover at HWS; they are in the red sector of St John's Point auxiliary light. Between these rocks and St John's Point there are other rocks closer inshore. There are three oval yellow buoys in the centre of the bay marking a firing-practice area. If a red flag is flown from No 8 flagstaff (*see Dundrum plan*) firing from the army ranges about 2 miles E of Dundrum is taking place or will shortly start and yachts should keep away from the area. Red flags on other flagstaffs do not concern the mariner unless there is one on No 8 also.

Newcastle Harbour. HW +0015 Dover. Rise: 5·1–4·1–1·5–0·5 m. This is a small artificial harbour at the S end of the town with Fl R WG Red 232°–240° White 228°–232° Green 180°–228° on end of pier. A strong wind between SE and NE makes the entrance difficult and causes scend in the harbour. However, in summer a fleet of dinghies and motor-boats lie on moorings there and take the ground at LW. It dries completely, even at neaps. The approach is shallow, but otherwise free of danger. The entrance faces N. The best berth is at the N pier anywhere between the end and the steps, clean sand bottom, 2·7 m HWN. Watch out for rock amouring which extends 15 m S from S pier which covers at HW. A sewage outfall extends 240 m due E from the sewage works to S of S pier, and is barely covered at LW. In settled weather a yacht could put in here at HW and perhaps risk drying out subject to local advice. The Newcastle SC, with showers when open, has premises beside the RNLI house and there is a slip for launching dinghies at HW. The town stretches for a mile along the shore. Harbour Master: Hugh Paul (22106).

Dundrum Harbour (*see plan*). HW +0010 Dover; it has been found that HW Liverpool gives the closest prediction for HW Dundrum. Rise: HW reckoned to be

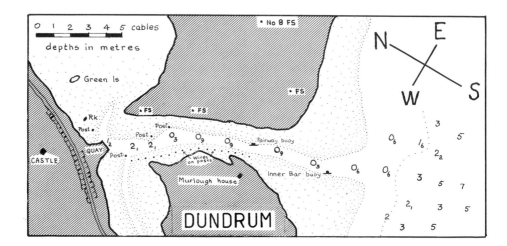

0·3 m less than at Newcastle and LW 0·3 m more; the rise is notably increased by S winds and reduced by N winds. This is a pretty estuary surrounded by sandhills at the head of Dundrum Bay. Though used by small coasters it cannot really be recommended for keel-yachts because the narrow bar, which is completely exposed to the S, has only 0·3 m, and there is nowhere very suitable for lying afloat. It would be interesting to visit in a twin-keel yacht or a motor cruiser. The channel is liable to change so be prepared to deal with going aground when entering or leaving.

Directions. Entry should only be attempted in reasonable sea conditions, good visibility and with a rising tide. An old castle on a small rounded hill behind the town bearing about 330° leads to the entrance. Steer for a small round buoy which marks the outer end of the narrow entrance channel and leave this buoy about 11 m to port. Next steer for the fairway buoy, a small buoy on the E side inside the entrance and leave it close to starboard. (Both buoys are black, and may remain so.) There are two posts to be left to starboard passing half-way between the second of them and the poles along the shore to port. From here carry on towards the last post (port-hand diamond topmark) and when about 45 m from it alter course to starboard for the quay. The only anchorage with over 2 m is in the reach between the last two posts but the tide there runs very strongly. On the W side of the fairway and just S of the quay is a better place but the depth there is only 0·3 m which might however enable a small yacht to lie afloat at LWN. Drying out at the quay is not recommended, chiefly because of the strong tidal streams. **Facilities.** Garages, shops, PO, a small hotel. EC Thur.

Light. St John's Point, the E tip of Dundrum Bay, is easily recognisable by the prominent lighthouse, 40 m high, black with two yellow bands, which stands near the end of the long low point. Main light: Q (2) 7·5 s 37 m 23 M; auxiliary light Fl WR 3 s 14m 15/11 M, with FW sector from 064° to 078° and a FR sector from thence to shore. Horn (2) 60 s, Fog Det. Lt.

50

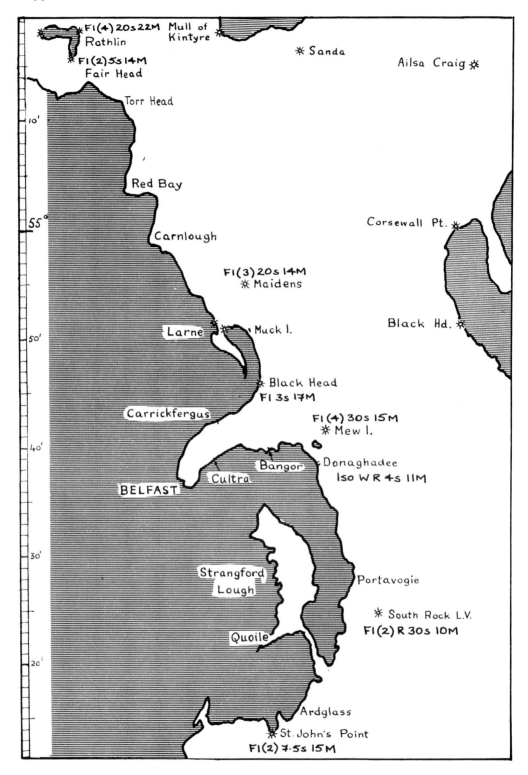

Fl(4)20s22M Mull of Kintyre
Rathlin
* Sanda
Ailsa Craig *
Fl(2)5s14M
Fair Head

Torr Head

10'

Red Bay

55°

Carnlough

Corsewall Pt. *

Fl(3)20s14M
* Maidens

Black Hd. *

50'

Larne • Muck I.

* Black Head
Fl 3s 17M

Carrickfergus

Fl(4)30s15M
* Mew I.

40'

Bangor Donaghadee
Cultra Iso WR 4s 11M
BELFAST

30'

Strangford
Lough

Portavogie

* South Rock L.V.
Fl(2)R 30s 10M

Quoile

20'

Ardglass

* St John's Point
Fl(2)7.5s 15M

CHAPTER III

St John's Point to Fair Head

Charts. The S part of this coast is included on chart 44 (which covers Chapter II). It is possible to manage with three other charts: 2156, Strangford Lough and the coast E of it, and 2198 and 2199 covering the N Channel. Charts 2156 and 2198 just join, at different scales, so 2093, S Approach to N Channel, might be desirable also. 1753 is useful if going to Belfast, but not essential. 3709 is only needed for investigating the Copeland Island shores. It is possible to anchor in Larne Lough without 1237. The entrance to Strangford Lough is now on chart 2159.

General. Ardglass Harbour is safe and a handy terminus for a day's sail to or from Co Dublin. Strangford, just N of it, is undoubtedly the best lough for yachting in Ireland. At present there is nowhere sheltered in onshore winds on the rock-strewn shore between Strangford and the neighbourhood of Belfast Lough, which is also a popular yachting area with anchorages in offshore winds but rather exposed to the E. Larne Lough has no closely sheltered spot but plenty of space for anchoring in suitable depths and safe conditions. From Larne to Fair Head the handsome coast with bold heads offers no security in onshore wind; advice about crossing from there to Scotland is given in Chapter V Part I.

Tides. The flood tide runs SE and S, following the trend of this coast, while the tide is rising at Dover; the ebb flows out to the N during the falling tide at Dover. In the entrance to the North Channel both the flood and the ebb can reach 4·5 kn at springs. The tides run strongly in the Channel till it widens S of Belfast Lough and becomes weak near St John's Point, SE of which the flood streams from N and S meet and divide. The time of HW along this coast is nowhere much different from HW Dover. The tidal range decreases from S to N. More detailed descriptions of local tidal streams are given where necessary.

Killough Harbour, 1¾ miles NE of St John's Point. Killough Pier has been rebuilt but has no depth of water alongside nor facilities. A new marina is planned. The harbour is officially closed. Anchorage in the bay outside the harbour and W of Ringfad Point is not particularly attractive as most of the bottom is rock; it is therefore not recommended. The only danger just outside the bay is Water Rocks which dry 3 m and are marked by a red mast. There are more rocks inside. If wishing to go in there the plan on chart 633 gives full details.

Ardglass (*see plan*). HW +0015 Dover. Rise (HW), probably: 4·7–4·0 m. VHF Call 16, Work 14, 12. This busy fishing harbour is 3 miles NE of St John's Point. It consists of a rocky inlet partly sheltered by substantial breakwater with quays on its inner side.

Further in there is a completely sheltered old tidal dock. Approaching from seaward the white roof of the fish shed above the pier is a useful landmark. Coming from the S one sees a tower on the conical hill S of Ardglass and a water tower nearer Ringfad Point outside the hill. **Lights.** The principal lighthouse is on the end of the inner pier and shows Iso WRG 4 s, 6 M G shore −310°, W 310° −318°, R 318° to shore. On the end of the breakwater there is Fl R 3 s 10 m 5 M. (*see photo*)

Directions. Keep well away from the rocks on both sides of the shore outside the harbour entrance and go in between the breakwater and an iron tripod marking the rocks on the NE side. At night approach the harbour in the white sector of the inner light. The best place to anchor is between the outer quay and the red iron beacon on the rock NW of it, in 2 to 2·5 m. This is a safe anchorage but uncomfortable in fresh winds between E and S, it can also be disturbed by heavy fishing traffic. In quiet weather or offshore winds it is suitable to anchor between the entrance and the inner entrance, NE of the two beacons.

Berths. During the day while the fishing fleet is at sea yachts may go alongside the quays but should consult the HM about staying there. The foundation of the N-facing quay protrudes 0·6 m in places; when the shed on this quay is closed it is not possible to go ashore past it. Small yachts might dry out alongside the inner W-facing quay, firm bottom. Beyond the inner lighthouse pier the harbour dries and is mostly rocky. The dock there is normally only worth using in a E to S gale. It is about 3 m deep at HW over a bottom of deep mud. To reach it keep close to N of the Wall W of the lighthouse till it bends towards the entrance. Good fenders are necessary as the quays are built of stones and yachts are apt to move when settling down in the mud.

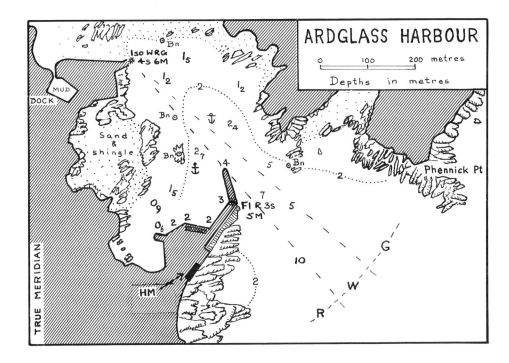

Facilities. Report arrival to the HM whose office is in the Northern Ireland Fishing Harbour Office on the pier (0396-841291). Shops often stay open in the evening. One hotel. Public phone in fish-market on the quay. Fresh water from tap in fish market. Petrol and derv conveniently available; bulk diesel by arrangement. Buses to Downpatrick and Belfast. Minor harbour dues. Major works to extend pier during 1991/2.

Coast. Between Ardglass and Guns Island 2¾ miles further NE there are are few outlying rocks within a cable of the shore. Guns Island is 30 m high and has a white obelisk on its SE side. Ballyhoran Bay (Charts 2156 and 2159) north of Guns Island is foul but Benderg Bay is a pleasant and useful anchorage in suitable conditions. Beware Craiglewey Rocks south of Killard; if rounding Killard Point lay-off to pass E of them; if heading for Benderg Bay give their S end a very wide berth (approach holding the Lattice Radio Mast on 287° sighted between two conspicuous dwellings on cliff top, turning in when Benderg Beach is well open to N).

Strangford Lough. (Chart 2156, Strangford Narrows 2159). The largest inlet on the E coast, is naturally suited for yachting, having a sufficient area of unobstructed water for racing and many islands with sheltered anchorages behind them along the W shore. There is little commercial traffic in the lough. Being within easy reach of Belfast there are many yacht clubs and fleets of dinghies and keel-boats. It is also a very pleasant place for day sailing in largely unspoilt pastoral surroundings. For the visitor the only drawback is the number of drying and submerged patches, known as pladdies, only some of which are marked by poles and beacons. The entrance known as the Narrows is about 5 miles long and quite straightforward both by day and night, using the main channel to the E of Angus Rock (*see plan*). The West Channel should not be attempted without local knowledge. A fair tide is necessary both for entering and leaving as the streams run from 4 up to 7 kns. It is alway safe to enter but it is dangerous to leave against a fresh onshore wind (*see caution below*). The anchorages in the narrows make excellent overnight stops if HW happens to be in the small hours. The lough itself is well worth a visit for any passing stranger with a day to spare. It abounds in sheltered anchorages which can easily be chosen from chart 2156. A new chart 2159 Strangford Narrows has recently been issued, and is strongly recommended.

Lights. Bar Pladdy S Card Buoy Q (6) + Fl 15 s (this buoy is now in position from Angus Tower 144° 7·8 cables). Angus Rock Tower Light Fl R 5 s 15 m 6·5 M. Dogtail Point beacon Oc (4) 10 s 2 m 5 M. Salt Rock beacon Fl R 3 s 8 m 3 M. Gowland Rocks beacon Oc (2) 10 s 6 m 5 M. Swan Island NE beacon Fl (2) WR 6 s. Swan Island SSW Fl (3) 10 s. On Watch House Point to S of Swan Island the perch has been replaced by a beacon FR (2 VERT). In fairway immediately NNW of Swan Island a beacon Q. Church Point Fl (4) R 10 s. In addition there are leading lights for the ferry into Strangford Quay. Portaferry Ferry Pier Oc WR 10 s 9 m 9–6 M. Ballyhenry Island Q G 3 m 3 M. Limestone Rock Beacon Q R 3 M (this rock is well above the narrows and is very dangerous as it lies in the fairway).

Tides. HW Killard Point as Dover. (N.B. HW Dover relates closely to HW Belfast). HW Strangford Narrows and Strangford Lough as for Strangford Quay +0140 Dover. Rise at Strangford Quay 3.6–3·1–0·9–0·4 m. Outside the entrance the stream runs NE

54

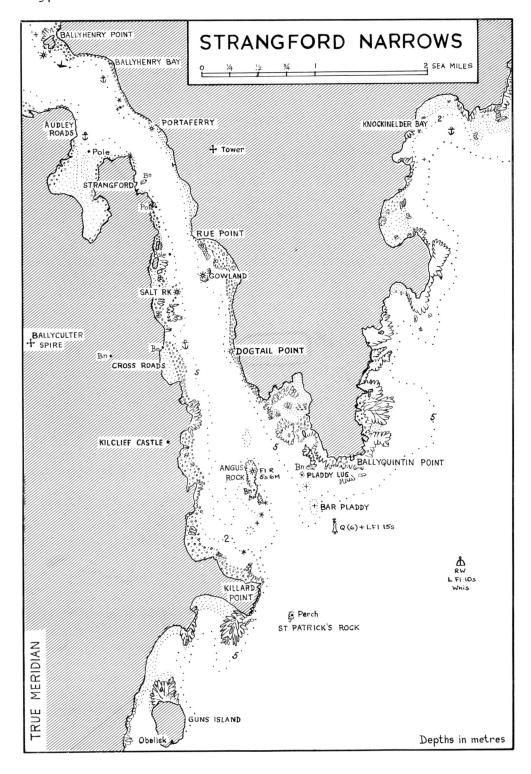

STRANGFORD NARROWS

0   ¼   ½   ¾   1   2 SEA MILES

BALLYHENRY POINT

BALLYHENRY BAY

KNOCKINELDER BAY   2

AUDLEY ROADS

PORTAFERRY

+ Tower

• Pole

Bn

STRANGFORD

Pole

RUE POINT

Pole •

GOWLAND

SALT RK

BALLYCULTER SPIRE

Bn •   Bn

CROSS ROADS

5

DOGTAIL POINT

5

KILCLIEF CASTLE •

5

ANGUS ROCK   Fl R 5s 6M

Bn

PLADDY LUG

BALLYQUINTIN POINT

Bn

+ BAR PLADDY

Q(6)+LFl 15s

2

RW L Fl 10s Whis

KILLARD POINT

Perch
ST PATRICK'S ROCK

5

TRUE MERIDIAN

GUNS ISLAND

Obelisk

Depths in metres

from +0200 to +0500 Dover, and then SW for nearly 8 hours. The stream in the Narrows runs in from +0200 LW (Belfast) and out from +0200 HW (Belfast), about six hours each way and at speeds of up to 7 kns in places.

Caution. Beware the overfalls at the bar and in the SE approaches out to a distance of 1½ miles, which only occur when there is ebb in the Narrows. These overfalls though bumpy at the best of times become severe in strong onshore (E to SSW) winds. It is alway safe to attempt entry (though few will wish to do so against a strong ebb), as the attempt can readily be abandoned and safer water regained. It is not however always safe to depart and the danger lies in this not becoming apparent until it is too late for a yacht to regain safe water. A departing yacht approaching the white water at the bar may wish to make back for shelter but be unable to do so against the ebb and so be drawn out into the overfalls against its will. These are the only circumstances in which Strangford Lough is actually dangerous.

Dangers at the entrance. St Patrick's Rock, 4 cables off Killard Point, is steep-to with deep water on either side and is covered within 2½ hrs of HW. It is marked by a 9 m high red perch with can topmark so by day it presents no problems but at night it must be carefully avoided. **Bar Pladdy,** with 0·6 m over it, is near the end of a rocky shoal running out S from the W side of Ballyquintin Point, which is marked at its S end by the Bar Pladdy Buoy Q (6). **Pladdy Lug,** which dries 1 m, is near the end of a reef which runs out W from Ballyquintin Point. It is marked by a white beacon made of glazed tiles which should be given a berth of at least ½ a cable. **Angus Rock,** most of which dries, lies in mid-channel ½ mile within the entrance. Covered rocks run out S and SW of it but its E side and N end are steep-to. Near the N end of the rock there is a square white tower Fl R 5 s 13 m. On the tail of the rock, about 1½ cables S of the tower, there is a truncated obelisk. **The Meadows,** an unmarked rocky shoal with 2·3 m lies 3 cables N of Angus Tower and should be given a berth. N of the Meadows the centre of the channel is free of dangers. There are a good many rocks on either shore, those which project into the fairway being marked by beacons. **Routen Wheel,** a whirlpool on the E side of the fairway between Rue Point and Salt Rock beacon Fl R 3 s, could be dangerous to small yachts but there is no difficulty in sailing clear of it. The Narrows has many other whirls and tide rips but these should be enjoyed rather than feared.

Directions. The entrance is marked by a Safe Water spherical buoy. L Fl 10 s, whistle (known locally as Craigs or the Moaning Boy) moored about 1½ miles SE of Ballyquintin Point. The position was modified some years ago so that it, the Bar Pladdy Buoy and Angus Rock Tower all line up on 144/324°. Coming from the S, St Patrick's Rock may be passed on either side, but do not head in till Portaferry is seen on the right of Angus rock. Coming from the N leave Bar Pladdy buoy to starboard. Having passed between Angus Tower and Pladdy Lug beacon, keeping at least a cable away from the latter, leave the Meadows to port by keeping the building at the N end of Portaferry just open of Rue Point, a prominent buff, till Kilclief Castle is well abeam. Thereafter keep mid-channel.

Though not recommended some local yachts both enter and leave through tricky passages closer to the entrance corners. Their chief advantage is that going out in onshore winds they avoid most of the overfalls. Leaving to go N a popular short cut is between Pladdy Lug and the Bar Pladdy holding a transit Angus Rock Tower/Kilclief Castle. It should be noted that the new chart 2159 shows this to take one directly over the Knob, charted depth 1·8 m. **Leaving to go S** enter the half-way between Angus Tower and Mullog Point opposite it on the W shore. Then head S and soon Kilclief Castle will come in line 314° with the vertical left end of a conspicuous grove of trees on the skyline. Go out strictly on this transit (see note in text below) and, as soon as the obelisk on the tail of Angus comes in line with Rue Point, bear to starboard steering first towards St Patrick's Rock beacon and then between it and Killard Point. (Note: Before leaving the 314° transit which leads between shallows there will, in onshore wind, have been a couple of breaking seas, but after bearing to starboard there should be no more breakers.) **Approaching from the S** inside St Patrick's Rock, head for Pladdy Lug beacon till turning in on the 314° transit described above. It is possible to make some progress W of Angus rock before the ebb has finished as the streams there are weaker than in the main channel. (Note however that the transit leads across a depth of 2 m and there is considerable weed; note also that LW occurs about 1½ hours before the ebb in the narrows stops.) Entering during the flood, which flows strongly towards the tail of Angus Rock, you would at first have to steer to port of the transit to keep on it. Therefore whenever you enter do not rely on the wind, but keep the engine going, as safety depends on a certain speed. The transit must be watched without interruption. Keep on it till the obelisk bears NE, then head for Rue Point.

Above the Narrows many of the dangers which have poles or perches have been marked with reflecting tape by the local Inshore Life Boat crew as follows:

Location	Marking
Skate Rock	1 Narrow
Barrell Rock	2 Narrow
Selk Rock	3 Narrow
Limestone Pladdy	4 Narrow
Brown Rock	1 Broad
Verde Rocks	1 Broad, 1 Narrow
Long Sheelagh West	1 Broad, 2 Narrow
Long Sheelagh East	2 Broad, 1 Narrow
Sand Rock Pladdy	2 Broad
Hadd Rock	Silver/metal disc on a short pole
Janes Rock	No marking
Dead Mans Rock	1 Narrow
Rig Pladdy	2 Narrow
Newton Rock	3 Narrow
Dullisk Rock	1 Broad
Michael's Rock	2 Broad
Craigyouran	Narrow, broad, narrow

Anchorages

Cross Roads on the W side is the nearest anchorage to the entrance and is a suitable place for anyone who does not wish to go ashore. The lead into the anchorage is marked by two stone beacons (once white), one on the bank at the top of the foreshore and the second in a hedge about ½ mile inland.

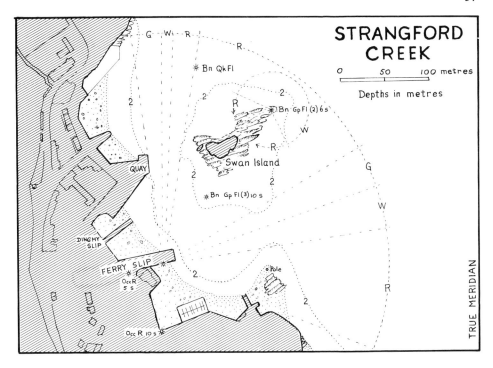

Strangford Creek (see plan, which also shows the lights). This small area is sheltered by Swan Islet and out of the main stream, the tide there running N except from −0100 to +0100 HW. It was always fairly crowded and is now more so as a result of the car ferry service. The ferries operate from the slip but one of them frequently lies alongside the end of the quay. A ferry is also often moored fore and aft between the two buoys N of Swan Islet. If the quay is unoccupied a yacht might berth there temporarily but should remain ready to leave at once when requested to do so. If the height of the tide allows it is possible to berth elsewhere on the quay. **Approach.** The white stone beacon Fl (2) WR 6 s near the NE end of the reef around Swan Islet should be given a berth of 40 m. Pass either S of the beacon Fl (3) 10 s situated 40 m SSW of the islet, or N of the beacon Q 100 m NNW of it. **Facilities.** Victuals and stores, restaurants, water at quay, diesel (cans), gas. Electrical or other repairs. Bus to Downpatrick. Ferry to Portaferry. Some visitors moorings—apply Ferry Superintendent/Harbour Master Ch 16 or (039-686637). Anchor in fairway NW of Swan island. 2 slips. (*see photo*)

Caution. Church Point on the W side about 1½ cables N of Strangford Creek has a white stone beacon with a light, Gp Fl (4) R 10 s; the beacon, and the shore S of it which is foul, should be given a berth of at least ¾ cable.

Audley Roads, NW of Church Point, is an excellent anchorage. It is within walking distance of Castleward House (National Trust), but there are no shore facilities. Anchor in 4·5 m between the small stone pier under the ruins of Audley Castle and a pole which marks the end of a long spit stretching across from the SE side of the bay; the inlet is all shoal further in. There are yacht moorings and some racing marks belonging to Strangford Sailing Club on the W shore. The scenery and shelter make it very popular with local yachts so at weekends it may be necessary to anchor outside them in up to 10 m. (*see photo*)

Caution. It is not advisable to sail further into the lough without chart 2156. Careful pilotage is necessary as so many of the islets and rocks are of a similar appearance. Compass courses cannot be relied upon owing to the set of the tides. Many rocks and pladdies are marked by poles or perches but these are unreliable. East Down YC is situated inside Island Taggart and is marked on chart 2156. Approach with care. There are two visitors' moorings and a pontoon which will receive four yachts. Showers available in the clubhouse which is active on race nights and at weekends when the bar is open. Facility to haul out 32 ft yachts.

Quoile. Another well sheltered spot is the limit of navigation of this river which enters the lough at its SW corner. The approach is betwen Barrel and Skate rocks, both marked by perches. The transit to pass clear N of Skate Rock is to keep Portaferry pier open of Chapel Island. Keep on this transit till you see between Green and Salt islands so as to avoid the shoal 3 cables W of Skate Rock; this shoal sometimes has a small perch on it. When entering the estuary favour the port shore and leave the perch on the Toadstone and the iron beacon beyond it to starboard. Anchor off the moored yachts; the depth is suitable anywhere between Castle and Gibbs islands. Close W of Gibbs Island is very well sheltered but probably occupied. Quoile YC, on Castle Island close to the dam, offers its facilities to visitors from recognised YCs. There is a slip and quay suitable for drying alongside and scrubbing. Water hose at end of quay. Phone in clubhouse 0396-612266. Approaching the quay leave the perch just off the end of the jetty to starboard. Shops are 3 M away in Downpatrick. 4 visitors buoys—yellow—at NE edge of members moorings.

Killyleagh, HW +0145 Dover. Rise (HW): 3·8–3·3 m. This town, on the W coast at the entrance to the Quoile, is approached by the same transit. There is ample space to anchor in 2 to 4 m SSW of Town Rock beacon, a red brick cylinder Qk Fl R 3 s. It is handy to land at the YC pontoon jetty, W of the beacon, from which the shops and a garage are easily accessible. Showers and bar in YC. The town quay, NW of the beacon, is frequently visited by coasters. A yacht drawing 2 m could go alongside it at −0200 HW and should approach with the spire a little open W of the quay. It is safe to dry out there but not recommended because of the smell. Fresh water hose, fuel and gas. A 5 ton crane is usually available. Victuals and stores, chandlery, pubs and restaurants. Taxis and buses. Plans for a marina. 5 visitors moorings—yellow buoys property of Down County Council in line 260°. **Caution**: the area has become wooded and the rear beacon though visible when on the correct transit is much obscured and difficult to identify. Anchor as soon as the depth corresponds to 3·5 m. Rather subject to tide.

Ringhaddy Sound, the headquarters of the Ringhaddy Cruising Club, is splendidly sheltered and most attractive. Unfortunately it is mostly rather deep and moorings extend the full length of Islandmore. The flood tide runs N at 2 kn. **Directions**. After rounding Ballyhenry beacon steer 337° for the conspicuous Scrabo Tower 14 miles away. This leads to the Limestone Rock which is marked by a beacon, QR, on its E end, plus two perches on the N and W ends, and covers at 4 hours flood. Leave this beacon to port and steer 318° for a ruined windmill just on the skyline 4 miles away; astern on the E shore will be a white cottage in Marlfield Bay which should be kept just open N of the beacon. Hold this line right in. It passes between Rathgorman Pladdies on the NE side, marked by a perch, and Brownrock Pladdy and Brown Rock on the SW side which are not marked; they cover at half tide but their seaweed often shows. Black Rock, a grass-topped islet, is one cable SW of Brownrock Pladdy. When Pawle Island and Islandmore come abeam to starboard keep about mid-channel. When Ringhaddy Sound opens up swing round to starboard. There are two rocks awash at LWS about ½ cable offshore, slightly S of a jetty below a green wooden bungalow on the SW end of Islandmore. Entering the sound keep towards the SE side as the spit on the opposite shore extends half-way across. Proceeding up the sound avoid the bays, which are shoal, and keep mid-channel to clear moorings. (*see photo*)

Berths—Facilities. On the W shore one cable S of Ringhaddy quay there is a floating pier and concrete slip belong to the Ringhaddy CC. Visting yachts are welcome and those requiring temporary use of a mooring should secure alongside and contact Mr Bob Scott who lives beside the entrance gate to the club. The floating pier should be approached with caution as there is less than 1·8 m at LWS. The bottom is soft mud. Yachts may only lie alongside for a short time. Water tap on the pier. Ringhaddy Quay is a stone pier which dries; the bottom there is firm and yachts normally berth on its N side. Between the floating pier and the quay there are private facilities for hauling out. No stores are available as Ringhaddy is remote from any village.

Whiterock is the headquarters of the Strangford Lough YC. The direct approach is up the middle of the lough, course J on the chart, leaving the perch on Dead Mans Rock to port before turning NW leaving Trasnagh to port. The approach from Ringhaddy is between Darragh and Parton. A spit extends 2 cables W of Parton; it dries a cable from Parton, where it is marked by a pole, and deepens to 1·2 m a further cable W. Always keep closer to Darragh than to the pole. At LW keep 60 m off Darragh shore round to its NW point, whence head straight for the E end of Sketrick Island (345°). Anchor outside the moored yachts. **Facilities**. The club boatman can advise whether a mooring is free and also about obtaining stores, which are available 2 miles away. There is a new pontoon jetty at the Clubhouse, with 2 m 3 hours either side of HW. Water hose available. There is a bar in the clubhouse open on Wednesday, Friday and Saturday after racing. Daft Eddie's pub and restaurant is near the castle on Sketrick Island, and there are plans for a landing pontoon (least depth 1·7 m) on the N shore close to the pub. Boatyard in Conly Bay (S of Whiterock) with a slipway for yachts up to 25 tons and some repair facilities; the proprietor Mr W Smith lives ½ mile from Whiterock.

Down Cruising Club (Ballydorn) has its headquarters in a converted lightship moored afloat in the narrow channel W of Rainey Island and connected to the shore by a gangway. In summer there are usually members on board and visitors are welcomed. The entrance between Rainey and Sketrick Islands is only 1·5 m deep but inside there is 3 or 4 m. There is 2 to 3 kn tide through the channel and numerous moored craft so there is really no room to anchor. A visiting yacht might berth temporarily alongside the club ship which has facilities including a bar, waterhose and diesel fuel. Three visitors moorings. There is also a derrick for mast lifting. (*see photo*)

Newtownards Sailing Club lies on the E shore of Strangford Lough about 1 M N of the village of Greyabbey. The club which is mainly involved in dinghy racing does have 4 visitors moorings. Showers and bar facilities are available when the clubhouse is in operation. The jetty has water laid on but dries out at LWS.

Kircubbin lies on the E side of the lough and its completely exposed to the west. The approach is strewn with pladdies. From the E end of Long Sheelah steer 035° for 1·5 m leaving Gransha Pt to starboard 3 cables then 005° into the bay. Watch for Sand Rock pladdy. There are two passages from the W, S of Skart Rock, and S of Bird Island respectively but neither is recommended to strangers. The harbour dries and is of no value but there is a slip at the sailing club on the north shore of the bay. Anchor off in 2·1 m. Sheltered from N through E to S. Limited stores in village.

Ballyhenry Bay ¾ mile NNW of Portaferry provides good anchorage easy of access and convenient to the town. At the S end of the bay give a good berth to Walter Rocks which dry 2·1 m and are marked by a perch; the tide runs strongly across them. Anchor off the cottage among the trees. A number of yachts moor here permanently. Beware the remains of a wrecked ship at the NW end of the Bay, 2½ cables SW Ballyhenry Point beacon, which is partly covered near HW.

Portaferry is on the E side of the narrows opposite Strangford Creek. There are boat moorings off the town but nowhere suitable for a yacht to anchor. There is a T-shaped pier near the S end of the town which, while it has adequate depth alongside its outer quay, is unfortunately built on piles against which it is awkward for a yacht to berth without a plank. Approach the pier with caution as there is probably an eddy inside the main stream. **Light**, on a mast on the ferry pierhead which is near the N end of the town, Oc WR 10 s, W 335°–005°, R 005°–017°, W 017°–128°. **Facilities**. Water, petrol and diesel in cans, gas, victuals, stores, hotel, several restaurants, taxis, buses, banks.

Leaving Strangford Lough (*see caution and directions on page 55*) is dangerous in fresh onshore winds when the ebb causes a heavy breaking sea right across the approaches, and indeed there can be dangerous sea during the ebb in any strong winds except perhaps between W and N. There is never any damaging sea at or N of Angus Rock. In bad weather the best procedure is to approach Angus Rock at +0150 LW Belfast and if the stream is still ebbing wait until it is slack and then sail out, aiming to get NE of Bar Pladdy or S of St Patrick's Rock as soon as possible. Slack water only lasts for about 15 minutes but the streams are not very strong for 15 minutes before and after slack water. It is also possible to leave at HW slack, and local yachts do so if necessary, but this involves the difficulty of getting down the narrows against the flood, the disadvantage of being unable to go back if the weather seems too bad, and the danger of being delayed and not getting clear before the sea starts breaking; it is therefore not recommended in difficult weather. In normal circumstances locals going north plan to leave Strangford Creek an hour before HW (Strangford Quay) aiming to reach the bar at slack HW and thus work the outside tidal stream to maximum advantage. Southbound the effect of outside tide is less significant, and the likely state of the overfalls at the bar is the critical consideration.

Coast. Ballyquintin Point is very foul and should be given a berth of ½ mile. Kearney Point, 3¼ miles NE of Ballyquintin Point, is a low shelving point foul for 2 cables all round. Butter Pladdy, a cluster of rocks with least depth 1·8 m and 2 cables in extent lies 1 mile SE of Kearney Point and is marked by a red buoy moored E of it. On the NW side of these rocks there is a steel wreck which uncovers at LW and whose position is difficult to fix. It is therefore advisable to pass E of the buoy unless the wreck is clearly visible, when it would be safe to pass at least a cable W of the wreck. **Anchorage.** Knockinelder Bay, inside Kearney Point, is sheltered in winds from NNE through W to SW when it is a good anchorage on sand in 3 to 4 m.

South Rock, barely covered at HW, is part of an extensive group of covered rocks 1¾ miles NE by E of Kearney Point; it is marked by a disused lighthouse 18 m high. Privateer Rock, with 2·1 m over it is ½ mile SW of the old lighthouse. The Breast is a rocky patch with 2·1 m about 9 cables N by W of South Rock. Crooked Pladdy, with 2·1 m and deep water around, lies ¾ mile S by W of the South Rock. The Ridge extends about a mile E from South Rock where it is 2·4 m deep; it is marked by a red buoy off its E end; the buoy is small and difficult to spot.

South Rock LV, with red hull, 2 masts and lantern amidships, is moored 2 miles E of South Rock. **Light**, Fl (3) R 30 s 12 m 20 M, horn (3) 45 s. The light is shown in fog or bad visibility. Radio beacon, *see Appendix 5* Fog Detector Lt. **Tides.** At South Rock LV the flood starts running S at LW Dover and the ebb N at −0015 Dover; the max speed at springs is 1·4 kn. The flood and the ebb flow SW and NE between South Rock and North Rocks. The flood flows S across The Ridge and close E of South Rock but the ebb flows ENE past the S side of South Rock and The Ridge and turns N outside The Ridge.

Inside Passage. In clear weather there is a good short cut inside the South Rock and between it and North Rocks. It is also advantageous if the tide is foul. Chart 2156 is recommended. There is a yellow buoy 1·5 M W of South Rock LV. It is in 11 m so can be passed close to on either side.

North Rocks, a large bank nearly all covered at HW, is over 1½ miles ESE of Ringboy Point; there is a spit between it and the point. It is marked by a red pillar 12 m high about ¾ cable inside the E drying edge. Yachts should pass at least 1½ cables E of the pillar.

Portavogie. HW as Dover. Rise: 4·7–3·9–1·4–0·6 m. VHF Call 16, Work 14; 12; (working hours only). This is a small, well sheltered fishing harbour. It is very congested at times, particularly at weekends; it should only be used for an overnight stop or in an emergency. Fuel and water are available, but supplies are limited. Engine, hull and electrical repairs can be arranged. No hotels or pubs. **Warning**. The entrance was always liable to be dangerous in strong onshore winds.

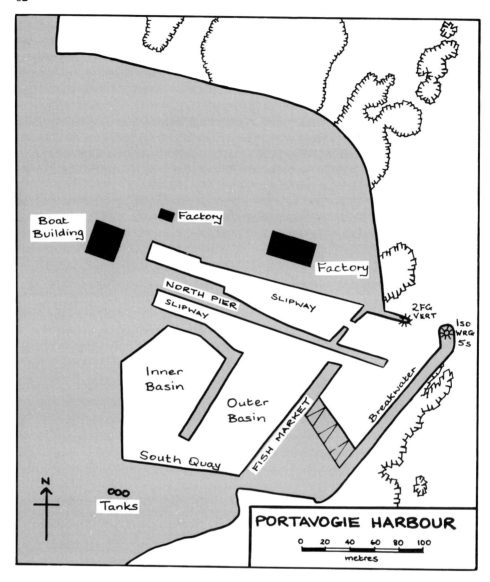

Dangers. SE of the harbour there are several rocks, the outer one being Plough Rock which dries 3 m and is marked by Plough buoy NE of it, a red bell buoy showing Q R. For ¾ mile N of the harbour there are unmarked rocks which extend up to ½ mile offshore. **Directions**. Approaching from the S do not go inside the transit of the North Rocks pillar and the South Rock old lighthouse till Plough buoy is seen; then turn in towards the buoy and having left it to port steer in towards the pierhead. Approach from the N, after passing outside Burial Island steer S till Plough buoy is seen, then steer towards the buoy till the harbour bears at least 250° when it is safe to go straight towards it. The final approach is through a short 24 m wide dredged channel which runs out due E from outside the harbour entrance, which faces N. **Light**, from a steel tower 5 m high on the outer pierhead, Iso WRG 5 s 5 m 9 M green shore to 258° white 258° to 275° red 275° to 348°. Inner pier light 2 FG Vert. The white sector indicates the approach but yachts coming from the N are advised to follow the directions. **Facilities**. There is water at the central quay, a couple of good shops and a ship's chandler with many supplies including diesel and petrol. EC Thur. No licenced premises.

Burial Island, the E point of Ireland, lies 2 cables E of Burr Point. It is 8 m high and small at HWS but is surrounded by a reef which seldom covers and extends 3 cables N and 2 cables E and S of the island; the reef is steep-to on its N and E sides. There is a clear channel inside the island and using chart 2156 it would be possible to go straight through in not less than 2 m. However yachts are recommended to pass outside keeping at least 3 cables E of the top of the island.

Ballyhalbert Bay is clean with a good temporary anchorage in W or SW wind a cable N of the pierhead in 5 m. The pier is just inside Burr Point and has a yellow diamond top on the new breakwater to W of pier. This small sheltered harbour dries out. **Facilities**. Water 100 m from pier. Good shop, petrol (open Sundays) ½ mile NW of pier. Phone further away in High St (2nd turn left). Pub a mile NW of pier.

Skullmartin Rock is 3 miles N of Burial Island and a mile offshore. It dries 1·2 m and the passage inside it is very foul. It is marked by a red mast with cage and flag topmark 11 m high. **Light Buoy**. Skullmartin Safe Water spherical buoy, L Fl 10 s, whistle, is moored 1½ miles ESE of the red mast. **Tidal streams** near the buoy: the flood runs SSE starting at +0540 Dover and the ebb starts NNW at −0035 Dover, max rate 1·2 kn at neaps, 2·3 kn at springs.

Ballywalter, a mile WNW of Skullmartin Rock, has a quay facing NW which dries. There is temporary anchorage off it with shelter in winds from S to NW. It is advisable to have chart 2156 as there are rocks near the pier and around the part of the bay NE of it. However it is quite clear to go straight in with the church spire in line with the pierhead bearing 272°; anchor 1½ cables E of the E corner of the pier in 4 or 5 m, sand. **Light**, on the NW end of the breakwater from a metal column 3 m high, Fl WRG 1·5 s, 7 M G 240° to 267°, W 267° to 277° shows the safe approach, R 277° to 314°. **Facilities**. There is a water tap on pier and a coin operated electricity supply half way along pier. Coast guard shed with equipment. Shops, hotel, pub and phone ¼ mile in from pier. Petrol ¼ mile S of road junction.

Coast. Between Ballywalter and Donaghadee there are rocks drying up to ¾ mile offshore for a mile N of Ballywalter and up to ½ mile offshore further NW. Give it a good berth by day and at night keep in the white sector of Donaghadee light (*see below*). There is a small drying harbour under construction at Millisle (1991).

Donaghadee Harbour (*see plan*). HW as Dover. Rise: 4·0–3·4–1·1–0·5 m. This is a small harbour formed by two massive piers. Heavy scend frequently sets into it. It is very congested and has been gradually silting, so now there is scarcely space for a visiting yacht to anchor. It can only be recommended for a temporary visit in the absence of scend when a yacht should be able to berth alongside the SE quay, or more

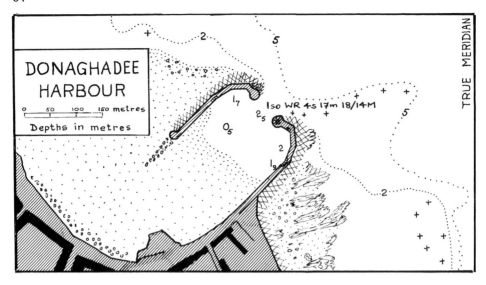

likely outside other vessels there, not further in than the steps about 60 m in from the pierhead. It is a very convenient place to go ashore for shopping as all provisions are available in the town close to the harbour. Report to the Harbour Master, who can also advise about taking a yacht into the marina (*see below*). **Light**. The white tower on the S pierhead shows Iso WR 4 s 17 m 18/14 M, R between 326° and the dangerous coast already described, W elsewhere. Siren 12 s, only if a vessel is expected.

Directions.—Dangers. A sunken ledge with less than 2 m in places extends 1½ cables ENE from the S pierhead. Coming from the S, do not approach within 2 cables until the landward end of the N pier is well open of the S pierhead, in fact nearer the N pierhead. There are similar rocks a cable N of the harbour; they are inside the normal approach from the sound with the entrance open and bearing more than 180°. By night keep the pierhead light bearing well between 180° and 240°. When approaching the entrance, which is only 45 m wide, allow particularly for the S-going tide; fortunately it runs N for 9 hours from −0300 Dover till +0600 Dover. It is of course preferable to motor in, but if you have to sail in beware of the blanketing effect of the piers. HM can be called on VHF 16 working 6 or 8. Telephone 882377. There are local engineers and electricians. Water on pier and fuel at harbour yard. Electricity available on S pier. Normal supplies in town—short walk. Hotels, restaurants and pubs. Places of interest include the Moat and Commons. Bus to Belfast. Taxis. Harbour dues £2.00 per day or £5.00 per week. One visitor's mooring—yellow buoy inside harbour mouth during summer season. Lifeboat.

Marina. This is completely sheltered in a small inshore harbour 3 cables S of Donaghadee Harbour. It is fairly fully occupied by local yachts and boats and is very well equipped. The approach is extremely narrow between drying rocks and is only deep enough at fairly high tide. Anyone cruising who wishes to leave his yacht there or put her in for any other reason should first apply for permission to do so and then arrange for a pilot from the marina to take his yacht in, and also in due course to take her out. It is a tricky entrance, new leading marks have been established. A pay telephone is available in office.

Donaghadee Sound (*see plan*), inside Copeland Island just N of Donaghadee, is the normal passage for yachts sailing along the coast. It is very satisfactory with a fair tide but quite possible to get through against the tide with a fair wind or a good engine.

Dangers—Buoys. There are many rocks 2 or 3 cables offshore between Donaghadee Harbour and the red perch off Foreland Point. Foreland Spit, with less than 1·8 m, is between the perch and Foreland red buoy, Fl R 6 s. Governor Rocks with 2·7 m are between the perch and Governor red buoy, Fl R 3 s. NE of Deputy green buoy, Fl G 2 s, Deputy Reefs have less than 1·8 m and beyond them over the deeper Magic Rocks there are heavy tide rips. There are a few rocks off the shore NW of Foreland Point. Off Carn Point, the SW point of Copeland Island, a drying reef extends 1½ cables S with Bush Rock 1 m high at the S end and rocks with less than 1·8 m almost ½ cable W and SE of Bush Rock. The very dangerous Rid Rock, awash, is just one cable S by E of Bush Rock.

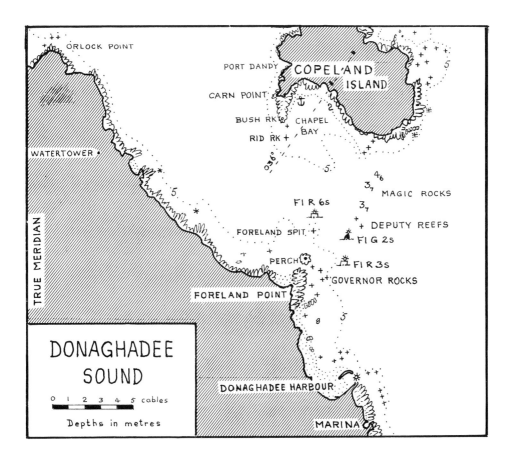

Tides in the sound change earlier than at sea, the flood starting SE at +0445 Dover and the ebb NW at −0115 Dover, max rate 4·5 kn, probably near the buoys; details on chart 3709. From Ballyferris Point 4 miles S of Donaghadee an eddy starts running N along the coast from about −0300 Dover till the ebb starts; it widens gradually to 1½ miles NE of Donaghadee where it runs out E of the sound and the Copelands.

Directions. Going NW through the sound leave the two red buoys to port and the green buoy to starboard; do not go SW of a line between the red buoys. Keeping the red buoys in line (which should be 147°–327°) leads well clear of the rocks off Donaghadee and also of Rid Rock off Copeland Island. NW of the buoys the coast as far as Orlock Point should be given a berth of 2 cables. Going SE against the tide it is best to enter the sound along this coast till it is necessary to turn out E towards Foreland red buoy. Beating through with the tide, which would be safest using chart 3709, there is good space for a tack NE of Foreland buoy, but if going SE with the tide be careful not to let Deputy buoy get in line with Governor buoy. The Coastguard Station on Orlock Point is to be relocated in Bangor Marina Buildings during 1991.

Anchorage. Chapel Bay (*see plan*) is well sheltered in W to NE winds. Great care must be taken to avoid Rid Rock. Approaching from the S keep Donaghadee lighthouse halfway between the two red buoys. Coming from the N keep these two buoys in line and turn in when the long grey cottage on the shore comes in line with the white cottage on the skyline, 036°. Anchor in the W half of the bay about a cable E of the outer HW rock on Carn Point in about 3 m, gravel and clay, not particularly good holding but out of the tide. If rowing in to land on the steps beside the grey cottage take care to avoid a rock which dries about ½ cable SW of these steps. There is a small jetty behind the steps.

Copeland Islands (*chart 3709 or 1753*) comprise Mew Island and Lighthouse Island which almost touch each other, and Copeland Island divided from them by Copeland Sound. The sound is navigable but not recommended as there are no marks to lead between the groups of rocks across its E end. The only guide to pass between them is to keep the red buoy outside bearing 101°. Unless passing 2 or more miles outside Mew Island yachts should go through Donaghadee Sound. Only pass close to Mew Island when the following races are not in operation, giving it a berth of at least 2 cables. Races extend N and S from up to ½ mile E of Mew Island. The N-going eddy (*see above*) meeting the S-going main stream causes the dangerous Ram Race from −0230 to +0015 Dover; it curves SSE and then S for 1½ miles. The N race takes place between +0330 and +0600 Dover and extends NE and then NW for almost 2 miles. **Mew Island Lighthouse** on the NE end of the island is a conspicuous 37 m high black tower with a white band and shows Fl (4) 30 s, 15 M. Diaphone (4) 30 s. Radiobeacon, *see Appendix 5*. (*see photo*)

Anchorages. A pleasant day can be spent in fine weather exploring the islands. Chapel Bay has already been described. The following three anchorages are only suitable for temporary use in settled conditions and chart 3709 is necessary. **Port Dandy** on the W side of Copeland Island is a useful though very restricted anchorage in E and SE winds. It is a small bay with a grey sandy beach. A reverse transit leading to it is the water tower S of Orlock Point in line with a white flat-topped cottage on the shore. Anchor just inside the arms of the bay in 4·5 m, out of the tide. The N side is nearly steep-to; some rocks extend a bit from the S side. Off the **N side of Copeland Island** between Bessy Point and Port Rammon is a pleasant anchorage in light S winds, out of the tide. This must not be approached from the E. Give Bessy Point a berth of at least 2 cables and then close the shore to 2 or 3 m and anchor. There are rocks off the inlet marked Port Rammon on the chart; if you open up its sandy beach you have gone too far SE. There is a well behind Port Rammon beach. **Lighthouse Island** is steep-to on its NE side at the entrance of the gut between it and Mew Island, off which there are some rocks. Anchor there in 5 or 5·6 m not more than ½ cable off Lighthouse Island with its N side bearing about W. There are two boat landings on the N and SW sides of Mew Island. Lighthouse Island has a bird observatory in the original buildings.

Belfast Lough, 6¾ miles wide at the entrance between Orlock Point on the S and Black Head on the N, is free of dangers in its navigable area which has an average depth of 11 m. The S shore is rocky and much indented but may be approached to within a few cables except off Orlock Point, about ½ mile NW of which are South Briggs rocks; a red buoy, Fl (2) R 10 s, is moored N of these rocks and yachts should pass outside it. **Tides**. In the middle of the outer half of the lough the streams are always less than 1 kn and are rotary in a clockwise direction; they run between 160° and 260° during the rising tide and between 330° and 080° during the falling tide. On the N side between Black Head and White Head there is hardly any stream. Along the whole shore SW of White Head and on the S shore SW of Grey Point the streams are very weak, the flood running in and the ebb out of the lough. Along the shore E of Grey Point it is also very weak but starts running W at half flood and E at half ebb.

Bangor (*plan on chart 1753*) is a well known sailing centre and the HQ of the Royal Ulster and Ballyholme Yacht Clubs, both of which have extensive premises and welcome visiting yachtsmen. Telephones: RUYC Bangor 270568 and 271467. RUYC has a permanent secretary, where there are showers, meals and bar. The town has excellent shops with all kinds of stores.

Ballyholme Bay was the principal yacht anchorage at Bangor and lies 1½ miles W of South Briggs buoy, however it has been superceded by the marina at Bangor (*see below*). It offers a good anchorage in 3·5 to 5·5 m in offshore winds but is very exposed to winds from NW to NE. Approaching from the E, Ballymacormick Point is foul and should be given a berth of at least 2 cables. Lukes Point on the W side of the bay is also foul and should be given a berth of 1 cable. There are two visitors' moorings in the bay, which may be used free of charge off the BYC premises on W side of the bay. At HW yachts drawing up to 1·8 m can be alongside the club wall in order to take fuel and water. There are two slips at which to land. Bangor Shipyard also has a patent slip and can handle large (21 m) vessels. All types of repairs. BYC offer showers, meals at weekend and bar in the evenings and weekend. RUYC—a large red brick building—is close by and also offers their similar facilities. VHF channel M. Supplies are all available in Bangor about ¾ M away. Number of ICC members live locally.

Bangor Bay, Marina and Harbour. The bay lies ½ M W of Ballyholme Bay. It now

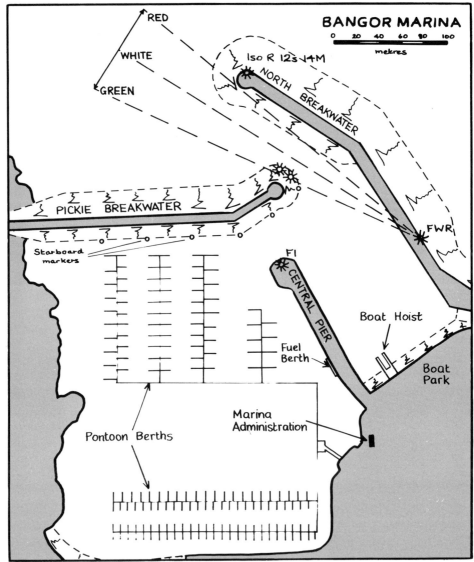

BANGOR MARINA

(Camper Nicholson)

has a large marina in the W side of the old harbour. The bay itself is exposed to winds from W through N to E and is not recommended for anchoring. Yachts may lie alongside the N breakwater, but are subject to the interest of the locals and visitors. The marina is sheltered by a new breakwater—Pickie and an extension of the old Central Pier. **Light** on the N breakwater Iso R 12 s 14 M. The marina has all facilities, including a travel hoist for 50 tons, all repairs, fuel 24 hours per day. VHF channel 37 and 80 c/s "Bangor Marina" or "Bangor Harbour" on channel 11. Telephone 0247-453297. Marina charge (1990) 85p per metre per day including VAT. Marina Manager and HM—Captain A. P. Jaggers. Bangor is a major holiday town with all its attendent features—hotels, pubs, restaurants, dance halls, etc. Good shops. Bus and rail connections to Belfast. Tourist office. Taxis. Inshore lifeboat. Note: Permanent marina buildings are under construction and will be in use by the end of 1991. They will also house the main Coastguard Station for Northern Ireland. **The Long Hole**, a pool immediately E of the harbour, offers complete shelter to small shallow draught boats which take the ground easily. It is only accessible around HW and should not be entered without a pilot who can be engaged at the harbour. (*see photo*)

Grey Point 2½ miles WNW of Bangor is a bluff point 23 m high. For a mile W of Bangor the shore should be given a berth of a cable; nearer Grey Point and between it and Cultra a berth of 4 cables is recommended to avoid foul ground. **Temporary anchorage** may be had in suitable weather off Helen's Bay immediately E of Grey Point.

Cultra, 2½ miles W of Grey Point, is the headquarters of the Royal North of Ireland YC. In offshore wind there is good anchorage in 3·5 to 4 m outside the yacht moorings, some 4 cables from the shore which is very shoal. In S winds there is less roll here than in Bangor but it is exposed from WSW through N to E. **Facilities**. Water and diesel are available, as are showers, bar and meals, during the summer months. More limited during winter. It is possible to lie alongside the club jetty at HW 3·3 m in order to take fuel and stores. Nearest good shops—Holywood—are about 1½ M away. Taxis are available. Small shop about ½ M. Boatyard and patent slip for 15 tons. Full-time secretary, telephone 0232-420841. Number of ICC members live locally.

Holywood. There is a drying anchorage off this town about 1M W of Cultra, but one must be prepared to take the ground near existing boats. Holywood YC have showers and a bar. The town has good shops, pubs and restaurants.

Belfast Harbour (*see plan*). Chart 1753 has a very much larger plan. HW −0015 Dover. Rise: 3·5–3·0–1·1–0·4 m. VHF Call 16, Work 08, 11, 12, 14. This is a very large commercial harbour and should not be visited unless in dire emergency as the new marinas at Bangor and Carrickfergus give very adequate shelter from all quarters, and all facilities. The following entry instructions are still included in case of such

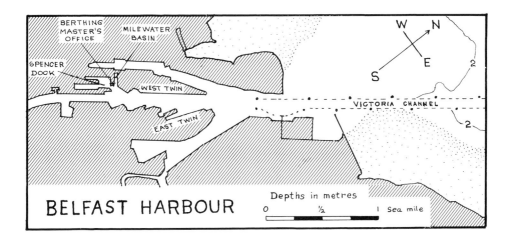

BELFAST HARBOUR

emergency. Yachts do not need to use the seaward part of the dredged channel which starts at a buoy between Carrickfergus and Grey Point but should enter it between the buoy and the beacon N of Cultra. Inside this buoy it is marked by pile beacons with lights, red and even numbers on the SE side, green and odd numbers on the NW side. It is very dangerous to leave the channel inside beacon No 12, the 3rd beacon on the port hand when entering. Go straight in between East Twin and West Twin and after passing the 200 tonne crane to starboard and then a light column, Fl (2) G 12 s, bear to starboard and go straight past the entrance of Milewater Basin into Spencer Dock. Tie up where directed by the Berthing Master at the office on the NW side of the dock entrance. **Belfast Harbour radio** maintains a 24 hour watch on VHF Channel 16 (working channel 12) and yachts with VHF should ask for permission to use the harbour before entering the channel. If intending to do so when in a previous port you should phone 234422. **All facilities** including a sailmaker are available in Belfast.

NW shore. The N point of Belfast Lough is Black Head which is steep-to and 62 m high with a prominent white **lighthouse**, Fl 3 s, 45 m, 17 M. **Whitehead town**, about a mile SSW of Black Head, is the headquarters of the Co Antrim YC and is only a temporary anchorage in offshore wind and settled weather. **Dangers**. Hailcock Rock which dries 0·9 m with other shallow rocks NE of it lies 1½ cables offshore and 2 cables ENE of the YC slip. A bit S of the slip between it and White Head there are more rocks, one with 0·3 m being ½ cable offshore. The anchorage off the slip, in 3 or 4 m, should therefore be approached heading W or NW. **Facilities**. Good shops, petrol, derv. Cloghan Jetty, S of White Head, is T shaped and 6½ cables long with Fl G 3 s lights on the ends of its long head; there is a green buoy, Fl G 3 s, ½ mile outside it, also a conical buoy Fl Y 10 s approximately 6 c SSW of the Jetty Head. SW of this is Kilroot jetty, 350 m long with a light Oc G 10 s on its outer end; ¾ mile W of the jetty Kilroot harbour reaches about the same distance offshore S of a 198 m high chimney. Between this harbour and Carrickfergus a drying shoal extends up to ½ mile out from the shore. Carrickfergus is described below. For two miles SW of it there are rocks on the sand a long way off the shore which should be given a berth of 3 cables. Beyond this, where the conspicuous obelisk on a hill bears around NNW, it is possible to anchor 2 cables off the shore in 2 m, well sheltered of course in NW wind. The North Belfast YC, about a mile SW of the little Green Islet, has a slip which is the only place for landing SW of Carrickfergus; the nearest shops are at Whiteabbey a mile away. This is about 2 miles NW of the RNIYC moorings at Cultra. Further SW there is plenty of anchorage space in between 2 and 3 m, but further offshore.

Carrickfergus Harbour (see plan). HW −0020 Dover. Rise: 3·2–2·7–0·9–0·3 m. Its position is mentioned above; it is 3 miles NW of Grey Point. It is easily recognised by the remarkable castle beside it. It normally provides adequate shelter in summer and is available to go ashore on the NW side of the lough. The harbour is tidal and is dredged along the W quay. In the dredged area and between the pierheads the depth is approximately 1·8 m. The approach is on a course of 347° with St Nicholas Church spire in the middle of the entrance; at night approach the FG light on the inner side of the harbour which bears 347° when halfway between the lights on the pierheads, which are Fl R 7½ s on the W pierhead and Fl G 7½ s on the E pierhead; the inner light will probably remain FG for the present. Yachts may be permitted to occupy a berth at the

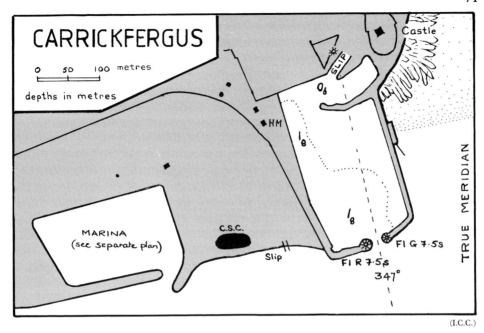

CARRICKFERGUS

0   50   100 metres

depths in metres

Castle

SLIP

0₆

HM

⁸⁄₈

MARINA
(see separate plan)

C.S.C.

Slip

⁸⁄₈

Fl G 7·5s

Fl R 7·5s

347°

TRUE MERIDIAN

(I.C.C.)

W pier but should not be left unattended. HM office is on the W pier (phone 62292—Hbr Security 62332 will relay a message); adjacent to it is the Ulster Sailing School. Belfast Pilot Station is on the E pier. Water obtainable on W pier. Yachts up to 1·5 m draught may dry out for repairs on the slipway with permission from the HM, Capt Heddlis. There is a boatyard capable of most yacht repairs. All stores obtainable in the town. Good road and rail communications to Belfast and Airports. Taxis.

Carrickfergus Marina (*see plan*) HW as Dover; Rise 2·9 m (9½ ft.) Sp: 1·8 m (6 ft.). Np: is situated on the Northern shore of Belfast Lough 330 m to the W of Carrickfergus Harbour. It is a purpose built Marina basin to accommodate 300 yachts behind rubble stone breakwaters and has largely taken over the requirement to enter Carrickfergus Harbour. The basin is dredged to give depths of 1·7 to 2·3 m at LAT. Manager's Office, Phone: 09603-66666. Carrick Sailing Club, Phone: 09603-51402 (limited food). VHF 16 and 37.

There is a red can buoy Fl R 10 s close W of Marina entrance.

The entrance to the Marina is situated at the E end of the basin and is open to the SW. The ends of the two breakwaters are marked with red and green beacons showing Qk Fl R and G. R not showing from 065° to 125°. A dredged entrance channel approximately 50 m wide, giving 2·3 m (7′6″) at LAT and marked by leading beacons on the breakwater 320°. Outside this channel other approaches to the marina have generally 1·7 m (5′6″) of water at LAT. On entering the Marina, visitors should check in at the Marina office (manned 24 hrs/day) which is situated at the head of the temporary E gangway, giving access to the pontoons.

Water and electricity are available at each berth. Carrickfergus is a good shopping town; stores of all kinds are available and there are several hotels and restaurants in the area. The Carrickfergus Sailing Club has its headquarters on the E side of the Marina.

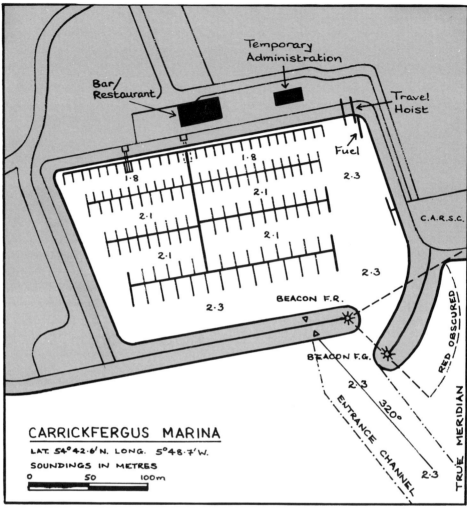

Temporary
Administration

Bar/
Restaurant

Travel
Hoist

Fuel

1·8   2·3

1·8

2·1

2·1   C.A.R.S.C.

2·1

2·1   2·1

2·3

2·1

BEACON F.R.   2·3

2·3

BEACON F.G.

CARRICKFERGUS   MARINA

LAT. 54°42·6'N. LONG. 5°48·7'W.

SOUNDINGS IN METRES

0   50   100m

ENTRANCE CHANNEL   2·3

320°   2·3

RED OBSCURED

TRUE MERIDIAN

(Carrickfergus B.C.)

In 1990 the following facilities are available—lavatories, showers, sail repairs, pontoon berths for 303 including 30 visitor berths, chandlery, fuel berth, boat and engine repairs, also very good cabin soft furnishing made to order; 30 ton travel hoist, and marine electrics servicing.

A new administration office, bar, restaurant, chandlery are under construction. Opening 1991.

Costs for visitors in 1991 expects to be 26p per ft. daily or £1.60 per ft. weekly or £4.00 monthly inc. VAT.

Carrickfergus is a very old town, with a well preserved Norman Castle—well worth a visit. Many local leisure pursuits. (*see photo*)

Coast. The E shore of the peninsula called Magee Island is steep-to for the 5 miles from Black Head to Isle of Muck, which is also steep-to on its E side. **Isle of Muck** is 1¼ cables off the shore to which it is joined by a narrow drying ridge of stones. There is a small temporary anchorage on either side of the ridge, in about 6 m on the SE side and 3·5 to 4 m on the NW side. At Portmuck (*see chart 1237*), 3 cables SW of the NW end of Muck, there is a small pier which dries; a drying spit extends ¾ cable NE of the pier. The coast NW of Muck has rocks close in and needs a berth of at least ½ cable as far as Skernaghan Point; this point (*see plan*) has a reef with a sunken rock outside it so it should be given a berth of at least 1½ cables when passing N of it.

Tides. In the middle of the North Channel the ebb starts flowing out NW at HW Dover and reaches 3½ kn at springs; the flood starts at +0600 Dover, max 4 kn. **Off Magee Island** the ebb starts 1¼ hours later than in the North Channel. Off Isle of Muck the streams are very strong, possibly up to 6 kn at springs. In the following description "N-going" and "S-going" means parallel to the shoreline. **At +0115 Dover** the main N-going ebb starts both off the peninsula and close inshore and continues thus till: **At +0300 Dover** a S-going eddy starts close inshore between Larne and Muck. The main stream and the stream inshore S of Muck still run N. This S-going eddy probably widens gradually and **At −0600 Dover** as counter-eddy starts running N inside it along the shore N of Muck. **At −0445 Dover** the S-going flood starts everywhere except along the shore N of Muck, where the new N-going eddy continues and runs on till it merges with the start of the ebb at +0115 Dover, but **At −0300 Dover** a N-going eddy starts running from Black Head to Muck. This eddy extends about 1½ miles offshore and causes a race off Muck and overfalls 1½ miles E of it where it meets the main flood stream; this continues till +0115 Dover when the eddy becomes part of the main N-going ebb, as above.

Hunter Rock, about 2¼ miles NNW of Isle of Muck, has a depth of 0·8 m and is steep-to all round. South Hunter buoy is a S Cardinal, Q (6) + LFl 15 s, Horn (3) 30 s. North Hunter buoy is a N Cardinal, Q. The R sector of Ferris Point lighthouse shows over the rock. There is magnetic disturbance in its vicinity.

The Maidens are two dangerous clusters of rocks mostly above water and separated by a clear channel a mile wide. They are within 4 miles of Ballygalley Head and their S end is 2¼ miles 015° from Hunter Rock. **The S Cluster** is composed of E and W Maiden rocks 7 and 9 m high and ½ mile apart. W Maiden is steep-to all round and has an unused stone lighthouse. E Maiden is very foul especially on its S side where a shallow reef with drying and above-water rocks runs out for 7 cables. The E Maiden lighthouse is a 23 m high white tower with a black band showing Fl (3) 20 s, 14 M; 14 m below this an auxiliary light Fl R 5 s is vis only between 142° and 182° over the N Cluster. **The N Cluster** forms a triangle up to 1½ miles N to NW of the E Maiden lighthouse. Highland Rock, the NE corner, dries 1·5 m and is marked by a 10 m high red mast with can topmark. Russel Rock, only 0·6 m above HW, is 6 cables W of Highland Rock. Allen Rock which dries 1·5 m lies 3 cables SE of Russel Rock. There are other rocks less than 2 m deep up to 3 cables ESE of Allen Rock.

Directions. A yacht under power or with a commanding breeze may pass safely between the two clusters of the Maidens with a fair tide (*see below*), but this has nothing to recommend it and it is far better to give the Maidens a very good berth, especially in poor visibility. Highland Rock is deceptively far N of the lighthouse. The S danger of the N Cluster is just a mile N of the W Maiden. To pass E of the rocks, E Maiden should not be brought to bear less than 206° while within 2 miles of it or more than 332° while within 1 mile of it. **Tides**. Between and around the Maidens the flood starts at +0610 Dover and runs ESE and the ebb starts at −0015 Dover and runs WNW. During the flood an eddy runs NW towards the S Cluster and during the ebb an eddy runs SE towards it.

Larne Harbour (*see plan*). HW −0100 Dover. Rise 2·8–2·5–0·8–0·4 m. VHF Call 16, Work 14. Call sign "Larne Harbour". This is a very busy commercial port occupying the ¾ mile long entrance to Larne Lough with 34 scheduled movements of ferries during each 24 hours, 7 days a week. It can be safely entered by day or night but yachts must keep clear of the ships entering and leaving. Much of the W side consists of the quays, which are not available for yachts. Beyond them off Curran Point there is a defined area fully occupied by local yachts. On the E side, off Ballylumford power

LARNE LOUGH
ENTRANCE

Depths in metres

stations, there is a large tanker jetty and further in an L-shaped wharf. N of the tanker
jetty there is a small boat harbour.

Tidal Streams are listed in detail on chart 1237. N of Barr Point the flood runs SE but
W of Barr Point it runs SSW towards the entrance. In the harbour channel the flood and
the ebb start at about LW and HW Dover, max rate 1·5 kn. Off Ballylumford L-shaped
wharf the flood starts about −0545 Dover but at −0215 Dover a weak eddy starts
running N till HW Dover when the ebb turns NW, max rate 1·1 kn. Further in there is
little stream.

Lights (*see plan for positions*). **Chaine Tower**, 24 m high, shows Iso WR 5 s, 11 M,
W 230°–240° leading S of Hunter Rock and N of Barr Point, R 240°—Magee shore.
Ferris Point light, on top of a watchroom on a white tower, shows Iso WRG 10 s, 18 m
17–13 M, W 345°–119°, G 119°–154°, W 154°–201°, R 201°–223° over Hunter Rock.
Barr Point has a red framework tower, Diaphone 30 s. **The leading lights** are on
structures on the S side of the lough; they show Oc 4 s 8 M between 179° and 189°, and
in line 184° lead towards and into the harbour. **Buoys.** No 1 E Cardinal buoy, Q Fl (3)
10 s. No 3 Green buoy, Fl (2) G 6 s. Nos 5 and 7 Green buoys, Q G. **Two red pile
beacons** mark the E side of the channel, No 2, Fl R 3 s and No. 4, Fl (2) R 6 s. The
other lights on the piers and jetty on the E side are 2FR (vert) except out the corner of
the L-wharf which is Oc R 10 s. Both lights on the W side quays are 2FG (vert).

Directions. Approaching from the E give Skernaghan Point a berth of 2 cables and
Barr and Ferris Points a berth of one cable. Coming from the N leave No 3 green buoy to
starboard and do not go W of a line between it and the quays. Approaching either way it
is best to head next for No 2 red beacon and leave it and No 4 fairly close to port. Then if
going towards Curran Point head across, or if going into the lough pass between the
jetty and No 7 green buoy and keep a cable off the NE shore all the way down to
Ballydowan anchorage.

Larne Lough (chart 1237 is useful but not essential). The lough is about a mile wide
for the first two miles, then it gets much narrower and mostly dries. A lot of the SW half
of the first two miles also dries. An area immediately S of the centre of the compass rose
on chart 1237 is going to be made into an island. Though not very snug the lough is a
safe place with plenty of room to anchor. Except for the first mile of the channel off the
NE shore it is mostly fairly shallow. Commercial traffic uses all the channels so in any
anchorage a riding light should be shown.

Anchorages

Brown's Bay, E of Barr Point outside the lough, is a good anchorage in winds
between SE and SW when it is the best place to stop for the night provided the wind is
not likely to veer NW. A depth between 2 and 4 m can be found fairly close to either
side of the bay or offshore in the middle, the head of the bay being shoal. Landing at SW
corner. Shop, PO, bus.

Near the port. The closest approved area for yachts is NW of a line from from Curran
Point to No 5 buoy, SW of a line from No 5 buoy to the S end of the ferry quays, and at
least 45 m away from the buoy. This space is so congested by local boats that a visitor

cannot really anchor within its limits; if a mooring were vacant a small yacht might pick it up and check ashore whether she might be left there. Another permitted anchorage is S of a line between the SE end of Ballylumford wharf and the beacon about 1¼ cables S of No 5 buoy, where there are anchors on the plan, E and W of which it is shallow. Its only advantage is that it is not too far from the landing place, but the bottom is usually thick with seaweed and the tide is fairly strong. **Alternatively**, near HW a yacht might berth alongside Wymers pier the end of which just dries; it is possible to dry out on either side of it if desired. **Facilities**. Landing at the East Antrim BC slip or at Wymers pier. Wymers pier has a fresh water tap and a hose is available. The EABC patent slip can haul vessels up to 150 tonnes. The club, which is used Tuesday, Thursday evenings and Saturday and Sunday, can usually arrange a spare mooring. Phone 0574-77204. Their VHF 16 is manned during the season on these days. Limited bar and meals. Showers. Harbour office, Customs, PO and bus terminus almost ½ mile distant at entrance to the docks. Petrol and all stores in Larne town, a short bus ride. Larne Harbour, VHF Channel 16, Work 12, is manned night and day. Larne port information service telephone 0574-74085. Cranes are available for commercial use only. A passenger ferry crosses between Chaine Quay and Magee shore every ½ hour till about 1800. **Ballylumford Harbour**, immediately S of the ferry quay on Magee shore, is a small boat harbour 60 × 40 m with least depth 0·6 m. It is pretty full in summer, but if there were room it would be a very handy place for a small shallow-draught yacht if a visit to Larne town were desired.

Anchorages inside the lough. **Yellow Stone**, painted occasionally, is on the edge of the NE shore a cable E of the L-shaped wharf. The anchorage, SW of the stone or further SE, is the traditional one for cruisers, perfectly suitable for spending a night and the only place inside the lough easily accessible in the dark. The depth is 3 m when the outer side of the wharf is a little open. There is some tidal stream. **Ballydowan** is the local name of the anchorage a mile SE of Yellow Stone where there are yachts moored outside a shallow bay off a ruined lime kiln. **Danger**. There is a sunken schooner ¾ cable off the shore of the bay and 1¼ cables SE of the NW tip of the bay; its masts no longer show at HW. There is good holding and very little tide-flow. It is best to anchor NW of the moored boats about ½ cable offshore in 2 to 3 m. Anywhere beyond this anchorage the lough is quite shallow, less than 1 m in places, so most yachts should only go further in within 3 hours of HW. About 2 cables SW of the S point of **Millbay** (which is ½ mile SE of Ballydowan) there is an area 2 m deep where boats sometimes anchor; there is a jetty in Millbay, a bay which dries and where the chart indicates stones, so it should only be approached towards HW. On the S side of the lough, just NW of the conspicuous cement factory, is **Magheramorne Bay** where a lot of local boats and yachts are moored. Head across towards it from the NE side of the lough when the bay bears about 170°. At present most yachts should not cross the lough much below half tide as there are 0·8 m depths here and there; however it is now proposed to dredge a 4 m deep channel reaching across 353° from the cement works harbour. Leading lights established into quay. Front OcR 7 s 9 m Rear Oc R 12 s 12 m. Anchor N of the moored boats, choosing a suitable depth which can vary rather suddenly because the mud is dredged out for making cement. It is very well sheltered except in N winds. Land at the wooden jetty with two triangular topmarks. Concrete slipway. Clubhouse up the road from the shore with showers and phone. Buses to Larne (3 miles) and Belfast.

Coast. Between Larne and Fair Head much of the coast is very clean. Shallow rocks extend up to a cable in a few places and a berth of 2 cables is safe everywhere. The only offshore danger is The Maidens, already described.

Tides. The main stream runs past Garron Point and Torr Head at up to 5 kn, the S-going flood starting at +0600 Dover and the N-going ebb at HW Dover. Between Ballygalley Head and Garron Point eddies extend up to ½ mile offshore during the second half of both main flood and ebb; so along this shore the S-going stream starts at +0300 Dover and the N-going stream at −0300 Dover. Between Garron Point and Cushendun Bay the eddy during the second half of the main ebb runs S from Cushendun to off Cushendall, then across Red Bay and E along the S shore to Garron Point; a weaker eddy runs the other way during the second half of the main flood. There is hardly any stream off the head of Red Bay. As shown on chart 2199 there is a strong local eddy ¾ mile NE of Tornamoney Point where the stream runs S for 4 hrs, max 3 kn, starting +0540 Dover, and then runs N for 8¼ hrs, max 4 kn, starting −0240 Dover. Between Torr Head and Fair Head there is an eddy during the second half of the flood; the SE stream runs about 2½ hrs, starting +0600 Dover, and the NW stream runs about 10 hrs starting weakly at −0400 Dover but soon increasing and by −0200 extending across the E entrance of Rathlin Sound.

Anchorages. There is only Carnlough harbour which is best approached towards HW. Mosts of the rest of the bays are only temporary anchorages in offshore wind and calm sea. **Ballygalley Bay** is clean with 4 or 5 m 1½ cables offshore and a possible anchorage in W or SW wind, but Brown's Bay 4 miles SE of it is much preferable (*see above*). **Glenarm Bay** is 9 miles from Larne and just W of Path Head which rises steeply to 137 m. it is also sheltered in W and SW winds. Anchor in 2 to 4 m due N of the harbour, which dries completely. **Carnlough Bay** is just NW of Glenarm; close off Straidkilly Point between the bays is the small Black Rock which never covers. There are fish farms about a mile offshore in an E direction. Keep a good lookout if approaching from the S. The head of Carnlough Bay is shallow and the place yachts usually anchor, in suitable weather, is one cable off the harbour at the N end of the bay.

Carnlough Harbour (*see plan*). HW −0010. Rise (HW) about: 1·8–1·5 m. This has always been a popular place for yachts to spend a night as it is the only sheltered harbour between Larne and Portrush. The new plan shows Carnlough Harbour, the entrance channel has been dredged to 2 m, which is to be redredged at the start of each season, however, it is inclined to silt up over the summer. Enter on a bearing of 310° accurately; there are lights on each pier, the entrance is 18·5 m wide. Do not enter with winds onshore above Force 6. Turn to port once inside, there are berths for visiting yachts or tie up to N breakwater as far up as arrow. A slip for dinghies is in the starboard spur. **Facilities**: PO, food, hotel, several small cafes, fuel, gas and water all near quay. Small shops. Bus to Larne. Hull repairs—contact Red Bay Boatyard Co, Cushendall. Engineers and electricians—A. McCormack (telephone 88531) in Carnlough. Tourist representative in PO. Good base from which to explore the Glens of Antrim. Taxis. The Harbour Authority is Larne Borough Council. Harbour Master: Mr Linton who lives at Glenarm, telephone 0574-841486. Charges: Up to 5 m £2.10 per week; over 5 m and under 10 m £3.60 per week; over 10 m £5.00 per wek (1991). (*see photo*)

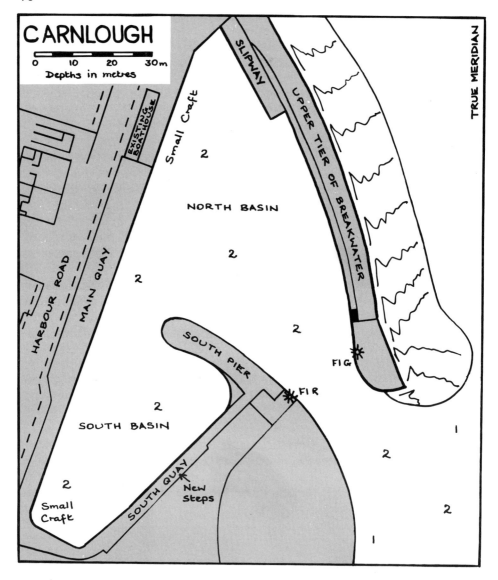

CARNLOUGH

0 10 20 30 m
Depths in metres

SLIPWAY

UPPER TIER OF BREAKWATER

TRUE MERIDIAN

EXISTING BOATHOUSE

Small Craft

2

NORTH BASIN

2

HARBOUR ROAD

MAIN QUAY

2

2

2

SOUTH PIER

FIG

FIR

2

SOUTH BASIN

1

2

SOUTH QUAY

New Steps

2

Small Craft

1

2

2

Red Bay. HW −0015 Dover. Rise: 1·6–1·5–0·3–0·2 m. This fairly deep bay is quite open to N and E but provides the best anchorages on this part of the coast, out of the tide, and safe in winds between SE and NW. Even in moderate S or SW winds there can be fierce squalls off the hills or down the glen, but the holding is reliable. Approaching from S keep 2 cables off Garron Point and the shore W of it where, as well as a couple of rocks, there are two ruined piers. Light established on Glenariff pier Fl 3 s 10 m 5 M. In S winds the best anchorage is in the S corner of the bay. The inner ruined pier extends 110 m off the shore ½ a mile from the head of the bay; E of it there is some tidal stream. Go in past this pier and anchor 2 cables off a white stone arch on the shore, depth 3 or 4 m. Yachts have ridden out a SE gale here. In W or NW winds anchor S of the small pier ½ mile NE of Waterfoot village, as close in as draught permits, depth 2 to 5 m. There is about 2 m alongside the outer part of the pier which is of open timber construction, the inner part being stone. Boats lie here all summer on moorings with stern warps to the pier, though in E wind it gives no protection from swell. Approaching from seaward the pier may be difficult to pick out and is best identified by getting it in line 255° with Lurigethan, a remarkable 350 m high spur with flat top and steep sides. **Facilities.** Some stores at Waterfoot. At Cushendall, a mile N of the pier, more shops, garage, hotel, hospital, but no shelter or landing facilities except a beach.

Cushendun Bay, 5 miles NW of Garron Point, afford temporary anchorage in fine weather off the hotel at the S end of the bay in 9 m, or 3·7 m fairly close in. Do not anchor more than a cable from the S end of the bay as the rest of it has a foul bottom and there is a wreck 2 cables offshore just N of the centre of the bay. Small local boats drawing 0·5 m can cross the river bar at HW and dry out on a convenient beach just below the road bridge. Hotel and shops. **Torr Head**, almost 5 miles N of Cushendun, has an ex-CG watch house on its 67 m high summit. In calm conditions it is possible to anchor just S of the head below the ex-CG house. Landing at a slip protected by a small breakwater; it has a salmon station and a power winch. **Murlough Bay** is immediately W of Ruebane Point, which is about 1½ miles NW of Torr head. At LW a sandy beach shows and at its W end there is a long cottage (occupied occasionally by holiday-makers) with a small boathouse to the right of it and a road leading up NW from the shore. The boathouse slip, which has a winch, gets some protection from the rocks which mark the W end of the bay. In offshore wind there is a possible anchorage SE of the outer rock, in about 2·5 m on clean sand and out of the main tide. A small yacht might find some shelter in light N winds S of this rock in 1·8 m. Inshore of the rock it almost dries. Beware of salmon nets.

Fair Head, the NE corner of Ireland 3 miles NW of Torr Point, is a magnificent headland 190 m high and of very distinctive shape. Its top is flat and surrounded by a vertical cliff which drops 90 m and from which an even 30° slope of boulders runs down to the sea. Its contour is almost identical as you gradually alter course 45° around it. It is steep-to all round. (*see photo*)

COASTAL SCENERY

From seaward the whole coast of Ireland is beautiful. In the north, beautiful beaches are backed by green fields and distant views of mountains; the headlands are bold and rocky. Donegal and Dundrum Bay and the Portrush areas sport vast uncluttered beaches. The Giant's Causeway is world famous and the aspect from the sea is breathtaking. There are cliffs and headlands in great variety, and often on a majestic scale, with high mountains beyond them. Offshore, in many places, there are spectacular rocks and islands; there are golden sands and picturesque anchorages. The colouring in sunlight is superb.

It is impossible to illustrate all this on 16 pages, but it is hoped that the photographs which follow of just a few of the harbours, bays and rocks will suffice to give the reader some idea of what he may expect and of the local craft he may see.

Credits for the use of photographs appear overleaf.

PHOTOGRAPHS

The photographs which follow are arranged in geographical order in which the subjects occur in the book. The list gives the page on which the place is described.

Number	*Subject*	*Photograph*
1	Wicklow Harbour	*Rex Roberts, ABIPP*
2	Malahide Inlet	*Rex Roberts, ABIPP*
3	Dun Laoghaire	*Rex Roberts, ABIPP*
4	Howth	*Rex Roberts, ABIPP*
5	Balbriggan	*Rex Roberts, ABIPP*
6	Rockabill Light	*Ronan Beirne*
7	Haulbowline Light	*W. Nixon*
8	Kilkeel	*Brian Black*
9	Ardglass	*Brian Black*
10	Ringhaddy	*W. Nixon*
11	Strangford Village	*Brian Black*
12	Ballydorn	*W. Nixon*
13	Audley's Roads	*Brian Black*
14	Mew Island	*W. Nixon*
15	Carrickfergus	*B. Black*
16	Bangor	*B. Black*
17	Carnlough	*W. Nixon*
18	Fair Head	*Tony Clarke*
19	Church Bay	*W. Nixon*
20	Portrush	*B. Black*
21	Portstewart	*J. R. Bainbridge*
22	Portmore	*W. Nixon*
23	Dunree Head	*W. Nixon*
24	Camusmore Bay	*W. Nixon*
25	Fanny's Bay	*Anne Woulfe Flanagan*

ERRATUM

Photograph No. 14

Change caption to:

Maidens Lighthouse,
just north of Larne.

1. *Above:* **Wicklow Harbour** showing the river. The anchorage is to the left and out of picture.

2. *Below:* **Malahide Inlet** with Howth in the background.

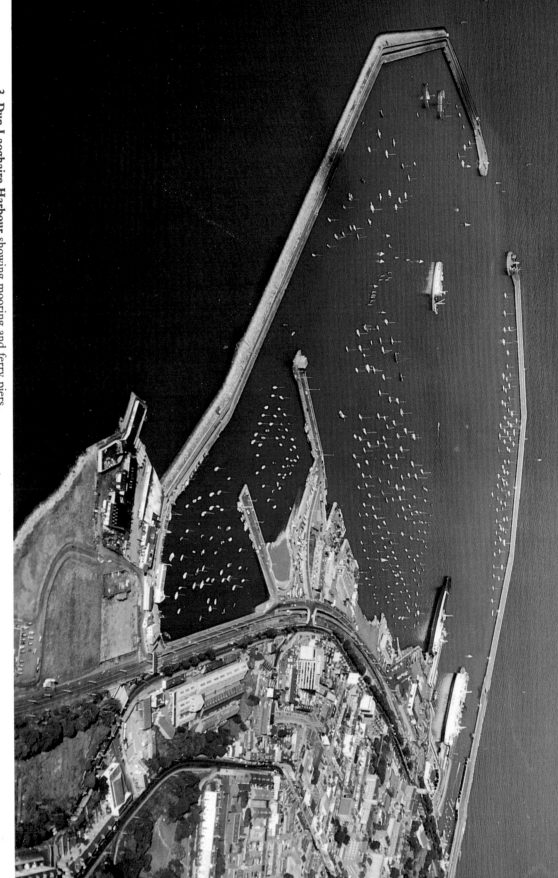

3. Dun Laoghaire Harbour showing mooring and ferry piers.

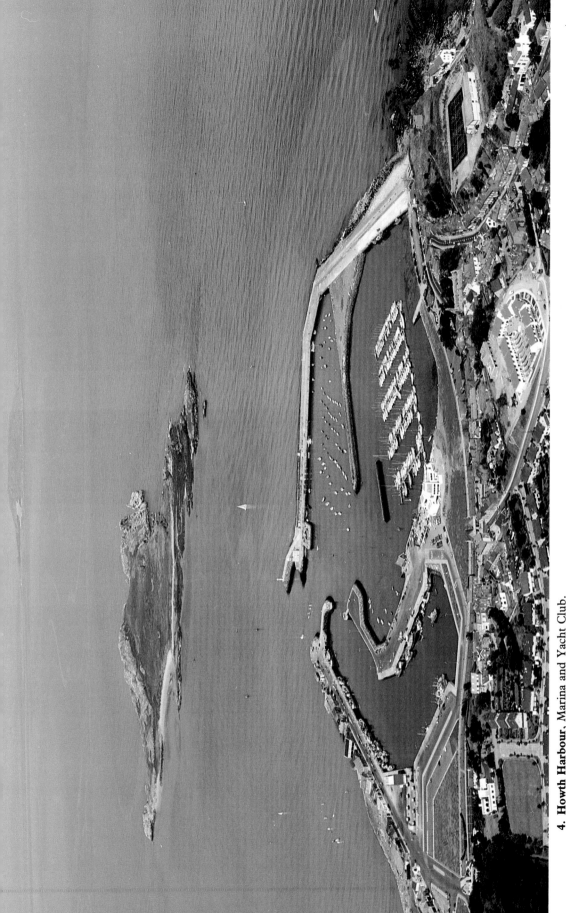

4. **Howth Harbour, Marina and Yacht Club.**

5. *Above:* **Balbriggan.**

6. *Below:* **Rockabill** from the S.

7. *Above:* **Haulbowline Light** at the entrance to Carlingford Lough.

8. *Below:* **Kilkeel Harbour** with fishing boats at weekend.

9. *Above:* **Ardglass Harbour** from S.

10. *Below:* **Ringhaddy Sound,** Strangford Lough.

11. Strangford Village with top end of Audley's Roads in background.

12. *Below:* **Ballydorn** – Down Cruising Club H.Q. in the Lightship.

13. **Audley's Roads** at the top of the entrance to Strangford Lough.

14. *Above:* **Mew Island Light** – one of the most powerful in the U.K.

15. *Below:* **Carrickfergus Marina** adjacent to the Harbour and Castle.

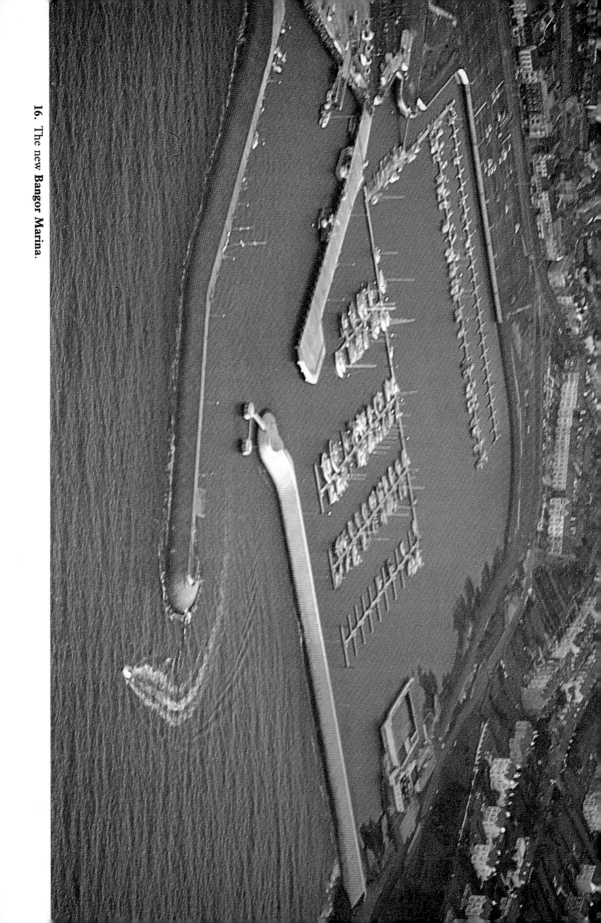

16. The new **Bangor Marina**.

17. **Carnlough Harbour** – there is always room!

18. *Above:* **Fair Head**.

19. *Below:* The new harbour at **Church Bay – Rathlin**.

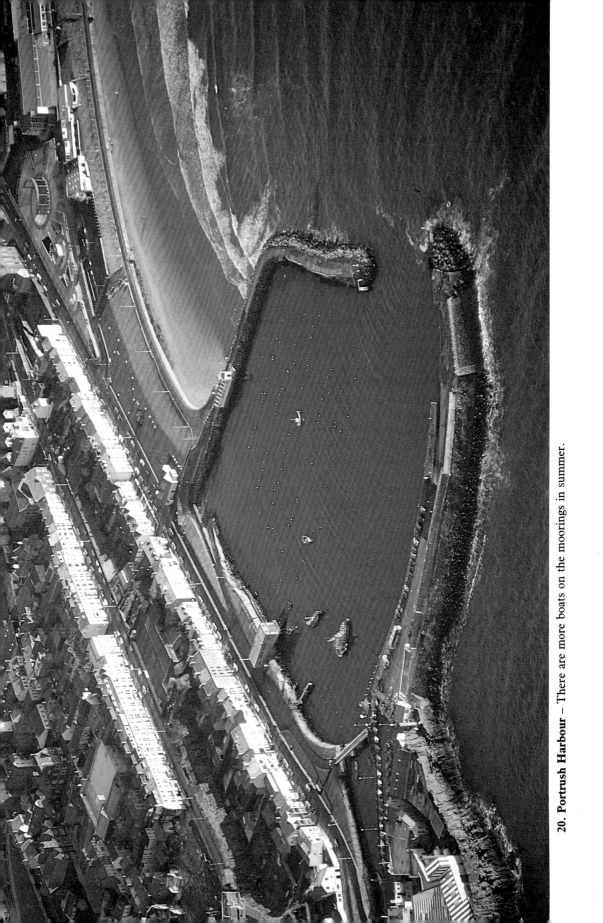

20. **Portrush Harbour** – There are more boats on the moorings in summer.

21. *Above:* **Portstewart Harbour.**

22. *Below:* **Portmore – Inishtrahull.**

23. *Above:* **Dunree Head – Lough Swilly.**

24. *Below:* **Camusmore Bay – Tory Island.**

25. **Fanny's Bay** at entrance to Mulroy Bay.

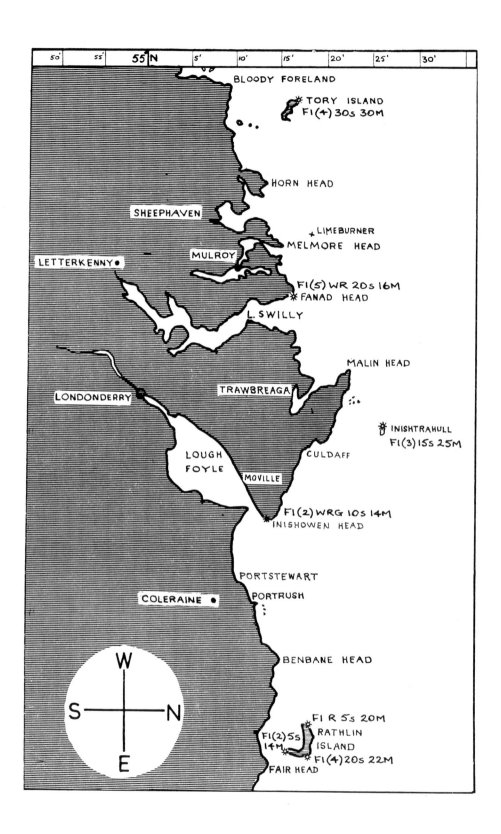

CHAPTER IV

Fair Head to Bloody Foreland

Charts. (*see Appendix I*) 2798 and 2811 cover the coast as far as Horn Head so the smaller scale 2723 is not needed if 2752 which includes Tory is carried. Yachts are also advised to have 2699 Sheep Haven and Mulroy, 2697 Lough Swilly, and 2499 Lough Foyle. 49 Portrush is not necessary.

General. The N coast is about 80 miles long with a great variety of headlands, cliffs, bays and inlets. It includes half a dozen anchorages secure against all summer winds: Portrush, the River Bann, Culmore (Lough Foyle), Fahan (Lough Swilly), Fannys Bay (Mulroy) and Downings (Sheep Haven). Many other interesting anchorages are available according to weather. Yachts sailing out W from the North Channel can have pretty tough beating against the predominant W wind, and in fresh onshore wind some anchorages are not accessible, but SW and S winds are quite frequent and then it is a most delightful coast to cruise along. Swell is much more prevalent W of Malin than E of it where the influence of the tide can kill it quickly. But between Rathlin and Inishowen Head a heavy swell at times accompanies the turning of the tide to the E; this subsides or disappears when the tide turns W. Fog is rare, on average less than one day per month, except in Rathlin Sound where it is not uncommon in summer. For crossing to Scotland see *Chapter V*.

Tides. The time of HW varies by only 1½ hours along the coast, the W parts being the earliest. HW at inland places such as Londonderry and Milford is of course later than on the coast. MHWS varies from a mere 1 m at Ballycastle to 3·9 m at Mulroy Bar. The tidal streams are strong near Fair Head but get progressively weaker further W. Maximum spring rate in Rathlin Sound is 6 kn, in Inishtrahull Sound 4 km and in Tory Sound only 2 kn. Of the three sounds Inishtrahull is the worst and can produce a steep and dangerous sea very quickly indeed when the tide turns against the wind; Rathlin can be pretty bad too. But even in W or NW wind up to Force 5 a well-found yacht should have no difficulty in going through either with a fair tide.

The period and direction of tidal streams is shown clearly in Admiralty Tidal Atlas No. 218. The table on page 84 gives the approximate directions of the streams as shown on the Atlas. When the tide changes W of Malin Head at −0430 and +0200 Dover it is in fact the beginning of an eddy which at first runs only within a mile of the coast but extends gradually seaward ending as part of the main tidal stream. There are tidal chartlets for Rathlin Sound overleaf and from Foyle to Swilly on pages 100 and 101.

It can be seen that a yacht coming in from the W with a fair wind and passing Bloody Foreland at +0230 Dover would probably have 10 hours of continuous fair tide. Likewise a yacht reaching to the W and leaving Rathlin at HW Dover should get to Malin Head before the tide turns and then have only 2 or 3 hours of foul or slack tide before picking up a further 6 hours of W-going tide. The ideal time to pass W through

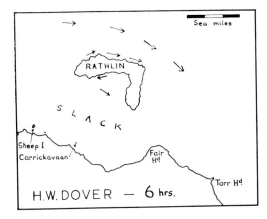

Sea miles

RATHLIN

SLACK

Sheep I
Carrickavaan

Fair Hd

Torr Hd

H.W. DOVER — 6 hrs.

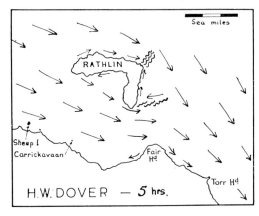

Sea miles

RATHLIN

Sheep I
Carrickavaan

Fair Hd

Torr Hd

H.W. DOVER — 5 hrs.

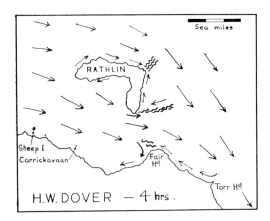

Sea miles

RATHLIN

Sheep I
Carrickavaan

Fair Hd

Torr Hd

H.W. DOVER — 4 hrs.

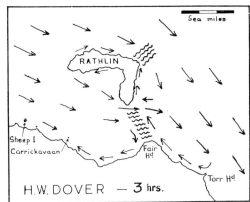

Sea miles

RATHLIN

Sheep I
Carrickavaan

Fair Hd

Torr Hd

H.W. DOVER — 3 hrs.

N.W.-going eddy extends from cliffs out as
far as Carrickavaan.

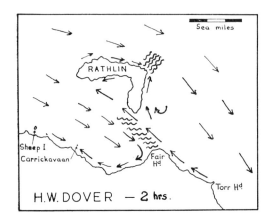

Sea miles

RATHLIN

Sheep I
Carrickavaan

Fair Hd

Torr Hd

H.W. DOVER — 2 hrs.

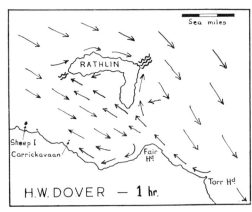

Sea miles

RATHLIN

Sheep I
Carrickavaan

Fair Hd

Torr Hd

H.W. DOVER — 1 hr.

83

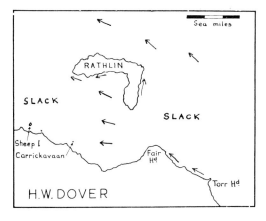

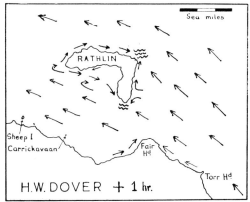

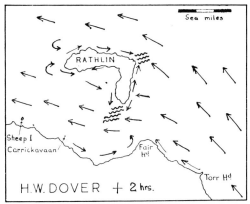

Slough-na-more is dangerous from Dover + 01.30 to Dover + 02.30

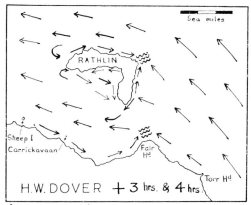

Streams and eddies run strongest at Dover + 3.

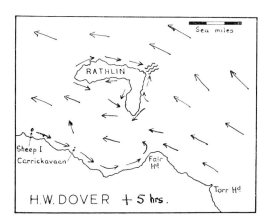

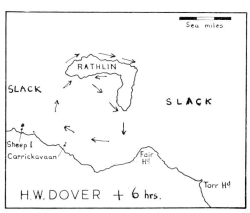

Rathlin Sound is +0330 Dover when the most turbulent 2 hours of tide there are over and this is just when a yacht might get there when making a fair-tide passage from Carnlough to Portrush. Voyaging from Portrush to Belfast you should leave at +0500 Dover, that is −0300 local HW. Quite good progress can be made by keeping inshore against the last half of the W-going stream and you should be able to get to Rathlin at LW Dover when there will be 6 hours of strong fair tide to take you through the sound and on down the North Channel. If you did not leave Portrush till local HW when the main tide had turned in your favour you would only have 5 hours of fair tide because S of Fair Head the tide turns an hour earlier than off the North Coast. This would scarcely give you time to get through the part of the North Channel where the tide runs strongest and you might if unlucky get swept back into Rathlin Sound. (*see photo*)

If working a foul tide along the E part of the coast it is worth remembering that the tides are much weaker between Ramore Head (Portrush) and Inishowen Head than elsewhere and that there is a useful eddy on both ebb and flood between Ramore Head and Barmouth, the River Bann entrance.

Rathlin Sound between Rathlin Island and the mainland is 2 to 3 miles wide and the normal approach to the N coast. Fair Head is quite clean to within a few metres of the boulders but between the head and Ballycastle the shore should not be approached closer than 2 cables as it is much subject to ground-swell and there are rocks close in. **Danger.** Carrickmannanon is the only offlying sunken rock in the sound. It is nearly always breaking and dries 0·3 m. It lies 3 cables NE of Kinbane Head and is easily avoided by keeping Bengore Head open between Ballintoy Point and Sheep Island, which leads ½ mile outside it. The tidal streams set with full force on this rock creating powerful eddies in its lee so it should be given a wide berth, particularly by sailing craft in light weather. Coasters regularly pass inside it and a line for this is to keep the N point of Carrickarade touching the S side of Sheep Island. Sheep Island Sound at the W end of Rathlin Sound is very shoal so yachts should always pass outside the island. On the shore inside the sound there is a white tower almost as high as the cliff behind it.

Tidal streams. The tides in Rathlin Sound are strong with several eddies. The excellent description in the Irish Coast Pilot should be studied by anyone making a stop in the area. The chartlets portray this information visually. For a passage through it is sufficient to know that the main stream in the centre of the sound runs W for 5 hours starting at HW Dover and runs E from −0530 to −0030 Dover. If going W it is best to pass through on the second half of the W-going tide and if going E on the first half of the

Tidal Stream Directions	Hours before HW Dover						Hours after HW Dover					
	5½	4½	3½	2½	1½	½	1	2	3	4	5	6
Rathlin to Malin Hd	Slack	——————— ESE ———————					——————— WNW ———————					
Malin Head to Bloody Foreland—Inshore	ENE		Slack	——— WSW ———					——— ENE ———			
Malin Head to Horn Head—Offshore	ENE	E	SE	Slack	SW		W		——— Slack ———			
North of Tory Island	E		SE	—— SW ——			W	WNW	N	NE	ENE	

E-going tide. Slough-na-more, the overfall SW of Rue Point, is dangerous from +0100 to +0300 Dover, otherwise the sound should not cause a well-found yacht any difficulty up to Force 4 or 5. It is essential to have a fair tide as the max rate is 6 kn Sp and 4 kn Np. The roughest water is usually between Fair Head and Torr Head.

Ballycastle. HW Sp −0445 Dover, HW Np −0200 Dover. Rise: 1·2–1·1–0·7– 0·2 m. This popular holiday town in the bay opposite Rathlin has a small pier running out NE which provides no shelter from the swell and is 2·5 m deep along its outer 11 m. Also there is now a new ferry pier about 100 m to the W of the old pier. Anchor 50 to 100 m off the pier, 5 m, sand, sheltered from W through S to ENE but liable to sudden swell, see *Church Bay* paragraph below. Good small hotels, shops and garages. EC Wed. **Light**, on high iron beacon on the pierhead, Fl R 9 s, 3 m 2 M.

Rathlin Island. Time and rise of tide are as at Ballycastle but both are irregular. The island is L-shaped and its W leg is surrounded by cliffs 60 to 120 m high. Population about 100. Telephone, PO, small general shop and pub. Water from a spring beside the Manor House in Church Bay. Only private stocks of petrol. There is a very large seabird nesting site below the Bull lighthouse.

Lights, shown on each of the three points. **Rue Point**: Fl (2) 5 s, 16 m, 11 M from a white tower with two black bands. **Rathlin West** (The Bull): Fl R 5 s, 62 m, 19 M from a lantern beside the base of a white tower 18 m high situated halfway down the cliff. Shore to 212° Red, 212° to Shore W. Diaphone (4) 60 s. Fog Det Lt. **Rathlin East** (Altacarry Head): Fl (4) 20 s, 74 m, 20 M from a white tower with black band 27 m high. Radiobeacon.

Anchorages
Church Bay (*see plan*) provides shelter in winds between NW and SSE through E. There is a large wreck in the middle of the bay a mile out from the harbour. There is usually 5 m over it but sometimes less, so yachts should keep well clear of it. A S Cardinal buoy lies 1½ cables SE of it. Approaching from the S either leave the buoy to port or if wishing to pass S and W of the wreck keep Rue Point open till Altacarry light disappears behind the high ground W of it, then steer in keeping it hidden. The best anchorage is a cable W of Sheephouse pier, or alternatively 70 m W of it, in about 5 m, good holding. The pier is convenient for landing. Approach and cross the Bow. It is not on the centre line of the lane running down to the centre of the beach at the harbour but very slightly to port (N) of the left hand (N) wall of this lane and keep on this line until just about half way from the Bow to the harbour wall on the port hand steering nothing to starboard (the ends of this semicircular reef can be seen at the shore on either hand).

Immediately alter course for a point about 1·5 m off the end of the pier on the port hand (the N pier) and keep this course until close to the pierhead, then alter hard to port and lie alongside the pier or another boat; there is little or no rounding up space inside the pier as only a narrow strip has been blasted and dredged out of the rock bottom to give a little over 1·5 m at low water (when there is almost 1·5 m at the Bow).

On leaving, steer from 1·5 m off the pierhead so as to arrive on the line just N of the near wall of the lane (see above) at about the halfway point to the Bow steering nothing to port, and then come out on this line (the reciprocal of the approach), until well

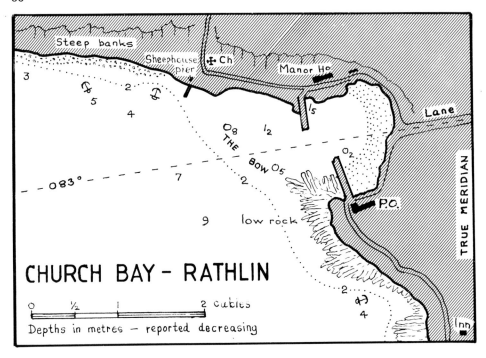

Steep banks

Sheephouse pier ✝ Ch

Manor Hᵒ

Lane

3

5   2

4

0₈
THE
BOW O₅
2

1₂

1₅

0₂

9   low rock

P.O.

TRUE MERIDIAN

CHURCH BAY - RATHLIN

083°   7

2

2 cables

4

0   ½   1

Depths in metres — reported decreasing

Inn

beyond the Bow. If there is any swell out at sea a N or NW wind will bring it into the sound during the E-going tide and it can break very heavily on the Bow; it is strongest at springs and during the first 3 hours of the E-going tide. In settled weather and provided there is not a big swell out at sea it is quite safe to cross the Bow when the tide is high enough. Work has commenced on the construction of an inner basin behind Manor House pier. The work will restrict the room available. Work is also in progress reconstructing the end of Post Office pier. (see photo)

Cooraghy Bay on the S shore near the W end of the island provides shelter in moderate N winds. Anchor in 4 m SE of the boat quay. Convenient for landing to visit The Bull.

Ushet Port is a rocky gut S of a ruined stone storehouse ½ mile up the E shore from Rue Point. It would provide emergency shelter for a small shallow draught boat in winds between SW and NE through N. Drop the anchor about 20 m within the E point and take warps to the boulders on either side. Leave immediately if the wind turns S.

Arkill Bay a little further N is the best anchorage on the E shore and is suitable in offshore winds between SW and NW. Anchor in about 5 m. Boulders on the shore make landing difficult.

Ballintoy Harbour (see plan) is on the mainland at the W end of Sheep Island Sound (see Rathlin Sound above). It is very small and only used by local open boats. The depth alongside the quay W of the boathouse is 0·8 m, therefore about 2 m at HWS. The

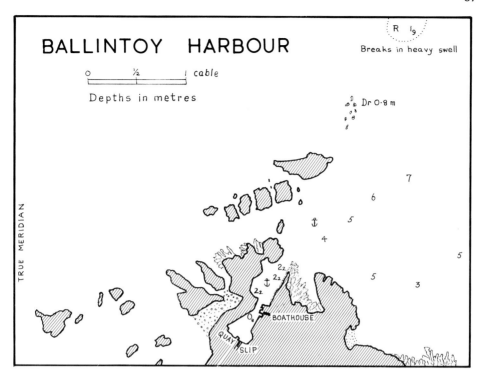

BALLINTOY HARBOUR

0   ½   1 cable

Depths in metres

R 19
Breaks in heavy swell

Dr 0·8 m

TRUE MERIDIAN

7

6

5

5

4

5

5

3

2₂
2₂
2₂

BOATHOUSE

QUAY

SLIP

rock-bound gut outside the harbour is about 70 m long and 40 m wide and makes an attractive temporary stopping place in settled weather and the gut has been dredged to about 2·2 m deep. It is simpler to anchor just outside, as shown on the plan, where the rocks provide some shelter. **Approach.** Head in to pass W of Sheep Island and having left its NW point about a cable to port turn to starboard towards the entrance. No supplies.

Coast. Portbradden at the W end of beautiful Whitepark Bay provides boat landing but no shelter except in moderate offshore wind. A mile further W **Dunseverick**, also known as Millport, has a boat slip and a small pier with 0·5 m alongside. A post with white triangular topmark stands on the outer end of the sea wall. Entering, leave the rocky islet which lies close N of the port to starboard. It should be approached with caution and only in settled swell-free weather. **Bengore Head** has quite a formidable tide race which can only be avoided by keeping 2 miles offshore; 2 cables E of the head Braddan Rock with 1·6 m over it lies 1½ cables offshore. Giants Causeway a mile W of Bengore Head looks quite insignificant from sea and provides no good landing.

Portballintrae (*see plan*) can be identified by a conspicuous row of houses above the small horseshoe bay which provides fair shelter in offshore winds. In N wind the swell breaks right across the mouth of the bay so do not chance getting caught there in such conditions. When approaching keep clear of Blind Rock on the E side. The best anchorage is NE of the W pier in 3 or 4 m with the gateposts of Seaport Lodge in line

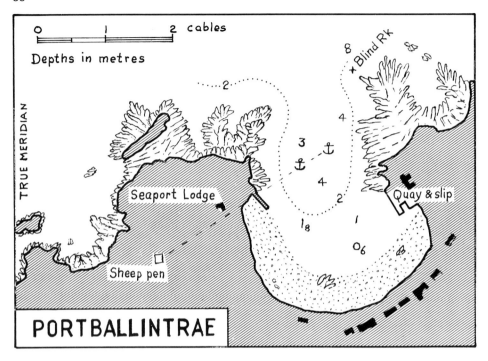

0   1   2 cables

Depths in metres

TRUE MERIDIAN

8 Blind Rᴷ

2

4

3

4

Seaport Lodge

Quay & slip

2

1₈

1

0₆

Sheep pen

PORTBALLINTRAE

with the inner end of the pier. Best landing is at the sheltered slip at the SE pier. Some supplies, hotels, PO.

Coast. Skirk Rocks (*The Storks* on the chart) ½ mile offshore at the E entrance to Skerries Sound are dry at half tide and clearly marked by a 11 m high red pillar with can topmark. They are steep-to on the N and elsewhere a berth of a cable clears the dangers. **Skerries Roads** provide shelter in moderate N winds. The best place to anchor is abreast the nick in Large Skerrie about 1½ cables from its E end; this is also the best place to land on the island. In a strong N breeze the swell would make this anchorage uncomfortable for yachts and in a N gale it would probably become dangerous. **Skerries Sound** (*see plan*) is a safe and convenient passage for yachts in moderate conditions. In strong onshore winds or high swell it is advisable to keep outside. There are two dangerous sunken rocks on the N side of the sound SW of the 5 m high Carr Rock. Give these a wide berth and remember that the E-going tide sets strongly onto them. Going through either way against the tide it is best to keep reasonably close to Reviggerly, a reef part of which always shows, and to Ramore Head. During the E-going tide there is a useful eddy off Curran strand and up to Reviggerly. Port-na-Dhu is a small boat harbour obstructed by a drying rock and of no interest to yachts. However, a set of leading marks have been established by HM Coastguard in position 55°12·59N 6°39·26WE. Upper beacon—Black cone apex down, 31 m to seaward. Lower beacon—Black cone apex up 230°T. These are to facilitate the launching of the local coastguard boat. **Caution.** Salmon nets are fixed in summer on both sides of Ramore Head and also off the curve of Curran strand S of the Large Skerrie.

Portrush (*see plan*). HW −0440 Dover. Rise: 2·1–1·4–1·1–0·4 m. This fair-sized artificial harbour lies on the W side of Ramore Head. Once inside it a yacht is secure from all summer winds though in heavy onshore winds the swell makes it uncomfortable. Unfortunately it is very congested and a yacht cannot be left there unattended unless the HM can allocate a vacant mooring. A berth will always be found for an overnight stay, either on the pontoon or on the N quay. (*see photo*)

Entrance. The ground swell, to which the bay outside is much subject, runs right across the entrance and a stranger should not approach in onshore winds of above Force 5. Once the entrance is known there should be no difficulty in entering unless it has been blowing hard from W or NW for some hours. In these circumstances Skerries Roads or preferably the Foyle offer shelter. A sunken breakwater runs out about 20 m SW from the N pier which should be given a good berth and the harbour mouth well opened up before turning NE to enter. The winds in the entrance are very fluky.

Lights. N Pier: Fl R 3 s 220°–160° and on S Pier: Fl G 220°–100°. Leading lights FR on red triangles 028°. These are difficult to pick out with the town lights.

Anchorage. The S side of the harbour is filled with local yachts and other craft while commercial vessels occasionally use the N quay and require the unoccupied part of the harbour for manoeuvering. The NW part of the harbour has depths of 3 to 5 m. On arrival a yacht should berth alongside the N quay and directions should then be sought from the Harbour Office on this quay. Alternatively call on VHF 16 working 14 or phone 0265-822307 for your previous port of call. The HM may be able to allocate a vacant mooring. There is now a pontoon at the E end of the N quay where stores, water and fuel by hose can be embarked. Overnight stay on this pontoon is permitted but yachts must be clear by 0900. Charge £3.50 per day.

Facilities. All stores including Calor and camping gas in the town. EC Wed. Rail and bus connections to Belfast and Londonderry. Hotels, good restaurants, wine bars and cafés. This holiday town has many attractions for young people. Lifeboat station.

Further information: Portrush YC adjacent to the Harbour Office has showers and is very helpful. HM Coastguard Sector Office (0265-823356) has a remote aerial connected to Belfast CG VHF 16 and 67. Admiralty Chart Agent (William Todd) has an office on the quay (0265-824176 and fax 0265-823077). Customs at Coleraine (0265-44803). Chandlery at Coleraine (0265-832086). For engine or electrical repairs consult HM. Coleraine is about 3 M inland and can be approached by sea up the River Bann, *see page 9*.

Coast. Portstewart Point is 2½ miles SW of Portrush. Black Rock 9 m high lies close offshore ½ mile NE of Portstewart Point and opposite a distinctive square rock on the shore. Lausons Rock which dries 1 m extends ¾ cable out from Black Rock which therefore must be given a berth of at least a cable. At night keep Portstewart light visible.

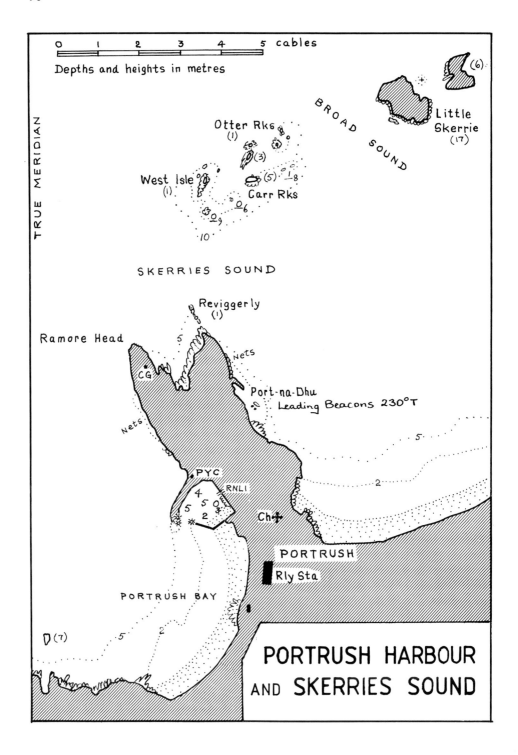

0   1   2   3   4   5 cables

Depths and heights in metres

TRUE MERIDIAN

BROAD SOUND

Little
Skerrie
(17)

(6)

Otter Rks
(1)

(3)

West Isle
(1)

(5) 8

Carr Rks

3 6
2 9

10

SKERRIES SOUND

Reviggerly
(1)

Ramore Head

5

Nets

CG

Port-na-Dhu
Leading Beacons 230°T

Nets

5

2

PYC

RNLI

4 5
5   2

Ch

PORTRUSH

Rly Sta

PORTRUSH BAY

D (7)

5

2

PORTRUSH HARBOUR
AND SKERRIES SOUND

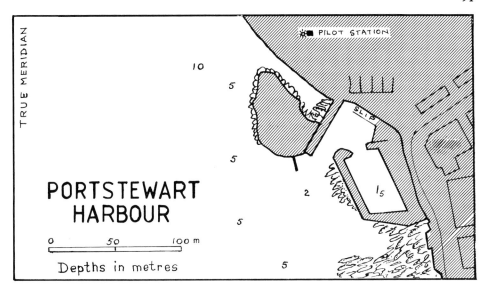

PORTSTEWART HARBOUR

0   50   100 m

Depths in metres

Portstewart (*see plan*) is a very small harbour 2 cables S of the point. The inner basin is 0·8 m to 1·7 m deep. In onshore winds the narrow entrance is difficult and the heavy run inside is liable to damage a yacht's topsides. In quiet weather it is very convenient for a temporary visit as it is right beside the town which has good shops and hotels, EC Thur. Berth alongside the S side of the inner basin. Water from a tap in the harbour. Gas but no fuel. Tourist Board Office in Town Hall. The patent slip takes out boats up to 12 m long and 1·8 m draught. River Bann pilots work from the port. **Light**. Oc R 10 s, 8 M from 040° through E to 220°; it is shown from the red pilot station on the point at a height of 21 m. (*see photo*)

Coast.—Tidal eddy. From Portstewart to River Bann the coast is rocky for the first mile, then a level sandy beach backed by sandhills. A berth of a cable clears any dangers. A tidal eddy runs along the shore during the second half of both ebb and flood between Ramore Head and the River Bann.

River Bann. HW Coleraine −0430 Dover. Rise: 2·1–1·6–0·7–0·3 m. The river mouth known as Barmouth is between stone training walls projecting 2 cables N from the beaches. The sand bar is constantly changing but appears to have a minimum depth of 3·7 m. It should not be attempted in strong onshore winds or swell. Do not try to enter if the swell is breaking noticeably on the pier ends. If in doubt consult Coleraine Harbour Radio (VHF Call 16, Work 12) or telephone 0265-2012. **Tidal streams**. The outgoing ebb runs at 3 kn and causes uneven seas and eddies up to 2 miles offshore. The ingoing flood is not strong. The coastal flood stream runs W fairly strongly across the entrance. It is best to enter at slack water or with the first of the flood (+0225 Dover).

Lights. E pierhead: Fl R 5 s 2 M from white concrete tower 5 m high. W pierhead: Fl G 5 s (occas) from black metal mast 3 m high. Leading lights: Oc Y in line 165° from piles on SW bank 4 cables inside. River Bann lights now operate all the year, Fl R 3 s on the NE side and Fl G 3 s on the SW side. There are 25 of them and also 6 unlit perches.

Entrance. Enter with the white leading light beacons in line. The channel is 45 m wide and is kept dredged to 3·7 m. It is well marked with beacons, red on the NE side and green on the SW side; the first red beacon appears very far over to the W and unless prepared for this a stranger might take it the wrong way. **Caution**. In summer there may be salmon nets fixed across the full width of the river during the flood tide. On sighting one, stop and shout for the men watching it who are then bound to lower it for you. But vessels may be held responsible for damage to nets.

Coleraine Marina VHF Ch 16 and 37 is now the normal place for yachts to stay in the river. It is on the NE bank 4 miles from the entrance and ½ mile downstream of the town. It has berths for 63 boats with depths of 3 m at the outer pontoons and 1·4 m near the bank. There is usually a berth available for a visitor but to make sure the supervisor may be phoned between 9 am and 5 pm, 0265 44768. **Facilities**. Water and electricity on the pontoons. Fuel. Showers and heads, chandlery, workshop, 15 ton travelift crane. Masts up to 15 m long can be stepped and unstepped. Shops are ½ mile away so it is probably necessary to phone for a taxi from the adjacent YC which welcomes visitors and has showers and a bar (limited hours). Marina charges 1991 are £3.00 per day up to 25 ft and £4.50 over.

Anchorage. If this is preferred the best place is on the NE side just upstream of a high scrubby sandhill which is ½ mile upstream of the old CG Sta. Anchor close in or moor to avoid swinging out into the channel and carry a riding light. This anchorage is known as Dougans Bay or Strawberry Hill. It is reputed to be calmer than the marina in certain cross winds.

Coleraine. Yachts do not normally go there now but it has a long commercial quay close to all the shops. Before going there phone the HM for permission and then phone the railway bridge (between the marina and the quay) to arrange to have it opened. (Phone Nos. HM 0265-42012. Bridge 0265-42403.)

Coast. From the Bann to Lough Foyle is all an open sandy beach except between Castlerock and Downhill where there is a mile of cliff on the edge of which there is a prominent classical temple. The shore is shoal and should be given a berth of at least 2 cables.

Tuns Bank, very shallow in places along its NW edge, extends 3 miles NE from the E side of Lough Foyle entrance. Approaching inshore from the E there is nothing to indicate the start of the bank so once W of Benevenagh Mountain you should either keep about 3 cables off the shore or head out for the Tuns buoy off the NE end of the bank.

Lough Foyle (*see entrance plan*). HW at Moville −0350 Dover. Rise: 2·3–1·8–0·8–0·3 m. A good stopping place for yachts bound W but otherwise there is not much to attract the average cruiser. The SE side is Northern Ireland and the NW side is the

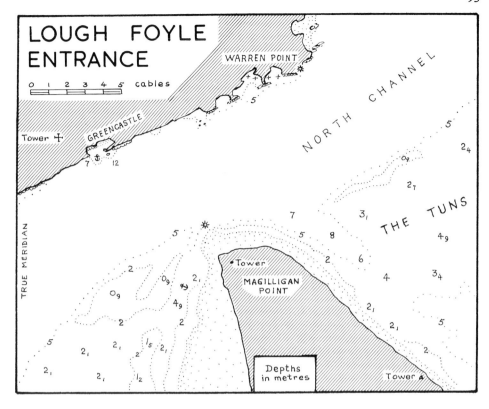

Republic. The lough is sheltered from the sea by the low-lying sweep of Magilligan Point which leaves an entrance about a mile wide. The E and S shores are low-lying and very shoal far out. The NW shore rises steeply. There is a good deal of commercial traffic.

At the top end of Lough Foyle on the starboard side just before entering the river is the border between Northern Ireland and the Republic of Ireland. Skippers should contact the Customs Authorities at the next port of call after passing the frontier. Flag Quebec should be flown close up at the Yard and courtesy ensigns as appropriate. If the Customs are not available easily report to the nearest Garda Station (R of I) or Police Station (NI) for clearance to proceed (*see page 153*).

Approach. The ship channel, about ¾ mile wide, lies NW of the Tuns Bank (*see above*). A berth of 2 cables clears all dangers along the NW shore from Inishowen Head. In June and July the channel is often obstructed at night by salmon nets. Coming from the E it is often more convenient to approach along the Magilligan shore particularly if trying to enter against the ebb in offshore winds. In these conditions you could if desired anchor anywhere off Magilligan strand to await the flood. The channel betwen Tuns Bank and the shore has a least depth of 4 m. Approach it about 3 cables offshore and when ½ mile from Magilligan Point move in to 2 cables offshore, take care to keep just this distance off till the point is abeam, if the tide is ebbing it sets strongly across the channel towards the bank.

Tidal Streams run through the entrance at 3½ kn at springs. The ebb commences −0320 Dover in mid channel and an hour earlier around Magilligan Point. On the NW side of the entrance from Warren Point to Moville there is a useful eddy extending from 45 to 90 m offshore on both ebb and flood. Between the entrance and Culmore the maximum speed is 2½ kn. Detailed information in Irish Coast Pilot.

Lights. Inishowen (locally called Strove) is a substantial white lighthouse with 2 black bands 23 m high on Dunagree Point (½ mile S of Inishowen Head). Fl (2) WRG 10 s, 14 M G from 197° to 211°, then W to 249° covering the ship approach, thence R to 360°. Horn (2) 30 s. Fog Det Lt. A disused lighthouse, white with one black band, 15 m high, stands ¾ cable E of the main lighthouse. **Lough Foyle Buoy**, a Safe Water pillar buoy, L Fl 10 s, whistle, lies about 2 miles NE of Inishowen Head. **Tuns Buoy**, red, Fl R 3 s, is about a mile E of Inishowen Head. **Warren Point**, Fl 1·7 s, 5 M from a white tower, from 232° to 061°, obscured close inshore. **Magilligan Point**, QR, from a pile structure off the point. The channel up to Londonderry is very well lit and beaconed as shown on the charts.

Anchorages

Greencastle (*see plan*) on the NW shore just within the entrance is a busy fishing harbour not very suitable for yachts as they would have to berth alongside fishing boats which are frequently on the move, particularly at night. The pier has recently been greatly enlarged and rebuilt, the plan on this page shows the new works which should be completed by 1991. It is now unwise to anchor in the middle of the harbour. In winds between NNE and WSW there is a convenient anchorage just outside the harbour. If

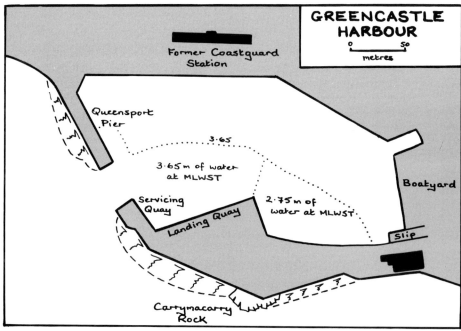

(Roinn na Mara)

anchoring outside the harbour in the bay it is well advised to be clear of the fishing boat route. If the wind comes onshore it is best to move without delay to a suitable place up the lough but if for some reason this is not possible tie alongside a fishing boat and ask for advice. Buoy the anchor as the bottom is foul with old moorings. Land either at Queen's Port pier which has 2·7 m alongside or in the harbour where there is a water tap on the pier and which is closer to the shops, garage and hotel in the village.

In E and NE winds there is a comfortable though remote anchorage in the lee of **Magilligan Point**. Approach with Magilligan light structure close to port and then keep it in line astern with Warren Point white tower. As soon as the low round tower on Magilligan Point comes abeam bear to port and keep Magilligan light structure bearing 021°. This leads down the centre of the gut which is not less than 2 m deep increasing to 4·9 m when the tower ashore bears 055°; do not go further in than this.

Moville pier (*see plan*) is about 3 cables NW of Moville Bank light structure, a white house on black piles. There is shelter on the inner side of the pier in winds from W through N to SE and it is 1·5 m deep near the end so that yachts can usually remain afloat there. As the bank is shallow in places the safest approach, especially near LW, is with the pier bearing 340°. It is close to the centre of the town which has most facilities including a boat builder. Shops closed all day Wed.

Carrickarory pier ½ mile SW of Moville is now in disrepair but the bay offers good shelter in winds from NNW to SW. The outer 25 m of the quay has a depth of 2 m. It is best to anchor NE of the quay and ask at the pilot office on the pier whether it would be possible to haul in closer to it, which is desirable in wind S of SW.

In SE winds there is no suitable anchorage until the lough narrows into the river at Culmore. There is complete shelter in **Culmore Bay** on the NW side. Anchor about 1½ cables W of Culmore Point in 2 to 3·5 m outside the moorings. Buoy the anchor. Stores at Londonderry, 4 miles.

Londonderry is 18 miles from the sea and the tidal streams are fairly strong in parts of the river; full details of the streams should be studied in the Irish Coast Pilot. A new bridge with 32 m clearance has been constructed just above Boom Hall and before

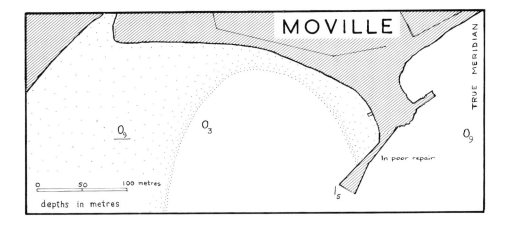

Rosses Point. Otherwise there are no difficulties for a yacht and the river is very well marked but it would be desirable to have chart 2499. Berth at the extensive new quay on the W side below Craigavon bridge. The city has all facilities including marine engineering however there is no yacht chandlery or boatyard. VHF Ch 16 and 14 c/s "Harbour Radio" Harbour Master 0504-263680. The main port operations are to be moved to Lisahally soon, work on new facilities is under way, see chart.

Coast. Inishowen Head to Culdaff Bay consists mostly of cliffs rising 100 to 200 m; a berth of 1½ cables clears all dangers. Kinnagoe and Tremone Bays provide boat landings on the beach in offshore winds but neither has any facilities ashore.

Passage timing for a yacht making 4 to 5 kn. **Foyle to Swilly**: leave Foyle entrance at HW Dover; this gives a fair tide round the head and should catch the last of the flood into Swilly. A yacht **bound W** along the coast can do well by arriving at Malin Head at −0500 Dover at the end of the fair tide; by keeping inshore W of Lough Swilly slack water followed by another fair tide will be picked up after 2 hours. **E bound**. For a coastal passage leave Melmore Head at −0600 Dover (−0100 Mulroy Bar) or leave Lough Swilly entrance at −0500 Dover. Going **to Foyle** leave Lough Swilly entrance at +0400 Dover or be at Malin Head at −0600 Dover; this should just enable you to catch the last of the flood into the Foyle.

Culdaff Bay (*see plan*). HW −0500 Dover. Rise (HW): 2·8–2·2 m. This is an excellent anchorage in winds between SSE and NNW and a convenient and pretty place to wait for tide or weather for rounding Malin Head. The strong coastal tides do not enter the bay and they cut off most of the swell but a yacht is sometimes tide-rode with resultant rolling.

Approaching from the E keep at least 2 cables off the beach and from the W keep 1½ cables off Bunnagee Point; this avoids the rocks shown on the plan. **Anchorage**. Bunnagee Port pier runs SSE and has 2 m at its head but shoals rapidly and dries at the bottom step. A 9 m yacht drawing 1·4 m can lie alongside afloat at LW neaps but not at springs. Anchor SSE of the pier in 3 to 4 m sand, good holding. Let go as soon as the inner side of the pier opens; in NW to SW wind with Dunowen house just open N of the most S ridge of rock; in S wind about ½ cable off the pier. **Facilities**. In the village, a mile away, shops, petrol, hotels. Water near the pier.

The coast between Bunnagee Point and Stookaruddan is rocky and mainly composed of cliffs. S of Glengad Head (locally known as The Rue) all dangers are cleared by a berth of a cable, NW of the head by a berth of 2 cables. During the flood a **tidal eddy** runs SE inshore of the line from Dunmore Head (the E of Culdaff Bay) to Glengad Head.

Portaleen is a small fishing pier inshore of the rocks on the SE side of Portnalong Bay which is a mile S of Glengad Head. Mullandoo Rock lies between 1 and 2 cables NE of the pier and is ½ cable wide; only parts of it dry and one part near the N side only just covers at HW. The berth is on the SE side of the pier, the depth 1·2 m at the head gradually reducing further in. It is not really suitable for yachts. However it can be

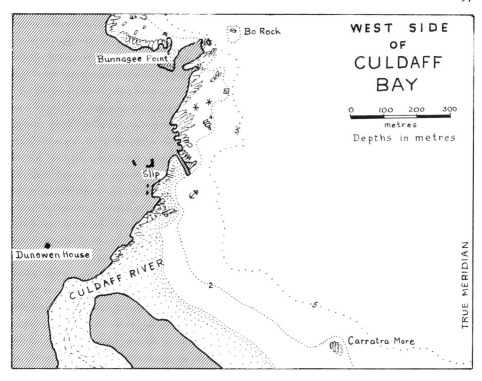

WEST SIDE
OF
CULDAFF
BAY

0   100   200   300

metres

Depths in metres

Bo Rock

Bunnagee Point

Slip

Dunowen House

CULDAFF RIVER

2

·5

Carratra More

TRUE MERIDIAN

approached directly from seaward by keeping half the slip just showing to the left of pierhead, which should bear 240°; this leads through a passage 50 m wide between Mullandoo Rock and a sunken reef S of it. Portnalong Bay is not as good a place as Culdaff but a yacht might anchor temporarily outside the small fishing boats which are moored there in summer. The approach between Mullandoo Rock and the NW shore is clear and 1½ cables wide. It is possible to go from the bay to Portaleen pier inside Mullandoo Rock by keeping 30 m off the point N of the pier where the depth is 3 m.

Tides near Glengad Head. A tide rip begins to form off the head at +0100 Dover, extends to the centre of Inishtrahull Sound at +0200 Dover, and starts to subside after +0300 Dover; it is particularly severe at springs and with NW wind, in which conditions a race extends ¾ mile E of the head. At +0400 Dover the tide is slack inshore at the head. At −0500 Dover it runs strongly SE within 2 cables of the head, but the direction changes to E as you go further out.

Malin Harbour or **Slievebane Bay** (*see plan*) 3 miles E of Malin Head offers temporary shelter in offshore winds but is much more subject to swell than Culdaff and not so easy to approach. The entrance is between Lackgolana and Rossnabartan (*see* Garvan Sound *below*). The small pier extends SSE and has about 1·2 m at its head. It is best to lay an anchor out to the S and tie a stern warp to the outer bollard. **Facilities.** Petrol, hotels, some supplies.

Inishtrahull. HW −0500 Dover. Rise: 3·3–2·55–1·6–0·4 m. This island lies 4 miles off the coast and 5 miles NE of Ireland's North Point. It is about a mile long and consists of two rounded hills about 40 m high forming the E and W ends and joined by a stretch of low ground. Except for the lighthouse keepers no-one has lived there for the last 50 years. All the shores are rocky. Torr Sound, between the W end of the island and Torr Rocks N of it, is ½ mile wide in the fairway which has quite a tide rip; it is foul on the S side where sunken rocks run out 3 cables N from Inishtrahull. On both sides of the E half of the island a berth of a cable leads clear of all dangers. **Light,** from a 23 m high slim white tower on the SW point of the island, Fl (3) 20 s, 18 M, obscured 256°–261° within 3 miles.

Portmore (*see plan*) is on the N side of the island. Coming from the W it is best to approach by going S of the island and round the clean E point. On the N side of this point there is a circular eddy with a whirlpool during most of the W going tide or flood; it commences shortly after LW. The port is sheltered from all winds except those between NNE and E. However even in offshore winds it should be approached with great caution if there is a swell running in Inishtrahull Sound. If arriving near LW it is quite convenient to anchor in 5 m in the mouth of the gut or further out in 8 m, *see plan*. The rocky gut is 170 m long and 25 m wide with a 20 m long quay on its S side. Off the quay there is a pool measuring 18 m by 24 m and about 1·7 m deep but the entrance is obstructed by a rock which dries about 0·5 m close N of the seaward end of the quay. Enter between the rock and the quay where the depth is 0·3 m; the rock will not be visible and the gap is much obstructed by weed; approach parallel to the face of the quay aiming to enter alongside it. Berth alongside the SW half of the quay. There is a

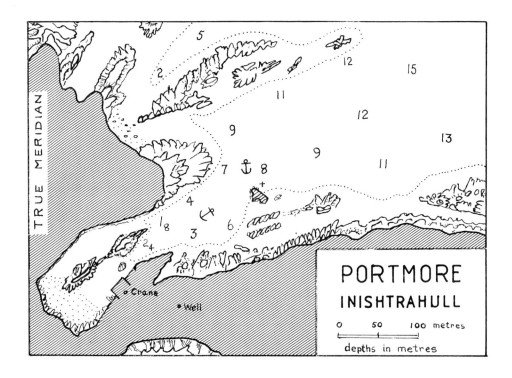

TRUE MERIDIAN

PORTMORE

INISHTRAHULL

0   50   100 metres

depths in metres

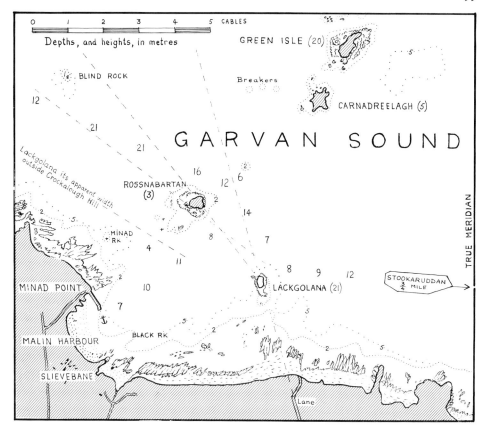

ring-bolt in the rock opposite the inner end of the quay and if remaining overnight it is best to use this and moor in the centre of the pool. (*see photo*)

Portachurry is a narrow gut on the SW side of the island. There is a small jetty with 1·5 m and a slip. It is exposed to swell and not recommended, but in N winds temporary anchorage is possible in 10 or 11 m in the mouth of the bay; beware of drying rocks close along the N shore. The tide runs strongly 30 m outside the SW point.

Inishtrahull Sound should be treated with respect if there is any sea running. If it is essential to make a passage round Malin Head in bad weather it is advisable to pass 3 miles N of Torr Rocks. Conditions in the sound can change extremely quickly, particularly of course at the turn of the tide. When the wind blows against the stream the swell is high and very steep. When heading W through the sound conditions often suddenly get worse as the N point of the Garvans is passed.

Garvan Sound (*see plan*) presents no difficulty in daylight unless there is a heavy swell and saves a considerable detour round Doherty Rocks. **From the E**, Garvan Isles should be approached with great caution in light weather unless you have a reliable engine, as the W-going stream runs between them with considerable strength and could

100

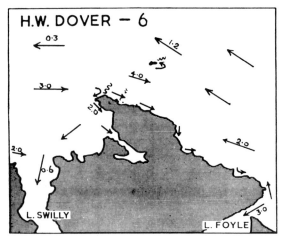

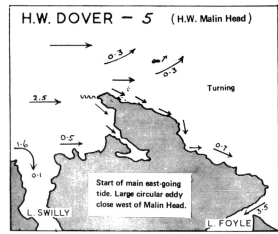

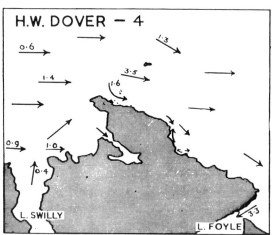

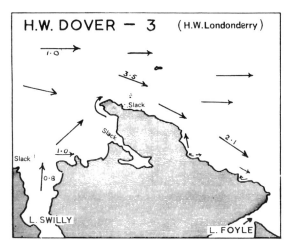

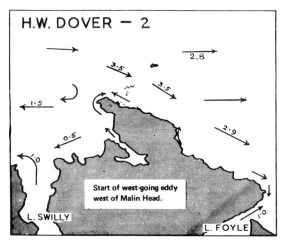

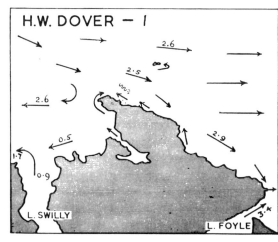

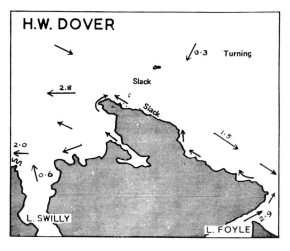

H.W. DOVER

0·3 Turning
Slack
Slack
2.8
1.5
2·0
0·6
2.9
L. SWILLY
L. FOYLE

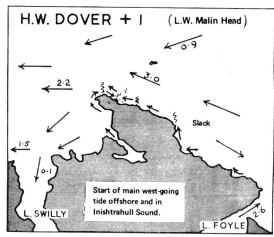

H.W. DOVER + 1 (L.W. Malin Head)

0·9
3·0
2·2
Slack
1·5
0·1

Start of main west-going tide offshore and in Inishtrahull Sound.

2·6
L. SWILLY
L. FOYLE

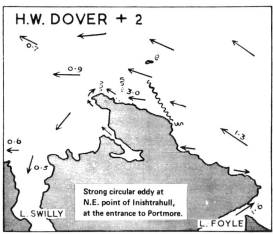

H.W. DOVER + 2

0·7
0·9
3·0
0·6
0·5
1·3

Strong circular eddy at N.E. point of Inishtrahull, at the entrance to Portmore.

1·6
L. SWILLY
L. FOYLE

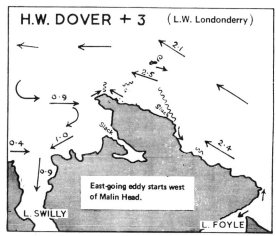

H.W. DOVER + 3 (L.W. Londonderry)

2·1
2·5
Slack
0·9
Slack
0·4
1·0
2·4
0·9

East-going eddy starts west of Malin Head.

L. SWILLY
L. FOYLE

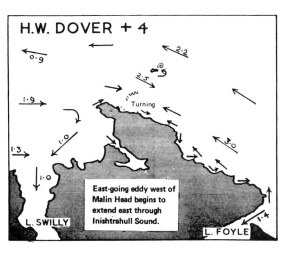

H.W. DOVER + 4

2·2
0·9
2·5
1·9
Turning
1·3
1·0
3·0
1·0

East-going eddy west of Malin Head begins to extend east through Inishtrahull Sound.

1·4
L. SWILLY
L. FOYLE

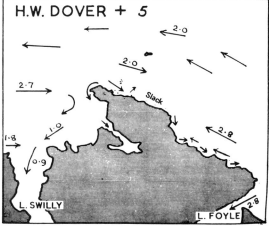

H.W. DOVER + 5

2·0
2·0
2·7
Slack
1·0
1·8
2·8
0·9
2·8
L. SWILLY
L. FOYLE

sweep a yacht onto the rocks. Approaching from the E, pass close outside the 70 m high loaf-shaped Stookaruddan; from there steer 275° for Lackgolana ("Saddle Rock") 21 m high and pass not less than ½ cable NE of it. From here the low flat-topped island Rossnabartan is unmistakable, bearing NW. It is best to leave it just one cable to port, or alternatively not less than 2 cables to port, so as to avoid a 2 m deep rock 1½ cables NE of it. When Rossnabartan is abaft the beam head directly towards Ireland's North Point for at least ½ a mile so as to pass well S of Blind Rock.

Transits. Lackgolana 162° in line with a lane leading to the top of the low cliffs leads between Blind Rock and the Garvan outliers and also between Rossnabartan and the rock NE of it. Lackgolana centered behind Rossnabartan leads closer NE of Blind Rock. Lackgolana open its own width S of Rossnabartan leads S of Blind Rock. Lackgolana its own apparent width outside Crockalough, the highest hill a mile S of Stookaruddan, leads safely betwen Rossnabartan and Minad Rock which dries 1·2 m.

From the W make the land at Ireland's North Point which is steep-to. From close off the point make a straight course, about 105°, to pass just a cable N of Rossnabartan and S of the 2 m deep rock 1½ cables NE of it. Thence head to pass close N of Stookaruddan. Yachts bound for Slievebane Bay should not be tempted to pass S of Rossnabartan unless the transit (*see above*) is definitely recognised as the clear passage is less than a cable wide.

Malin Head. The promontory consists of a rounded hill about 70 m high with a square derelict concrete tower on top of it. W of Blind Rock the outer parts of the shore are steep-to and a berth of 1½ cables clears all dangers, apart from Scart Rocks which never cover and lie about 2 cables W of Malin Head. An area of magnetic anomaly has been reported on a bearing of 250° *from* the head for a distance of approx. 1 M. Extreme caution should be exercised particularly in poor visibility. **NOTE CAREFULLY: the direction of lateral buoyage changes at Malin Head**.

Tidal Streams in Inishtrahull Sound and near Malin Head are complex and have not been investigated in detail. The tidal chartlets on page 100 and 101 represent an attempt to assemble and correlate available information. Rates shown in Inishtrahull Sound are interpolated from the maximum rate of 4 kn off Garvans (ICP). Rates in Garvan Sound are estimates. Other rates are from Admiralty Tidal Stream Atlas No. 218. At springs the tide inshore turns an hour later than shown. The time of slack water is liable to considerable unpredictable variation hereabouts, much more so than on other parts of the coast.

General Tide Pattern. The main stream runs W for only 3 hours in Inishtrahull and Garvan Sounds, that is from +0030 to +0330 Dover. However the W-bound navigator is not at a disadvantage as the main stream of the E-going tide is deflected by Ireland's North Point to pass N of the Garvan Isles. A W-going eddy starts in Garvan Sound on the second half of the E-going tide, that is at −0230 Dover. In fact the stream does not run E in Garvan Sound with much strength at any time. The streams in the passage inside Rossnabartan are not known but probably conform at most times to Garvan Sound.

Bound W you can therefore have a fair tide round the head from −0230 to +0330 Dover; if passing in the first half of this period use Garvan Sound, if in the latter half either Garvan or Inishtrahull Sounds. **Bound E** you can have a fair tide, by using Inishtrahull Sound, from +0330 to −0100 Dover; during part of this period, that is from +0500 to −0400 Dover, there would be a fair tide, though probably a much weaker one, through Garvan Sound.

Caution. At springs the stream reaches a rate of 3 kn near Malin Head and 4 kn in Inishtrahull Sound. In opposition to the wind it can create a steep and dangerous sea extremely quickly. The sound is much more exposed and more liable to produce a rough sea than Rathlin Sound.

Trawbreaga Bay between Malin Head and Lough Swilly is 6 miles wide and 3 miles deep. It is frequently subject to heavy ground swell. There is little attraction to sail into the bay unless the weather appears suitable to try entering Trawbreaga Lough, *see below*. Much of the coast is fringed with reefs which extend almost ½ mile offshore S of Whitestrand Bay so it should all be given a wide berth. The only offshore danger is Glashedy Island, cliffbound and rectangular in silhouette, which is surrounded by sunken reefs; it needs a berth of ¼ mile on the NE side, ½ mile NW and SE, and ¾ mile SW of it to clear Doherty Rock. There is a clear passage inside it, shown on chart 2697. In the NE corner of Whitestrand Bay there is a small pier; if dinghy landing is necessary it might be approached with caution in fine swell-free conditions, keeping towards the N shore and not attempting to anchor. At the SW of the bay chart 2697 shows anchorages in Tullagh and Rockstown Bays with a slip in the latter, but these bays are much encumbered with rocks and have little to attract yachts and the slip cannot be recommended.

Trawbreaga Lough (*see plan*). Shown on chart 2697; HW (at the bar) −0500 Dover. Rise (HW): 4·0–3·1 m. HW at Malin Bridge −0330 Dover, which is approximately when there is slack water on the bar. The lough locally called Strabreagy, offers complete shelter and good holding S of Doagh Point, 2 miles inside the bar. Further in the lough is extensive at HW but too shallow and subject to change for a keel boat to do more than proceed carefully direct to and from the anchorage. **Caution**. The tides run strongly, and because of the frequent ocean swell in Trawbreaga Bay the bar is often impassable. During the latter part of the ebb it breaks heavily in onshore breeze when there is no swell. It must be observed carefully before deciding to enter and strangers must bear in mind that they may have to stay in, or leave their yacht there, longer than intended.

Directions. Only approach in swell-free conditions and not in fresh wind. The time to enter is at about half flood, which is −0545 Dover. The position of the bar is indicated by an outcop of white quartz rock on the steep grass of the cliff S of it. Approach from the NW so as to keep well clear of Binderg Rock. Turn away if the bar does not look safe. The wind is inclined to baffle near the cliffs so have the engine running if not actually being used. Start crossing the bar not less than 2 cables offshore and steering SE across it, getting closer to the shore. The least depth on the bar is 0·6 m. When inside it keep between 100 and 150 m off the HW edge of Isle of Doagh, the S shore, passing S of

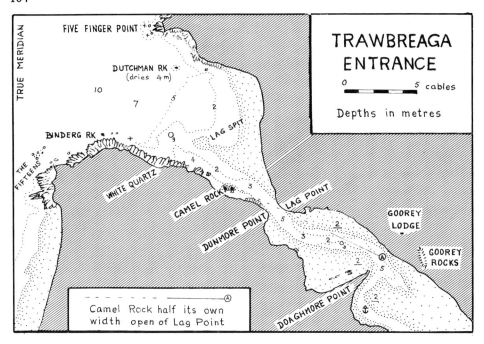

TRUE MERIDIAN

N

FIVE FINGER POINT

TRAWBREAGA
ENTRANCE

0   5 cables

Depths in metres

DUTCHMAN RK
(dries 4m)

10

7

5

2

BINDERG RK

LAG SPIT

9

THE FIFTEENS

+

4

2

WHITE QUARTZ

CAMEL ROCK

3

DUNMORE POINT

5

LAG POINT

GOOREY
LODGE

3

2

GOOREY
ROCKS

2

A

2

DOAGHMORE POINT

A

Camel Rock half its own
width open of Lag Point

Lag spit, generally marked by breakers, and head first towards Lag Point and then for the First Narrows between it and Dunmore Point. Both points are steep-to and the stream between them runs at up to 5 kn at springs. Beyond this the channel curves through a ½ mile wide area to the Second Narrows, which is marked by a conspicuous whitewashed farm on the N shore. It is not possible to give exact directions for this part due to the curve, also it may change a bit; someone should be watching the echo-sounder, but the colour of the water is the best guide, keep where it is darker and therefore deeper. As a general guide, after passing the First Narrows steer 150° for about ¼ mile and before the rocky outcrop on the S shore bears S start altering course to port and steer about 095° towards the N end of Goorey rocks on the N shore. Then look astern and when Camel Rock (a conspicuous twin-hump rock NW of Dunmore Point) appears half its own width SW of the abrupt left-hand edge of Lag Point alter course to starboard, keeping Camel Rock on this line astern (about 296°) which leads down the centre of the channel to the Second Narrows and clears the end of the sandspit off Doaghmore Point. Having passed through the Second Narrows turn about 90° to starboard and get the right-hand side of Goorey Lodge in line with the left side of the shed just S of the group of buildings near the shore; keep it astern on this bearing all the way to the anchorage, which is off the bend where the point joins the main body of the Isle of Doagh. The anchorage is in a depth of 4 to 5 m on stiff blue clay.

Departure. It is best to leave the anchorage about −0600 Dover, aiming to be near the bar at HW (−0500 Dover) when the flood will still run in for about another hour; then if there are breakers on the bar it should be possible to return to the anchorage. **Facilities**. None on Isle of Doagh. Some stores, PO, garage, in Malin village on the N side of the lough, 2 miles by road from Goorey farm.

Lough Swilly (*see plan*). HW Rathmullan −0500 Dover. Rise: 4·3–3·2–1·9–0·5 m. One of the finest natural big-ship harbours in Ireland or the United Kingdom, 25 miles long by up to 3½ miles wide with a clear entrance accessible in any weather. The best yachting area on the N coast. **Tidal Streams** do not run more than 1½ kn in the lough except between Rathmullan and Inch Island where they reach 2 kn at springs. In Fahan creek when the banks are uncovered near LW the streams can reach 3 kn. **Yacht Anchorages** listed below must be chosen carefully to obtain shelter. In spring and autumn swell can at times make all the bays N of Inch Island uncomfortable. There is now a fish farm approx. 3 cables ENE of Anny Point.

Lights. Fanad Head: Fl (5) WR 39 m 20 s 16 M, R from 100° to 110° and from 313° to 345°, W elsewhere. There is now a fish farm approx. 3 cables ENE of Anny Point. **Dunree Head**: Fl (2) WR 5 s 9 M, R from 320° to 328°, W thence to 183°, R thence to 196°. **Buncrana pier**: Iso WR 4 s, W 052° to 139°, R over Inch Spit and White Strand Rock. **Rathmullan**: Fl G 3 s on pierhead. **Buoys**, *see plan*. (*see photo*)

Approach. The ebb and flood in the lough appear to extend as far as Malin Head. If coming from the E it is therefore ideal to round Malin Head at +0130 Dover when the inshore tide has been running W there for about 3 hours and you then have 6 hours of flood into and up the lough. Dunaff Hill at the E of the entrance is 219 m high with steep sides. Fanad Head at the W side is very low. About 2 miles in from Fanad Head a G con Fl G 3 s marks Swilly Rocks and should be left to starboard; coming from the W round Fanad Head steer SE till the buoy is seen. When passing Dunree Head in heavy weather do not go E of mid-channel as the sea then breaks on Dunree Bar.

Dangers in the lough are relatively few but there are a number of unmarked rocks within a cable of the shore so keep further off than this until you have examined the chart. Four of the buoys mark other dangers which yachts should avoid. Colpagh red buoy Fl R 6 s marks a shoal and rocks drying 3 and 4 m; the shore from here to Buncrana should be given a berth of 3 cables. Kinnegar drying strand stretches out to within a cable of the green buoy Fl G 10 s and Kinnegar shoal with 0·4 m extends 4 cables N from the buoy. Two red buoys mark the W side of Inch Spit Fl R 3 s and Flat Fl (2) R 6 s which must be avoided except at HW.

Anchorages, W shore. Pincher Bay just inside Fanad Head is a possible temporary anchorage in 4 or 5 m, sand, for those not wishing to sail up the lough. It is less subject to swell than one might expect.

Portsalon Bay 4½ miles from Fanad Head is an excellent anchorage in W winds and quite suitable for an overnight stay in any reasonably settled weather. Anchor off the end of the pier or SW of it in 3 to 5 m. It is the best choice for a short visit to the lough. Large hotel. Shop, with bar, petrol and phone. There is about 0·5 m alongside the pier.

Scraggy Bay 2½ miles further in provides shelter similar to and perhaps slightly better than Portsalon but has no facilities ashore. The house is a Youth Hostel. Coming in from seaward give the shore a berth of 2 cables to avoid Yellow Rock which dries 0·8 m. Anchor at the S end of the bay beyond the beach in about 3 m.

106

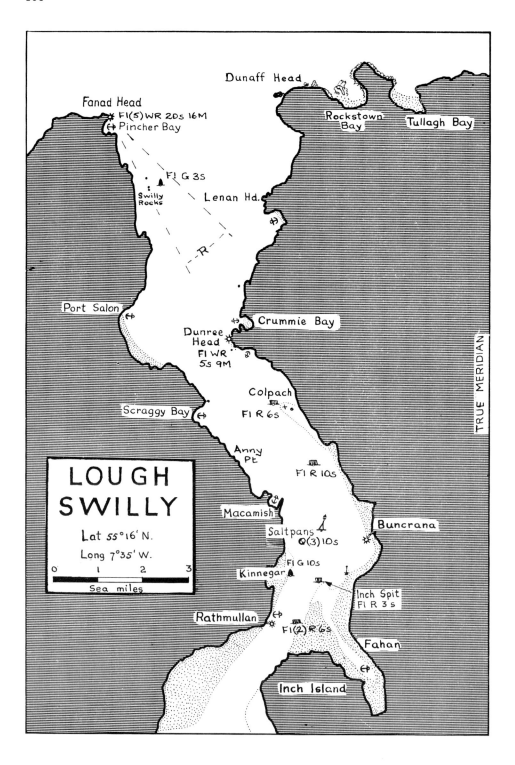

Dunaff Head

Fanad Head
✳ Fl(5)WR 20s 16M
⊕ Pincher Bay

Rockstown
Bay

Tullagh Bay

Fl G 3s
Swilly
Rocks

Lenan Hd.

—R—

Port Salon ⊕

Crummie Bay ⊕

Dunree
Head
Fl WR
5s 9M

Colpach
Fl R 6s

Scraggy Bay ⊕

Anny
Pt

Fl R 10s

LOUGH
SWILLY

Lat 55°16' N.
Long 7°35' W.

0   1   2   3
Sea miles

Macamish

Saltpans
Q(3)10s

Buncrana

Fl G 10s
Kinnegar

Inch Spit
Fl R 3s

Rathmullan ⊕
Fl(2) R 6s

Fahan

Inch Island

TRUE MERIDIAN

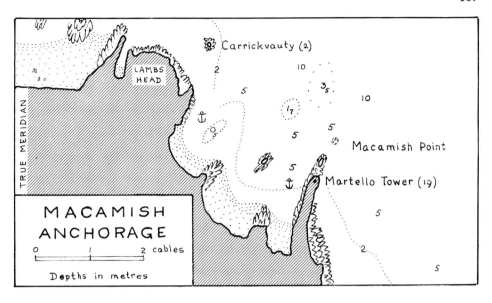

Carrickvauty (2)

LAMBS HEAD

TRUE MERIDIAN

Macamish Point

Martello Tower (19)

MACAMISH
ANCHORAGE

0   1   2 cables

Depths in metres

Macamish (*see plan*) is easily identified by the Martello tower on the point. It is a pretty place and well sheltered in winds between NW and SE. There are two small places for anchoring as shown on the plan. The nicest is beside the Martello tower; keep about 80 m off the point when entering to avoid the 1·7 m shoal NW of it; anchor just past the tower in about 5 m, sand. The other anchorage is close inside Lamb's Head in 3 m, sand; there is a shallow ridge about 0·5 m deep about 125 m away from the shore. Land on the beach. Shop on the main road ½ mile away. Home of Ottway Golf Club.

Rathmullan. Local craft remain on moorings all summer off the beach N of the pier. Visiting yachts should anchor outside or N of them. Well sheltered in prevailing SW to NNW winds. Land at the steps on the solid part of the pier or at LW on the beach nearby. It is risky to leave a dinghy at the steps at the open part of the pier because of the strong tide. The deepwater berths on both sides of the T-head of the pier being against open piles and in strong tide are not recommended except for large motor vessels. **Facilities**. There is a water hydrant at the pier-head and a water tap at the toilet at the root of the pier. Shops and PO in town, also fuel and phone. Two good hotels near the shore about ½ mile N of the town are most easily reached by outboard dinghy. Bus to Letterkenny and taxis.

Ramelton about 3 miles up the Lennan river can be reached on a rising tide by judicious sounding. Yachts drawing 1·5 m can enter at Whale Head at half-tide and go up to the town. It is a very pretty spot and well worth a visit for those who like a turn at "ditch-crawling". If staying it is best to dry out alongside the quay which fronts the town and has 3 m HWS. The port is very occasionally visited by coasters. **Facilities**. Hotel, shops, water on quay. EC Wed. Turners yard builds and lays up yachts and would take care of a yacht left alongside the town quay.

Anchorages, E shore. Leenan Bay 2½ miles in from Dunaff Head is a wide sandy bay facing SW. Beware of rocks off the N point of the bay and fishing nets on its N side. Anchor outside local boats. No facilities.

Crummie Bay is just N of Dunree Head. Anchor between the points of the bay; the inner part is all shoal. No facilities.

Dunree Bay is just S of Dunree Head. Note that there is a drying rock almost a cable SW of the head. None of shore of the bay is clear, so anchor not closer than a cable, depth about 4 m. On the W side of the head, 4 cables from the anchorage, there is a small pier much exposed to swell with 0·4 m alongside; permission to land required from CO of fort, phone Linsfort 404.

Buncrana. It is necessary to anchor a long way out to remain afloat so it is only suitable in calm weather. Alongside the SE side of the pier there is about 2·5 m at half tide but is made of open piles so a yacht is not safe there without someone on board. There is a water hose from the toilet on the quay and petrol at a store nearby. There are good shops in the town ½ mile away. EC Sat. Diesel fuel at garage ¼ mile up road to SE.

Fahan Creek (*see plan*) inside Inch Island is the most sheltered anchorage in the lough and many yachts are moored there but when a NW wind blows against the strong ebb it can be very uncomfortable. The entrance has been silting and the rise of tide is irregular so it is suggested that a visiting yacht should enter between 1½ and 1 hour before HW and turn out if she goes aground. Yachts drawing over 2 m should not attempt to enter. A new marina is being considered.

Directions: Fahan Creek offers sheltered anchorage for small craft and yachts, and is accessible to vessels of up to 2 m draft, at all states of the tide except Low Water Springs. The entrance lies between Lisfannan Bank and Inch Flats. Approaching from seaward, steer 150° from Inch Spit buoy till the conspicuous chimney (45 m) near the shore at Buncrana comes into transit with Barnan More (the Easterly and larger of the two prominent paps 6 miles to the NE), bearing 030°. Keep these in line steering 210° until Rathmullan Pier bears 252°, then steer 156° for the first low summit on the ridge west of Grianan Fort (the fort appears like a long shed on top of Grianan Mountain, 5 miles to the SSE). Keep this heading till abeam of the pole marking the end of the derelict Low Water Pier (55°05′15″N, 7°28′53″W). Give this pole a berth of 25 m, then steer between the lines of moorings into the upper creek. A sandbar with a maximum depth of 0·9 m at LAT crosses the creek S of Rinnaraw Point, and the deeper water lies on the Fahan side. Use of an echo sounder is recommended.

Anchor S or SE of moored yachts in 2 to 5·5 m, good holding, sand and mud. The Lough Swilly YC slip is just E of the pier. There is a pub and a PO beside the club but no shop. Bus service to Buncrana and Londonderry. Ferry to Rathmullan. Reliable boatman in whose charge a yacht could be left.

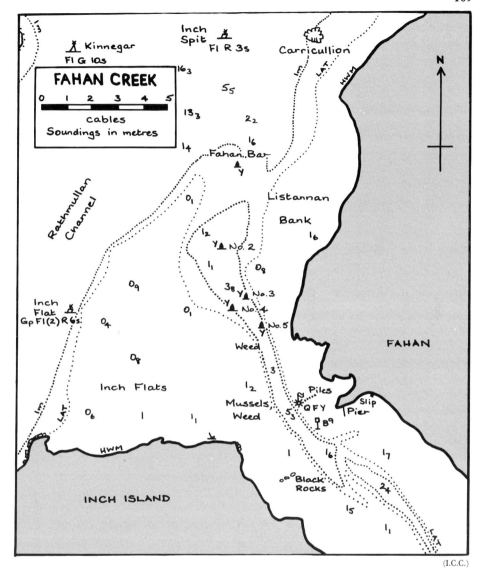

Kinnegar
Fl G 10s

Inch
Spit
Fl R 3s

Carricullion

FAHAN CREEK

0 1 2 3 4 5

cables
Soundings in metres

16_3

5_5

13_3

2_2

1_4

1_6

Fahan Bar

Listannan

Bank

1_6

0_1

Rathmullan Channel

1_2 Y▲ No. 2

1_1

0_8

0_9

3_8 Y▲ No. 3

0_1

Y▲ No. 4

▲ No. 5

Inch
Flat
Gp Fl(2) R 6s

0_4

0_8

Weed

3

Inch Flats

1_2

0_6

1

1_1

Mussels
Weed

Piles

5_3 QFY

B9

FAHAN

Slip
Pier

1

1_6

1_7

HWM

Black
Rocks

2_4

INCH ISLAND

1_5

1_1

N

(I.C.C.)

The Letterkenny Channel is pretty and interesting as far as Castle Grove. Above this the narrow channel winds through an expanse of very soft mud-flats to a small quay at the roadside outside Letterkenny, 3 m HWS, which is often occupied by a coaster.

Lough Swilly to Mulroy Bay. This coast is very foul. For clearing lines see below in Mulroy Bay *Approach* paragraph.

Offlying Danger. Limeburner Rock with a depth of 2 m lies 3 miles N of Melmore Head and has a N Card. QW (whistle) buoy. The red sector of Fanad Head light shows over the rock and the buoy.

Mulroy Bay. HW at bar −0500 Dover. Rise (HW): 3·9–2·9 m. Fanny's Bay 4 miles in from the open sea is the best anchorage on the N coast. Mulroy Lough extends some 10 miles inland and provides sailing on sheltered water in most attractive surroundings and with fairly intricate pilotage. There are now mussel rafts and salmon fish farms in the bay. A good look out is necessary. Chart No. 2699 is essential to really enjoy one of the most beautiful cruising areas of Ireland.

Approach. The coast between Lough Swilly and Mulroy Bay is very foul and should be given a wide berth using the clearing marks shown on chart 2699. Highest part of Dunaff Head open of Magheraguna Point (beside Fanad Head) is the clearest. Keep on this bearing until almost abreast of Melmore Head, the tower on which is in ruins but distinguishable. Then approach the entrance bearing S and keeping a bit nearer the W side. Blind Rock has 1·5 m over it (*see plan*). If approaching the bay from further offshore Limeburner Rock must be avoided. If approaching from the W *see paragraph* Mulroy to Sheephaven.

Lights. Ravedy Island, Fl 3 s, vis 177° to 357°. Dundooan Rocks, QG. Crannoge Point, Fl G 5 s. These are for the guidance of local boats. No stranger should attempt to enter in the dark.

Temporary anchorages if passing along the coast or waiting to enter the lough. **Ravedy Roads** is most convenient if wind is between NW and S. Anchor ¾ cable S of Ravedy Island in about 2·5 m, clean sandy bottom. It is surprisingly well sheltered from swell. **Portnalong** the bay S of Ballyhooriskey Island is better in winds between NE and S but is much more exposed to swell than Ravedy Roads. Anchor in 3 or 4 m with the S point of the island in line with its summit. **Ballyhooriskey Quay** is used by local lobster boats but is quite unsuitable for yachts. Anyone who nevertheless wishes to take a small boat in should only attempt this near HW and not if there is any swell. Pass close N of the beacon and note that the narrow channel between it and the quay has a rocky bottom which dries about 1 m.

Chart 2699 (or old chart 2698) is not necessary to reach Fanny's Bay but is essential for going further into the lough. The chart though based on a 1856 survey is accurate inside the lough, but not in the inner part of the bay N of the First Narrows as the Note beneath the title indicates. The channel shown on the plan on page 109 has been amended to show depths over the bar as taken in 1984.

The entrance has been E of Bar Rocks for at least 50 years. The shallowest part of the bar is SE of Bar Rocks where the depth is 2·8 m. If the sea is not rough one may enter at any time provided the yacht can progress against the tide which may reach 4 kn in the First Narrows at springs. If there is swell or N wind there may be breakers W of the Bar Rocks; in such conditions the bar should be carefully observed before approaching it and it would be prudent to enter with the flood or leave at HW.

Timing the passage. HW at the head of the lough is 2¼ hours later than at the bar and as this is about the time it takes to go in with the flood then if you enter as recommended at half flood it will still be half tide when you arrive at Milford. This

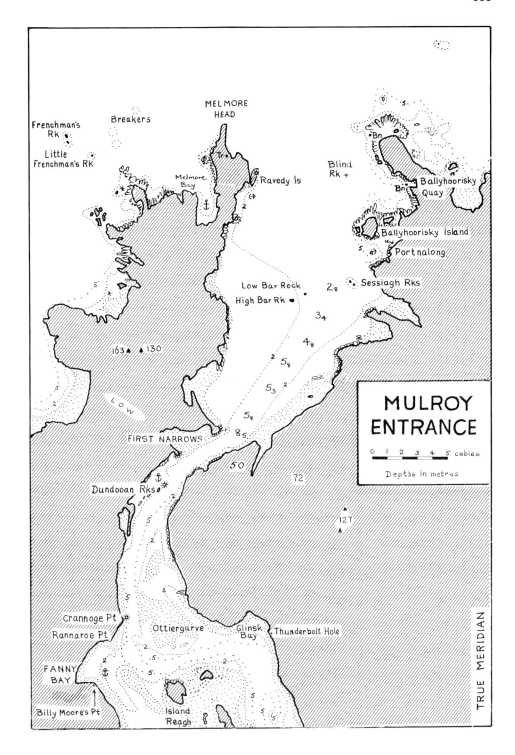

MULROY ENTRANCE

0 1 2 3 4 5 cables

Depths in metres

TRUE MERIDIAN

convenience when entering becomes the converse when leaving; it is then best to pass through the Third Narrows at HW or even a bit earlier in order to find a helpful depth of water in the Ottiergarve Bank area and later at the bar. As stated about half flood is the best time to enter if bound for the Broad Water or beyond. At springs it might be better to start an hour earlier and thus avoid the strongest flow at the Third Narrows and also have a good lift-off in the unlikely event, if you are a prudent navigator, of running aground or hitting a rock. Beating in or out under sail and with the tide is quite feasible but new visitors are advised to motor against head winds.

Directions. Before approaching identify High Bar Rock which at HWS is covered but marked by breakers. At half tide Low Bar Rock is visible. Leave High Bar Rock 2 cables to starboard, i.e. pass midway between it and the Sessiagh Rocks (named on plan) and a cable E of Low Bar Rock. Then steer towards the First Narrows, about 215°, and pass through it slightly nearer the SE side. Next steer towards the beacon on the N Dundooan Rock but when abeam of Dundooan Point aim to pass halfway between the beacon and the SE shore. After leaving all Dundooan Rocks ½ cable to starboard follow a curved course between ½ and one cable off the W shore till near Crannoge Point light tower which should be given a ½ cable berth.

From the light tower if making for **Fanny's Bay** steer about 192° for the left (SE) end of a row of houses SE of Billy Moore Point. When a small white beacon on this point comes in line 230° with a similar beacon on a rock on the skyline enter Fanny's Bay on this line. If the beacon cannot be seen head for the boatyard shed on the same bearing. (Anchorage described below).

If continuing up the lough, after passing Crannoge Point steer about 192° (see above) and when Rannaroe Point comes abeam steer for the middle of Island Reagh till on a line joining Billy Moore Point (or the left side of the boatyard shed) and Thunderbolt Hole which can be seen just S of where the road runs close to the Glinsk Bay shore and which is immediately S of the word Binderg on the chart. Hold to this line (076°) till about a cable from the shore, then head S to leave the high shore of Island Roy ½ cable to starboard and when this is well abeam start turning gradually to port so as to approach the **Second Narrows** heading about 085°. Pass through slightly nearer Rawross Point the S side of the narrows and continue E across Millstone Bay till a cable off its E shore, then turn SE to pass between the shore and Seedagh Bank. From here to the **Third Narrows** the E shore is all clear to within ½ cable (less in parts) and should be followed along accordingly. When within 1½ cables of the stone beacon on the rocks in the middle of the channel keep 15 m off the E shore and as soon as the rocks extending S of Marks Point (Umrycan Point on chart 2698) come abeam make good a due S course to the W shore. At this stage the tide may make steering seem peculiar to newcomers as maximum spring rate is 8 kn with a drop of 0·4 m causing rapids, so have the engine running even if there is a good wind. Keep the W shore close aboard (to avoid being swept onto Scalpmore Rock) until well into Pan Bay before turning out to pass the SE point of that bay. Pass 1½ cables off Deegagh Point (Cranford Point on chart 2698) and beyond Cranford Bay leave Cranford Rock beacon close to starboard. Next steer for a small islet 4 cables close in down the shore (a black dot on the chart inset, Otter I on chart 2698) and when it is nearly abeam turn to port so as to leave Greencastle Islet (a rock capped with grass) and Gowan Black Rocks (marked with a bent perch) ½ cable to port. When halfway between Gowan Black Rocks and Ranny Point (with a stone beacon) turn to starboard and steer about 205° towards an island a mile away covered with conifers; it is called Inishyweel. This course leads between the unmarked and dangerous Williamson and Ranny Rocks. When the first of the Long Islands comes abeam to port alter course to SW so as to avoid the spit off these islands. When Milford Flour Mill comes in line with the E side of Inishyweel steer to pass close NE of that island. Turn to starboard and pass midway between Inishyweel and McSwyne's Bed (the centre of the bed seldom covers and is marked with a stone beacon). Finally if bound for Milford Port pass midway between Hewitsons Island and the beacon SW of it off Ross Point; there is a rock pinnacle ½ cable outside this beacon.

ANCHORAGES

North of Dundooan Rocks in 3·5 to 5·5 m, sand. A well sheltered but isolated anchorage out of the main tide but with variable eddies which makes a yacht sheer about. Handy if leaving in the morning as it is only 1½ miles from the bar.

Melmore Bay inside Low and High Bar Rock to the W is reported to be well sheltered and to have good holding ground in 3 m. This bay is on the starboard side going in and is not the Melmore Bay which faces W.

Fanny's Bay (Fanny Hole on chart 2698). Approach described above. An excellent anchorage secure in all winds, uncomfortable only in SE wind and relatively calm in W and NW gales. Head towards the boatyard and anchor in 2 m when Crannoge Point touches the E shore of the seaward channel. It is advisable to buoy the anchor. The patent slip can be used for landing. No shops nearer than Downings a one mile walk across the hill. (*see photo*)

Rosnakill Bay just N of Broad Water is easily entered and well sheltered; anchor in 3·5 m towards the SE side. **Danger**: North Water is inaccessible due to a high voltage cable 6 m above HW which cross the N end of Moross Channel; ¼ mile S of this dangerous cable there is a low telephone wire.

Cranford Bay in Broad Water is a good anchorage. Towards the NW end at the 3·4 m chart sounding is a suitable place. A road along the shore but no facilities. The chart, and local moored boats, indicate other suitable places for anchoring.

Milford Port. HW −0245 Dover. Rise (HW): 1·4–1·1 m. There is 1·8 m alongside Milford Bakery quay which may be used with permission from the company office nearby; water is likewise available. Plenty of space to anchor SW of the quay in 3 or 4 m, soft mud. Small shop nearby. At Milford, a mile away, all stores, large garage, good small hotel, bus to Londonderry. EC Monday.

Coast. Between Mulroy and Sheep Haven there are many rocks and if coming in from seaward the coast should not be approached within a mile. However if going in good conditions from Mulroy to Sheep Haven or vice versa the passage inside Frenchman's Rock and between Carrickguill and Carnabollion is safe and interesting. Chart 2699 has useful transits.

Tranarossan Bay is a pleasant temporary anchorage in offshore wind. Anchor either in 8 m E of Carnabantry or not closer than in 5 m to Rosses Strand which is believed to extend somewhat further out than on the chart. No facilities. Tormore Rocks provide some shelter in NW wind but in general Ravedy Roads in Mulroy Bay is preferable in W and NW winds. Doagh Bay, used by curraghs, is very exposed and not recommended.

Sheep Haven. HW −0515 Dover. Rise (HW): 4·0–3·0 m. This bay is 4 miles wide. It is easily accessible in daylight and provides safe anchorage in all summer weather. Rinnafaghla Point on the E side is low-lying, rocky and foul for 3 cables off. The W point is Horn Head, the end of a peninsula with up to 200 m high cliffs. Tidal streams in the bay are weak except off Ards Bay.

Danger. Wherryman Rocks which dry 1·5 m and 2 m lie about a cable off the E shore 2¼ miles in from Rinnafaghla Point. Be sure to avoid them when approaching or leaving Downings. Duncap Head in line with Horn Head is a good clearing transit; the chart shows two others.

Lights. Portnablaghy pierhead Oc 6 s 7 m/12 m 2 M in line 125°15′. Downings pierhead Fl R 3 s.

Anchorages. Downings ("Downies" on chart) has a pier with about 1·5 m alongside its outer end which provides security against all summer winds but is subject to scend. Anchor SW of the pierhead; SE of it there is less depth than charted. **Facilities.** Grocery shop beside the pier. Water from pump. Petrol 300 m away. Hotels. Downings is a very busy holiday village. Bus to Londonderry. EC Wed.

Pollcormick Inlet, 2 cables W of Downings pier, provides excellent anchorage in peaceful surroundings in 3 m, sand. It is a short scramble across the point to the pier. Local boats remain here all the year.

Ards Bay, 1½ miles S of Pollcormick, probably provides the best shelter in Sheep Haven, but the bar can be dangerous if there is a big sea running in. The tide runs strongly over the bar and along the channel inside, the flood starting in at +0120 and the ebb at −0500 Dover. As well as the beacon (painted green) on Bar Rock on chart 2699 there are three perches along the NW shore inside: one on Yellow Rock, the second on the rock about 1½ cables SW of Yellow Rock, and the third on a rock just N of Bath Point. **Directions.** The least depth on the bar in the entrance is 2·4 m so in settled conditions most yachts can enter safely at LW. After passing half a cable E of Bar Rock beacon head S till the second perch opens to the left of the Yellow Rock perch (they are in line 220°). Then turn in and pass close SE of these two perches, anchoring outside their line about ½ cable beyond the second one. No facilities. The estate ashore belongs to a friary so one should ask for permission to walk through it. There is a slip. On the S side of Bath Point there is a quay which dries. The anchorage shown on the chart in the centre of the bay is intended for larger vessels. It should be quite safe for a yacht but is less convenient, not accessible near LW and probably rather difficult to find, particularly as the position of the channel is understood to have altered somewhat.

Marblehill Bay is ¾ mile wide and very pretty. In offshore wind and absence of swell it is a good temporary anchorage. Anchor towards the NW end in 3 or 4 m; the beach there is not as flat as elsewhere; it is frequented by holidaymakers and is the only place to land. No facilities.

Portnablaghy Bay is foul with rocks all round and is much exposed to swell which could be dangerous. There is temporary anchorage in the middle of the bay in about 4 m in suitable weather. Leading lights Oc 6 s 7 m/12 m 2 M bearing 125°15′. The pier dries alongside with rocky bottom. **Facilities**. Stores, petrol, hotel.

Dunfanaghy quay is accessible at HW but the bay dries out 7 cables to seaward of it and there is nothing to mark the way in. The bay is fully exposed to dangerous swell. The quay is therefore definitely not recommended, nor is the anchorage in the bay.

Coast. Half a mile SW of Horn Head Ummera Rocks, which dry at LW, lie 2 cables offshore with a reef inside them; to be sure of avoiding them keep Melmore Head in sight till past Ummera Head. From here a direct course to Inishbofin is clear. There are dangerous rocks N of **Tramore Bay**, a temporary anchorage in offshore wind. If heading there it is possible in calm conditions to pass inside all the rocks by keeping a cable off the cliffs S of Templebreaga Head. Otherwise pass 2 cables outside Carricknaherwy, which does not cover, and then steer for the SW end of Tramore strand till Marfagh Point at its NE end comes abeam, when it is safe to turn in.

Ballyness Harbour is too shallow for most yachts and can only be entered in very settled conditions. The bar is fully exposed and variable in position. The leading marks shown on chart 2752 are Iso W. Anchor off the pier, the wooden end of which is now ruined. Nearest stores at Falcarragh 1½ miles away.

Inishbofin, Inishdooey and **Inishbeg** are lowlying grassy islands extending from the mainland half-way towards Tory. Only Inishbofin is now inhabited. The passage between it and the mainland dries and should not be attempted. **Keelasmore Sound** the passage N of Inishbofin, is a good short cut if bound from Horn Head to Bloody Foreland. Reefs and rocks which dry extend from the SW side of Inishdooey, a cable off its S point and over 2 cables at the NE end of the sound. In the SE entrance of the sound keep just a little nearer the S end of Inishdooey to avoid Toberglassan Rock which has 1·5 m over it and at the NW end keep between 1 and 2 cables off the N end of Inishbofin.

Toberglassan Bay, the SW side of Keelasmore Sound, is most attractive in the absence of swell, to which it is fairly open. It is shelterd in winds from SSE through SW to WNW. Chart 2752 is necessary to avoid Toberglassan Rock when entering. Anchor in about 4 m, sand. Fresh water spring in the rocks on the SE side of the bay. Small shop on the SE side of the island.

Inishbofin Bay, S of the island, is exposed to swell and W winds. Magheroarty pier at the S end of the bay is used by the Tory Island mailboat; it sometimes is possible to anchor temporarily 3 cables off the pier in 4 m. The roadstead at the N end of the bay has somewhat better shelter; Inishbofin boats lie on moorings off the village pier W of the drying spit. Lt Fl 8 s 3 m 3 M on pier. HW −0530 Dover. Rise (HW): 3·9–3·0 m.

Coast between Magheroarty and Bloody Foreland is steep-to and a berth of 2 cables clears all dangers.

Tory Island is a slab of rock 2 miles long tilted towards Bloody Foreland with cliffs on its N side and a low S shore. The high torrs from which the island gets its name are a fine sight at its NE corner. As the most isolated inhabited island on the Irish coast it is an interesting port of call and, unless there is a high swell, it is usually possible to stop for a few hours or overnight. Local boats remain at anchor for much of the summer in Camusmore Bay and if the islanders are not pulling them up for the night it is usually a sign that it is safe to stay. However the weather is particularly liable to sudden change in this area so one must be prepared to leave quickly. Toberglassan Bay, described above, offers good shelter close at hand. The population is about 170. Mailboat three times a fortnight to Magheroarty. PO with telephone. Limited groceries. The island has a licensed club which opens daily at 1600. No fuel.

Lights. On the NW point of Tory Island Fl (4) 30 s, 40 m, 20 M from 27 m high black tower with one white band, obscured from 277° to 302°. Horn 60 s. Radiobeacon, *see Appendix 5.* On Camusmore Bay pier occas FW, 2 M.

Tidal streams in Tory Sound start running NE at +0230 Dover and turn SW at −0330 Dover, max rate at springs 2 kn. There is a tide rip off the NW corner of the island.

Danger. Between Camusmore Bay and the W of the island sunken ledges extend up to 3 cables offshore and outside their W end are Rinnamurreeny Rocks which dry. In bad weather there are breakers a long way outside the rocks so this coast should be given a berth of a mile. This danger is of course greatest when coming from the SW at night. Elsewhere round the island a berth of 2 cables clears all dangers.

Anchorages. There are three available to be chosen according to weather.

Camusmore Bay (*see plan*) is the most convenient for exploring the island in fine weather. It is sheltered from NW through N to ESE but open from SW to SE so you should not remain there overnight except in very settled conditions. Approach keeping the steps on the inner or E side of the pier open of the pierhead so as to avoid the reefs on the W of the bay. Anchor on this line in 2·5 to 5 m, sand and weed. There is 0·3 m at the outer end of the pier, rocky bottom. (*see photo*)

Port Doon, at the E end, is sheltered from SW through W to NNW. Anchor in the mouth of the bay in about 6 m, sand. In the bay there is a new quay 24 m long with a least depth of 1·5 m alongside, almost twice as much in places as the bottom is rock; if the sea is calm it is convenient for berthing.

Portnaglass (The Green Port) is on the N side ½ mile E of the lighthouse. It is sheltered from NW through W to SE. There is a small jetty and steps up the cliffs where the lighthouse stores used to be landed. Anchor off in 10 to 18 m.

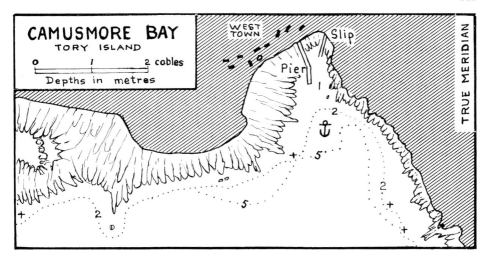

Portachulla (justs NNW of Port Doon and not named on the metric chart) is not recommended; it looks a possibility on the chart but is in fact a bad place much encumbered with boulders and difficult for landing.

Bloody Foreland, the NW extremity of Ireland, is a very low point from which reefs extend for a cable. It slopes up very gradually towards Bloody Foreland Hill which is 1½ miles inshore and 315 m high. Swell is apt to run high off the point so it should be rounded at a respectful distance. **Light**. A small concrete beacon near the end of the point shows Fl WG 14 m 7·5 s 6/4 M W to seaward between 062° and 232°, G between these bearings and the land on either side. The green sector should of course be avoided at night but note that it has a luminous range of only 4 miles which is less than the distance to Inishbeg which is within the sector. However if sailing round this coast at night it is simplest and safest to pass outside Tory Island.

The coast south beyond Bloody Foreland is described in a companion volume "Sailing Directions for the South and West Coasts of Ireland" published by Irish Cruising Club Publications Ltd. In order to assist visiting yachtsmen a fifth chapter has been added in this volume in two parts. (i) The passage NE across to Scotland. (ii) The refuge port of Dunmore East in case of bad weather when approaching Ireland from the SE.

Part 2

CROSSING TO SCOTLAND
and REFUGE PORT of DUNMORE E

NE Passage to Scotland and SE Refuge Port of Dunmore E

This chapter is divided into two sections:

(1) is the passage from the NE corner across to Scotland in order to connect up with the Clyde Cruising Club Directions for their area.

(2) is the area from the Tuskar Rock as far west as Dunmore E. It has been added in the interests of safety in case of yachtsmen approaching from the S find it difficult to make Arklow which is the best port N of Tuskar on the E coast. This section has been reprinted from the Club's South and West Coast Sailing Directions which should be consulted if intending to proceed further along the S coast.

CHAPTER V

Part 1—Crossing to Scotland

This is no more difficult than a coasting passage if you can pick your weather, but the following notes may help those making the crossing for the first time, or in small craft. (*see plan page 124*)

Distances. Nearest points: Torr Point to Mull of Kintyre 11 miles. Rathlin to Mull of Oa (Islay) 16 miles. **Shortest distance between fair weather landings**: Torr Point to Southend (Kintyre) 15 miles. **Port-to-port distances**: Donaghadee to Port Patrick 19 miles. Larne to Port Patrick 24 miles. Larne to Lock Ryan anchorage 30 miles. These are, however, not very attractive arrival points for those anxious to minimise exposure as there are still longish passages ahead to get to the Clyde, eg 43 miles from Port Patrick to Lamlash, or 34 miles from Loch Ryan. Ailsa Craig is an amusing stopping-place, particularly early in the year when the gannets are nesting; you can moor alongside at the NE corner, 34 miles from Carnlough, 18 from Loch Ryan.

More Practical Passages. From Carnlough to Southend or Sanda 22½ miles, to Gigha 41 miles, to Campbeltown 33 miles. **From Red Bay** to Southend 19 miles, to Sanda 21 miles, to Campbeltown 33 miles, to Gigha 37 miles. Adminish Bay in Gigha has ten Highlands Development buoys which are in a bay well sheltered from all quarters except E. It is also close to the hotel. Southend does not provide full shelter, but in offshore wind is a place to get the anchor down and relax; the same may be said of Sanda. A useful possibility is to head N from Carnlough and postpone deciding whether to go outside Kintyre or into the Clyde until you see what wind and tide conditions are like when abreast Fair Head. **From Portrush** to Port Ellen (Islay) 30 miles. Rathlin is an interesting place to stop, assuming you know the anchorages, and shortens the distance. **From E coast Rathlin** to Port Ellen 21 miles, to Gigha 28 miles. In the right conditions these passages from the N coast offer probably the simplest and shortest ways of getting to Scotland, and to attractive parts of it with many more possibilities close at hand. There are in every summer, times when the smallest boat can cross if you can pick your day.

Tides and Departure Times. Much more important than bare distances are the run of the tides. A passage which can be made with a fair tide all or most of the way, e.g Carnlough to Gigha, becomes substantially shorter, whereas a passage across the streams, e.g. Red Bay to Sanda, may be longer or, at best, the tide is of no help. The selection of the best state of the tide for departure is vital. This will vary with direction and strength of wind and the speed you are likely to make through the water. Rules of thumb are as follows. **For the Clyde**: Leave Red Bay at half-ebb. Leave Carnlough 1 hr earlier, ie 2 hrs after HW. **For Gigha**: Leave Red Bay at HW. Leave Carnlough one or two hours before HW. **Returning from the Clyde**: Campbeltown is much the best

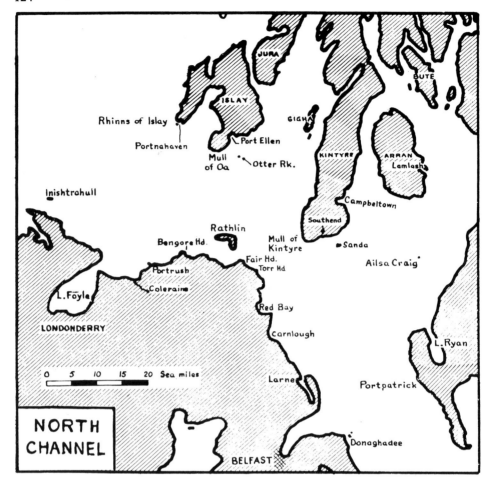

departure. Leave for Larne 6 hrs after HW Dover. Leave for Carnlough or Red Bay 5 hrs after HW Dover. This is because once past Sanda you will be cutting more or less across the tide, so you can take advantage of the ebb out of the Clyde for the first part of the passage. In W or NW wind you will do best with some ebb running N to allow you to sail freer. It is a mistake to leave too early as you might be pushed too far W along the S coast of Kintyre and get into the tide race of the Mull. **From Gigha**, leave at 4 hrs after HW Dover, against the tide, pick up a fair eddy close inshore at 6 hrs after and you should arrive at Carnlough before the end of the fair flood tide. **From Portrush to Islay**, wind direction will control your timing. In the old days the pulling boats used to leave an hour before local LW, go down to Bengore Head on the E-going tide and found they were pushed up to Islay by the W-going tide out of the Irish Sea. If you can sail at 6 kn or better, a good time to leave Portrush for Jura or Sound of Islay is 2 hrs before HW Dover (or 2 hrs after local LW). The E-going tide on your quarter will give some assistance and you should arrive off the Otter Rock just as the tide is turning N. You will be passing the overfalls and crossing the open water when the tide is slack. If bound for Port Ellen from Portrush with a commanding breeze sailing at say 5 kn, a good time to leave is 4 hrs before HW Dover; you can then steer the direct course to Port Ellen and the tide will change at about half-way and should even out; but you should be prepared to alter course depending on how you find you have been set at the half-way mark, keeping a bit in hand to the E to avoid being set W if arriving late at the S end of Islay. The total set of a tide in the outer part of the North Channel at springs usually works out at about 10 miles.

Winds tend to change direction a point or two and blow harder in the narrows between Kintyre and Fair Head due to the funnel effect of the land. NW and SE winds are most affected; NW winds in the Irish Sea often back a couple of points as you round Fair Head. The same funnel effect increases the speed of S winds between Jura and Kintyre.

Very Small Craft. Best departure point is Cushendun, for passage 16 miles to Southend (average 4 hours). Leave at −0130 Belfast, which is an hour before local LW. This gives you time to get clear of the overfalls which occur on Antrim coast on the first hour of flood, lets you be in the open water during the slack, then get a bit of help from the flood into the Clyde to work E. It is advisable in a small boat to keep at least 3 miles S of Deas Point, now called Sron Uamha, the S tip of Mull of Kintyre, as there is a tendency to ground swell and broken water round it, particularly near LW. Returning from Southend, an hour before local LW is again a good time to start to get clear of Sanda at slack water and have the help of the flood S along the Antrim coast. The rip extending 3 or 4 miles N of Garron Point on the ebb at +0200 Dover is bad enough to be troublesome to small craft and should be avoided if possible.

Places to Avoid, if there is any sea running, are the tide rip off the Mull of Kintyre, the close vicinity of Sanda, and, on the Irish side, the vicinity of Torr Point and Rathlin. If forced to cross the North Channel from Islay in bad weather, which should be avoided if at all possible, the fishermen say it is better to keep down the Kintyre coast as the sea runs a little easier there than farther W. The worst tide rip in the whole area is off the Rhinns of Islay and in a blow this should be avoided at all costs. However, Portnahaven at the SW tip of Islay inside Orsay Island is a good bunkhole and a good departure point for a visit to Donegal (29 miles to Inishtrahull). As it does not seem to be described elsewhere, directions are given below.

Portnahaven. HW −0110 Oban (roughly +0540 Dover). Rise: 2·6–2·3–1·3–0·5 m. The tide runs at 8 kn at springs outside Orsay where it can cause dangerous overfalls; it is fairly strong inside the island. Entry should not be considered except in reasonably quiet conditions. Old chart 3116 did not show great details and metric chart 2168 is slightly smaller scale. The NW entrance between unmarked rocks is impossible in on-shore winds. The entrance N of Orsay Island is used by locals but dangerous for visitors. Only the SE entrance can be recommended. Keep slightly closer to the Islay shore than to Orsay, follow it round N and anchor inshore off a new concrete pier in 3·3 m, sand. There is a completely sheltered pool with 0·8 m just inside the gut leading to Portnahaven village; it is best to pass N of the covered rock outside the gut. **Facilities**. Small shops, pub, PO.

Lossit Bay, 3 miles N of Portnahaven, is a good anchorage in off-shore winds, clean sand. No facilities.

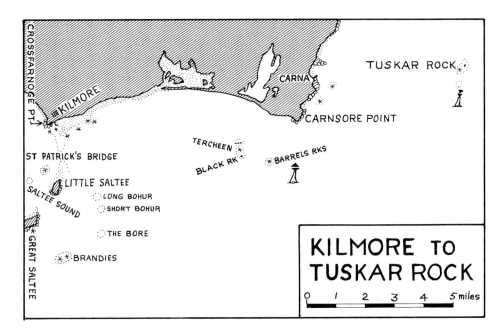

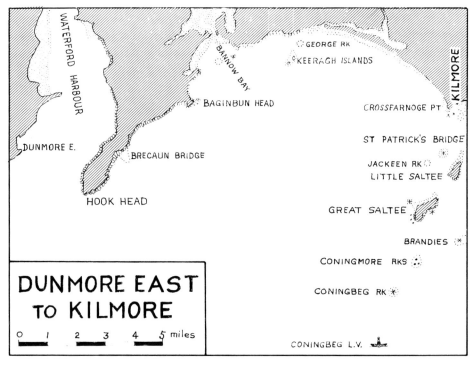

CHAPTER V

Part 2—Refuge Harbour–Dunmore East

A yacht coming from the S to cruise on the E coast of Ireland described in this book will normally pass outside Tuskar Rock and head for Rosslare or Arklow. In the event of strong N winds it may be advisable to leave Tuskar Lt, the Saltee Islands with Coningbeg LV to starboard and head for Dunmore East until the weather moderates. These directions are included in this edition in case of such an eventuality.

Warning. The sea area off the SE corner of Ireland is one to be avoided in bad weather. The tide runs strong right across the entrance to St. George's Channel, 2½ kn at springs, so it can be very rough even right out to sea. Between the Coningbeg and the Tuskar there are many rocks, shoals and irregular soundings up to 7 miles offshore. In gale conditions with wind against tide there may be heavy overfalls which could prove fatal for a small yacht. In recent years yachts have been lost in this area.

Tuskar Rock is 5 m high and lies 6 miles E by N of Carnsore Point, the SE extremity of Ireland. A tall white lighthouse and a radio mast stand on the island. It is clean on the E side but foul for a cable N and W. 2 cables NNW is Gypsy Rock with 2 m over it, 2½ cables SW is rock awash and 6½ cables SSW is South Rock with 2·4 m over it.

Yachts should give the Tuskar a good berth, especially in light weather for as well as the tide setting onto the rock there is probably an eddy running back towards it on the other side.

Light. A light is shown from a lighthouse on the rock, Q (2) 7·5 s, 35 m, 28 M. Fog signal Horn. (4) 45 s. Radiobeacon see Appendix 5.

Buoy. A light buoy, S Card Q (6) + LF 15 s, is moored almost a mile S of South Rock.

Shipping Lanes. There is a traffic separation zone off the Tuskar Rock which position is shown on chart 2049. The SW lane passes 2 to 5 miles outside the rock, the NE lane passes 7 to 10 miles outside the rock. The inshore zone is between the rock and the SW lane.

OFFSHORE PASSAGE. A yacht passing E of the Tuskar should continue S to the South Rock light buoy before altering course for the Coningbeg LV, on which line she should leave the Barrels buoy (see below) ½ to 1 mile to starboard. This is a straightforward trouble-free route and is obligatory in darkness, bad visibility or heavy weather from the S or SE. A yacht rounding Carnsore Point in the evening or with deteriorating visibility should also make for the Barrels buoy and Coningbeg LV. Greenore Point, some 5 miles N of Carnsore Point, seen 022° of Carnsore Point leads ½ mile E of the Barrels and rather less W of the buoy.

INSHORE PASSAGE. It is shorter, especially if bound for Waterford Harbour, to pass between the Saltees or N of them. It is only possible by day and in clear weather but it is more interesting and also often less rough, particularly with a head wind, than it would be out at the Coningbeg.

The many dangers surrounding this route are described below. The large scale chart, 2740, is almost essential for this passage. A yacht rounding the Tuskar and wishing to continue inshore should first round South Rock buoy and then make good a course to clear S of the Bailies Bank and then come in to, say, ¼ mile S of Carnsore Point. From Carnsore Point make for the N Saltee or for the gap between it and the mainland leaving Tercheen (N of Black Rock) and the wreck N of Tercheen and later the Bohurs to port; e.g. pass 8 cables N of Black Rock, 2 m high.

CARNSORE POINT is a low clay cliff (16 m) with rocky shelves below it. There are several rocks to the NE of it but on the S side it is fairly clear with a depth of 18 m 3 cables off. In rough weather with wind against tide there is quite a bad race off it around the times of high and low water; the stream is slack at about half tide. Approaching from S or E in clear weather the position of the point may be judged by Forth Mountain (224 m) just SW of Wexford town which may be sighted from 20 miles offshore, but yachts from the S should not plan to make a landfall on this dangerous corner of the Irish coast.

DANGERS BETWEEN CARNSORE POINT AND THE SALTEES. Inshore of the course there are some shoal patches which should be avoided if there is a big sea running. There is a 3 m patch ¾ mile W of Carnsore Point. Kilturk Bank with 5 m lies ¾ mile offshore 5 miles W of the point. A 6 m rock lies halfway between Kilturk Bank and the point.

Nether Rock with 5 m over it lies 1½ miles SW of Carnsore Point; it is clear of a yacht's direct course but should be avoided if beating.

The Barrels, a dangerous group of rocks which dry 1·5 m, lie 1½ miles SW by S of Carnsore Point. **Light buoy.** An E Card Q (3) 10 s, Horn (2) 10 s, is moored 1 mile SE of the rock.

Black Rock is a conspicuous rock 2 m high and ¼ cable long and lies 2 miles SW by S of Carnsore Point. **Tercheen Rock** lies 2 cables N of it and dries at LW. The latter rock will be ¼ mile to port on a direct course from Carnsore Point to Saltee Sound.

The Bohurs are 3 separate rocks. Long Bohur, the furthest N and shallowest of them, lies 1¼ miles E of the S end of North Saltee and has 4 m over it; it is on the direct course from Carnsore Point to Saltee Sound. SSE of it is Short Bohur with 7·3 m and ¾ mile S of this is The Bore with 5·5 m. There are tide races and broken water over these three rocks with wind against tide.

Rocks southward of the Saltees. About 1½ miles SE of South Saltee are **The Brandies**, two dangerous rocks 2½ cables apart; the W rock dries 2·5 m and the E rock dries 0·9 m.

Coningmore consists of 3 rocks within 1½ cables of each other, the largest 4 m high; they are steep-to and lie 1¼ miles S of the South Saltee; they are a most useful mark by day to a yacht which has been unable to avoid this dangerous area.

Coningbeg Rock which dries 2·8 m lies 1¼ miles SW of Coningmore and 2½ miles from the South Saltee. When covered its position can often be seen by its breakers but a yacht should keep well away from it.

Lightship. Coningbeg LV moored nearly 2 miles seaward of the rock is painted red and shows Fl. (3) 30 s, 12 m, 24 M. Fog Signal Horn (3) 60 s.

Red Bank with least water 7·9 m, lies 1½ miles W of Coningmore. It extends ¼ mile N and S and there is a tide rip over it.

Tidal streams. Between Carnsore Point and the Saltees the stream starts running ENE at −0110 Cobh (+0525 Dover), spring rate 2·4 kn. The WSW-going stream begins at +0510 Cobh (−0040 Dover), spring rate 2·6 kn. S of the Saltees the streams are rotary—clockwise. The E-going stream begins N at −010 Cohn (+0535 Dover), is at its greatest rate of 1·7 kn (springs) to the ENE at +0200 Cobh and ends SE. The W-going stream begins S at +0530 Cobh (−0020 Dover) reaches 1·9 kn (springs) W by S at −0355 Cobh and ends NW. Slack water lasts about 1 hour. There are ripples near and over all the shoals.

SOUTH SALTEE ISLAND is about 1 mile in length, ⅓ mile in breadth and is 57 m high at its S end. It is fringed by outlying rocks. The NW side of the shore has a boulder beach and these boulders continue out into a spit to the N of the island for ¼ mile called Sebber Bridge. Least water 4 m at its N end and 0·6 m at its S. Power's Rock lies 3 cables NW of centre of island and has 0·3 m over it while Whitty Rock, which is awash at LW lies 3 cables W of the centre of the island. 2½ cables S of the S point of the island lies Shoal Rock with 0·9 m over it, but its position is usually indicated by a tide ripple. Panstown Rock, close to the SW side of the S point of the island, shows above HW and Molly Hoy lies a little over 1 cable to NW of Panstown and shows. There is a group of drying rocks close to the E side of the S tip of the island called the Seven Heads. Makestone Rock shows and is close to the shore on the E side of the island.

NORTH SALTEE ISLAND is 35 m high and 1¾ miles off the shore. The beacon shown on the chart at its SE end is a cairn of loose stones. There are a number of rocks off the island. There is a ledge extending N which almost joins Kilmore Spit, a ledge running S from the shore, which together are called St. Patrick's Bridge, described below. Murroch's Rock, awash at LW, lies over ½ mile NW of the North Saltee and there is a rock with only 0·2 m over it ¼ mile W of the centre of the island. Jackeen Rock lies a mile to the WNW of the S of the North Saltee and has 1·5 m over it. Galgee Rock, awash at LW, lies ¾ cable to the SW of the S point of the island. Goose Rock which dries 2·5 m is ¼ mile NW of Galgee Rock and ¾ cable offshore.

130

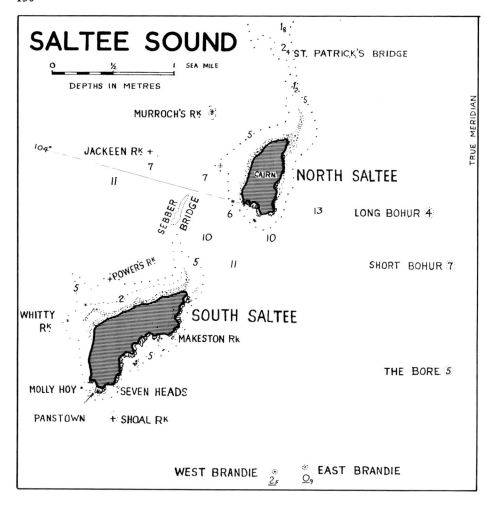

SALTEE SOUND

0 ½ 1 SEA MILE

DEPTHS IN METRES

MURROCH'S Rᵏ ✳

JACKEEN Rᵏ +
7
104°
11

7

SEBBER BRIDGE

CAIRN

NORTH SALTEE

13 LONG BOHUR 4

6
10 10

5 11 SHORT BOHUR 7

+POWER'S Rᵏ
5
5 2

WHITTY Rᵏ

SOUTH SALTEE

MAKESTON Rk

THE BORE 5

5

MOLLY HOY · SEVEN HEADS

PANSTOWN + SHOAL Rᵏ

WEST BRANDIE 2₅ O₉ EAST BRANDIE

1₈
2₄ ST. PATRICK'S BRIDGE
1₂
5
5

TRUE MERIDIAN

SALTEE SOUND (*see plan*) must be approached with caution owing to the numerous outlying rocks. Making the sound from the E steer from the N tip of S Saltee until you are nearly midway between the two islands and then steer 330° through the sound so as to avoid Sebber Bridge and the shoal soundings running N from S Saltee. Do not carry on too far on this course as it leads up near Jackeen Rock so alter course for the Hook when the cairn of stones on SE corner of N Saltee is in line with the SW point of that island, bearing 104°. Generally keep closer to the N Saltee when going through but not within 2 cables of it. Tidal streams in the sound are strong, reaching 3½ kn at springs, but do not set fairly through.

ST PATRICK'S BRIDGE is the shortest and simplest route from Carnsore Point to Hook Head and is constantly used by fishing boats but unfortunately there is no mark to guide the stranger. The deepest water is only 2·4 m and is about half-way between Kilmore Quay and N Saltee, a little nearer the latter. It can only be recommended to a W bound yacht with a fair and therefore rising tide or to an E-bound yacht above ½ tide, otherwise Saltee Sound is to be preferred.

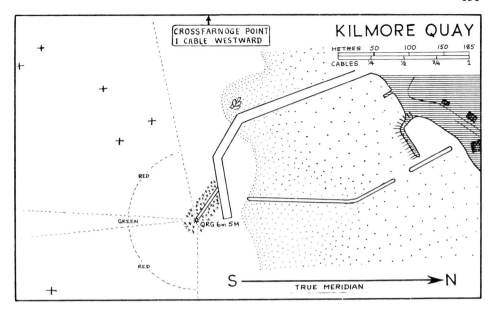

KILMORE QUAY (*see plan*) is just E of Crossfarnoge (or Forlorn) Point and just W of St. Patrick's Bridge. The harbour consists of a pier with 0·3 m alongside protected by a breakwater. It is in active use by locally owned fishing boats. Because of its lack of depth, indifferent shelter and the rocks and shoal water in the approach it is not recommended to yachts but in some circumstances it might suit to put in there.

Directions. Do not approach without sufficient rise to berth in 0·4 m. Coming from the W take care to pass at least ½ mile S of Crossfarnoge Point so as to avoid Forlorn Rock with 1·5 m over it which is ½ mile SSW of the point. When the E end of the breakwater (with light beacon) comes in line with Ballyteige Castle bearing true N steer in on this line. Coming from the E this line will be picked up almost immediately after crossing St. Patrick's Bridge. It leads in safely between the rocks called Lings on chart 2740 (but known as the Blackberries locally) which never dry but have very little water over them. A light, QRG 6 m, 5 M is shown from the end of the breakwater, visible between 269° through N to 077°. The G sector which leads safely in being from 354° to 003°. The fishermen use the village church instead of Ballyteige Castle as the day mark for entering. This gives a line of about 354° coinciding with the E edge of the green sector. This line leads over a charted depth of 1·3 m on Kilmore Spit. Berth at the pier or alongside a trawler. There is one berth on the breakwater side of the pier. A yacht should not be left unattended. If wishing to dry out consult a fisherman.

Facilities. Water and diesel on quay. Petrol, PO and groceries in village, also chandlery at fishermans' co-op. A RNLI lifeboat is stationed here.

SALTEES TO HOOK. The rocks W of the islands have already been described. Ballyteige Bay lies W of Crossfarnoge Point, and while its E end is clear, there are rocks and shoals in its NW end. The Keeragh's are two islets 6 m high and are 1 mile offshore with a reef extending from them in to the mainland. George Rock over ½ mile NE of the Keeragh's has only 1·2 m over it and is ½ mile offshore. Bannow Inlet W of the Keeragh's is very shoal and has a bar with only 0·3 m of water over it. Selskar Shoal is in the centre of the entrance and has 0·3 m over it while Selskar Rock dries 2 m and lies ¼ mile off Bannow Point on the E side of Bannow Bay. Baginbun Head is conspicuous with its Martello Tower and is SW of Bannow Bay. If beating down for the Hook the tides are slack inshore. Do not go too close in between Baginbun Head and the Hook as the shore here is foul for a few cables off and Brecaun Bridge 2 miles from Hook Head extends 3 cables off the shore and has a depth of only 1·4 m at its outer extremity. Forth Mountain, the only high point in SE Wexford, open to Baginbun Point 048° clears Brecaun Bridge.

Offshore anchorage. Baginbun and Bannow Bays are completely exposed to the SE but give good shelter in fresh W wind, so in these conditions, when the Hook Race is a formidable obstacle to any small yacht, they might provide a welcome overnight stopping place. The recommended anchorage is at the SW end of Bannow Bay just N of Ingard Point off the small drying dock there in 3 m sand, good holding. Ingard Point, 1 mile N of Baginbun Point, is foul for 1½ cables offshore; the mark to clear this is the largest house in Fethard village open N of the dock. Selskar Shoal, mentioned above, is ¾ mile ENE of Ingard Point so if beating in do not go too far in that direction. The dock has been dredged, exposing the rock in places; it has a depth of 1·5 m at half tide except towards the head; the best berth is just within the E pier. **Supplies**. Water at the dock. Petrol, diesel, provisions at Fethard, 1 mile.

Baginbun Bay also offers excellent shelter and holding. Watch out for lobster pots up to a mile offshore between the Hook and Baginbun Point, a salmon net extending from this point and more pots about 2 miles SE of it.

HOOK HEAD is the end of the low peninsula at the E side of the entrance to Waterford Harbour. A rocky ledge extends 2 cables SW of the point. There is a dangerous wreck 1¼ cables W of Doornoge Point, or about ½ mile NW of the Hook. **Light**. The Hook lighthouse is very distinctive consisting of a massive 12th century tower, 24 m high and about 12 m wide, white with two black bands, upon which stands a shorter modern light-tower. It shows Fl 3 s, 46 m, 24 M. Horn (2) 45 s.

Tidal Streams. From the Hook to the Saltees the tidal streams set E and W. The E-going stream begins at −0050 Cobh (+0545 Dover) and the W-going stream at +0553 Cobh (−0015 Dover). The rate near the Saltees is about 2 kn.

Off the Hook itself, especially in strong W winds there is a dangerous tidal race known as Tower Race, which extends about 1 mile S of the head. In general it is at its strongest from +0420 Cobh to −0455 Cobh (−0130 to +0140 Dover). If the race is expected to be bad a yacht should keep outside the 20 m line, when rounding Hook Point.

Distances.	Carnsore Point to Coningbeg Light Vessel	..	..	14	miles
	Coningbeg Light Vessel to Pollock Rock buoy (near Cork)			56¼	miles
	Carnsore Point to Hook (via Saltee sound)	..	..	21½	miles

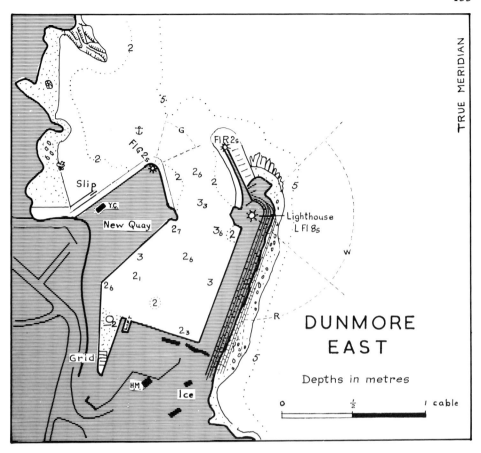

DUNMORE EAST (*see plan*) is a small artificial harbour on the W side of the entrance to Waterford Harbour. The village of Dunmore East is a popular holiday resort. The harbour is the base for the important autumn herring fishery during which it is crowded with fishing boats. Recent major improvements have given it a depth of 2 m to 3·4 m and made it safe in all summer weather, though there may be a swell along the NW wall in S winds. It is a popular port of call for yachts which are made welcome, though owners are reminded that it is primarily a fishing port and they should take care not to inconvenience fishing boats.

Lights. The large granite lighthouse on the pier shows L Fl WR 8 s, 13 m, 12–9 M. W from 224° to 310°, R thence to 004°, obscured elsewhere. A pillar on the end of the breakwater which forms an extension of the pier shows Fl R 2 s from 310° through S to 000°. On the N point of the W quay a light Fl G 2 s shows from 165° to 246°.

Directions. By day the white pilot look-out on Black Nob just S of the harbour is conspicuous as is the ice plant and the pier itself. Enter under power or much reduced sail and berth at the E pier, then report to the HM for instructions. The Waterford Harbour SC has a clubhouse on the NW quay. There are yacht moorings outside the harbour in the bight N of the NW quay which is a good sheltered berth in fine weather and W winds; these moorings are allocated by the HM. There are two baulks of timer with tyre fenders alongside the New Quay to facilitate yachts, 3 m at LAT.

By night approaching from the E, give Hook Head a berth of ½ mile or more depending on the state of the sea. Alter course for Dunmore East light when in the red sector. From the W hold course for Hook Head until the red sector of Dunmore East light is entered then alter course for it. The white sector of the light shows across the estuary and up it and clears Creadon Head.

Facilities. Water from tap on the pier. Diesel obtainable at the quay. Good shops and hotels and PO in the village. Bus to Waterford. The Waterford Harbour SC has its clubhouse on the New Quay and is most helpful to visitors. RNLI lifeboat lies afloat. There are good public heads on the N quay near the grid where there are showers with plenty of hot water; open at 0800.

Admiralty Charts and Publications

Chart No.	Title of Charts (most plans larger scale)	Scale 1:	Publication Date
1123	Western Approaches to St. George's Channel and Bristol Channel	500,000	21-12-84
1121	Irish Sea and St. George's and North Channels ..	500,000	30-9-88
1410	St. George's Channel	200,000	24-10-80
1787	Carnsore Point to Wicklow Head	100,000	27-7-84
1772	Rosslare and Wexford Harbours with approaches ..	Various	15-5-81
1468	Arklow to the Skerries Islands	100,000	24-8-84
633	Plans of Arklow, Wicklow, Malahide, Rogerstown, Skerries Killough and Ardglass	Various	11-11-77
1411	Irish Sea—Western Part	200,000	14-12-84
1415	Dublin Bay	25,000	23-9-88
1447	Port of Dublin and Dun Laoghaire Harbour	7,500	20-12-85
44	Howth to Ardglass	100,000	20-12-85
1431	Drogheda and Dundalk	Various	28-7-88
2800	Carlingford Lough (plans of Entrance, Warrenpoint and Kilkeel)	20,000	7-7-89
2093	Southern approach to North Channel	100,000	14-10-88
2156	Strangford Lough	37,500	24-6-88
2159	Strangford Narrows	12,500	2-2-83
2198	North Channel—southern part	75,000	25-9-87
3709	Copeland Islands and Donaghadee Sound	12,500	7-12-73
1753	Belfast Lough (with plans of Belfast Docks and Bangor Bay)	3,750	9-5-86
1237	Larne Lough and approaches	10,000	30-6-89
2199	North Channel—northern part	75,000	13-1-89
2798	Lough Foyle to Sanda Island including Rathlin Island	75,000	2-9-88
49	Portrush and approaches	15,000	7-2-75
2499	Lough Foyle	40,000	13-6-86
2811	Sheep Haven to Lough Foyle, including Inishtrahull ..	75,000	25-9-87
2697	Lough Swilly (including Culdaff Bay, scale 10,000) ..	37,500	27-2-76
2699	Horn Head to Fanad Head with Mulroy Bay	30,000	11-11-77
2752	Bloody Foreland to Horn Head, including Tory Island	30,000	12-12-75
2723	Western Approaches to the North Channel	200,000	16-2-79

Publications:
Irish Coast Pilot (12th edition, 1986).
Admiralty Tide Tables, volume 1.
Admiralty List of Lights, volume A, 1991.
Tidal Stream Atlases: No. 256 Irish Sea.
       No. 218 N Coast of Ireland and W Coast of Scotland.
Chart No. 5011: Symbols and abbreviations used on Admiralty Charts (Book Edition 5).

Agents for Admiralty charts:
Union Chandlery Ltd., Anderson's Quay, Cork. (021) 21643. Telex 24914.
Galway Maritime Services, New Docks, Galway. (091) 66568.
Windmill Leisure and Marine Ltd., 3 Windmill Lane, Dublin 2. (01) 772008. Telex 24511.
James Tedford & Co. Ltd., 5 Donegall Quay, Belfast 1 (0232) 326763.
Todd Chart Agency, Ltd., North Quay, The Harbour, Portrush, Co. Antrim BT56 8DF. (0265) 824176. Fax (0265) 823077.

APPENDIX 2

For Calculating Times of Local High-Water and Low-Water

Difference of time between secondary ports and the local standard ports.

Standard port DUBLIN (North Wall)	H.W. at GMT 0000 & 1200	0700 & 1900	L.W. at GMT 0500 & 1700	0000 & 1200
Secondary ports	Time differences			
Rosslare Harbour	−0440	−0710	−0440	−0710
Wexford Harbour	−0350	−0720	−0325	−0725
Polduff	−0321	−0431	−0340	−0414
Courtown	−0300	−0400	−0315	−0345
Arklow	−0215	−0255	−0225	−0245
Wicklow	−0035	−0047	−0038	−0044
Greystones	−0008	−0008	−0008	−0008
Dun Laoghaire	−0006	−0001	−0003	−0002
Howth	−0005	−0015	+0005	−0005
Malahide Inlet	−0019	−0013	+0006	+0014
Balbriggan	−0021	−0015	+0002	+0010
River Boyne Bar	−0025	−0015	0000	+0110
Dundalk (Soldiers Pt)	−0010	−0010	+0045	0000
Cranfield Point	−0027	−0011	−0007	+0017
Warren Point	−0020	−0010	+0040	+0040

Standard port BELFAST	H.W. at GMT 0100 & 1300	0700 & 1900	L.W. at GMT 0000 & 1200	0600 & 1800
Secondary ports	Time differences			
Kilkeel	+0010	+0010	0000	0000
Newcastle	+0025	+0035	+0020	+0040
Killard Point	+0011	+0021	+0005	+0025
Killyleagh	+0157	+0207	+0211	+0231
Portavogie	+0010	+0020	+0010	+0020
Donaghadee	+0020	+0020	+0023	+0023
Carrickfergus	+0005	+0005	+0005	+0005
Larne	+0005	0000	+0010	−0005
Red Bay	+0022	−0010	+0007	−0017
Cushendun	+0010	−0030	0000	−0025

Standard port **LONDONDERRY**	H.W. at GMT		L.W. at GMT	
	0200 & 1400	0900 & 2100	0700 & 1900	0300 & 1500
Secondary ports	Time differences			
Ballycastle Bay	+0053	−0147	+0056	−0125

Standard port **LONDONDERRY**	H.W. at GMT		L.W. at GMT	
	0200 & 1400	0800 & 2000	1100 & 2300	0500 & 1700
Secondary ports	Time differences			
Portrush	−0105	−0105	−0105	−0105
Coleraine	−0020	−0130	−0020	−0110
Moville	−0046	−0058	−0052	−0108
Culdaff Bay	−0136	−0156	−0146	−0206

Standard port **GALWAY**	H.W. at GMT		L.W. at GMT	
	0200 & 1400	0900 & 2100	0200 & 1400	0800 & 2000
Secondary ports	Time differences			
Inishtrauhull	+0100	+0100	+0115	+0200
Trawbreaga Bay	+0115	+0059	+0109	+0125
Rathmullan	+0125	+0050	+0126	+0118
Mulroy Bar	+0108	+0052	+0102	+0118
Fanny's Bay	+0145	+0129	+0151	+0207
Mulroy Broad Water	+0329	+0313	+0351	+0407
Downings Bay	+0057	+0043	+0053	+0107
Inishbofin Bay	+0040	+0026	+0032	+0046

If a tide table for the standard ports Dublin, Belfast, Derry or Galway is available these time differences, from the Admiralty Tide Tables, enable H.W. at the corresponding secondary ports to be found more accurately than in relation to H.W. Dover as indicated in the text. If the tide table gives L.W. this can also be determined. For example: To find the time of L.W. Rosslare. Supposing L.W. Dublin is 2130 BST, i.e., 2030 GMT, this is half-way between the GMTs 1700 and 0000 at the head of the L.W. columns. Between the two Rosslare L.W. time differences, −0536 and −0620, there is 44 minutes so deduct 0558 (0536 + 22 minutes) from L.W. Dublin and L.W. Rosslare is 1532 BST.

Shortest Distances between Ports (Nautical miles)

Upper chart (ports listed diagonally: Carnsore Point, Rosslare, Arklow, Wicklow, Dun Laoghaire, Howth, Lough Shinny, Boyne, Greencastle L. Carlingford, Kilkeel, Ardglass, Ringhaddy, Portavogie, Donaghadee, Larne, Red Bay, Fair Head)

From	2	3	4	5	6	7	8	9	10	11	12	13	14	15	16	17
Carnsore Point	7	39	52	71	76	85	98	114	115	129	144	145	155	173	187	196
Rosslare		34	47	66	70	79	92	108	109	123	138	139	149	167	181	190
Arklow			14	33	37	46	59	75	76	90	105	106	116	134	148	157
Wicklow				21	25	35	48	63	64	78	93	94	104	122	136	145
Dun Laoghaire					8	16	29	46	47	61	76	77	87	105	119	128
Howth						9	22	39	40	55	70	71	81	99	113	122
Lough Shinny							13	30	31	46	61	62	73	91	105	114
Boyne								21	23	41	56	57	68	86	100	109
Greencastle L. Carlingford									6	24	39	40	51	69	83	92
Kilkeel										18	33	34	46	64	78	87
Ardglass											15	16	27	45	59	68
Ringhaddy												21	32	50	64	73
Portavogie													12	30	44	53
Donaghadee														18	32	41
Larne															17	26
Red Bay																11

Lower chart (ports listed diagonally: Fair Head, Church Bay, Benbane Head, Portrush, Greencastle, Culdaff, Inishtrahull, Ireland's North Point, Trawbreaga Bar, Port Salon, Fahan, Mulroy Bar, Downings, Tory Island, Bloody Foreland)

From	2	3	4	5	6	7	8	9	10	11	12	13	14	15
Fair Head	4													
Church Bay	12	10												
Benbane Head	18	17	7											
Portrush	29	28	18	11										
Greencastle	34	33	23	18	12									
Culdaff	39	36	28	24	19	9								
Inishtrahull	43	41	31	27	21	10	6							
Ireland's North Point	48	46	36	32	26	15	11	5						
Trawbreaga Bar	57	55	45	41	35	24	20	14	12					
Port Salon	64	62	52	48	42	30	27	21	20	9				
Fahan	60	58	48	44	38	27	23	17	16	11	19			
Mulroy Bar	66	64	54	50	44	33	29	23	23	18	26	9		
Downings	73	71	61	57	51	40	36	30	30	25	33	16	14	
Tory Island	78	76	66	62	56	45	41	35	34	29	37	19	17	6

Longships to Wicklow Head	... ...	173
Longships to South Rock L.V.	... ...	260
Dun Laoghaire to Port St. Mary	... ...	68
Dun Laoghaire to Holyhead	... ...	52
Dun Laoghaire to Dunmore East	... ...	100

Donaghadee to Port Patrick	... ...	19
Larne to Campbeltown	... ...	38
Carnlough to Gigha	... ...	42
Portrush to Port Ellen, Islay	... ...	30
Portrush to Gigha	... ...	43

APPENDIX 4

Way Points

These positions have been prepared to give approximately 1M clearance of prominent headlands, buoys, etc. or approximately ½M off the entrance to harbours, when visual fixing should be possible in average visibility. They should be very carefully checked before entering any of them to an electronic means of assistance to the navigator.

Place	Way Point Positions	Way Point	
Carnsore Point	1M SE	52 09 70 N	06 20 60 W
Tuskar Rock Lt.	1M N	52 13 20 N	06 12 40 W
Rosslare Pier	½M N	52 16 00 N	06 20 20 W
E Blackwater Buoy	1M E	52 28 00 N	06 06 40 W
Cahore Point	1M E	52 33 90 N	06 09 85 W
Arklow Harbour	½M E	52 47 60 N	06 07 35 W
Arklow Lanby	1M E	52 39 50 N	05 56 40 W
N Arklow Buoy	1M E	52 53 90 N	05 53 40 W
Wicklow Head	1M E	52 57 90 N	05 58 25 W
Wicklow Harbour	½M NE	52 59 30 N	06 01 25 W
W Codling Buoy	1M W	53 06 95 N	05 56 20 W
Muglins Lt.	1M E	53 16 05 N	06 02 70 W
Kesh Bank Lt.	1M N	53 19 65 N	05 55 40 W
Dun Laoghaire Harbour	½M N	53 18 60 N	06 07 50 W
Baily Lt.	1M E	53 21 70 N	06 01 40 W
Howth Harbour	¼M N	53 23 85 N	06 03 90 W
Lamby Island	1M W	53 29 35 N	06 03 70 W
Rockabill Lt.	1M W	53 35 80 N	06 01 80 W
Drogheda Entrance	1M E	53 43 25 N	06 11 90 W
Clogher Head	1M E	53 47 70 N	06 11 20 W
Pile Light Dundalk	1M SE	53 57 85 N	06 16 50 W
Hellyhunter Buoy	1M S	53 59 25 N	06 02 05 W
St John's Point	1M S	54 12 60 N	05 39 50 W
Ardglass	½M SE	54 15 25 N	05 35 50 W
Strangford Lough Whistle Buoy	½M W	54 18 65 N	05 29 50 W
South Rock LV	1M E	54 24 45 N	05 20 20 W
Mew Island Lt.	2M E	54 41 90 N	05 27 30 W
Bangor Bay	½M N	54 40 50 N	05 40 18 W
Carrickfergus Harbour	½M S	54 42 15 N	05 48 30 W
Black Head Lt.	1M E	54 46 00 N	05 39 52 W
Larne Harbour Buoy	½M N	54 52 20 N	05 45 55 W
Maiden Light	1M E	54 55 70 N	05 41 90 W
Carnlough	½M E	54 59 57 N	05 58 30 W
Red Bay Lt.	½M E	55 03 95 N	06 02 20 W
Fair Head	1M N	55 14 65 N	06 08 85 W
Altacarry Lt.	1½M E	55 18 12 N	06 07 60 W
Bull Point Lt.	1M W	55 18 05 N	06 18 45 W
Portrush Harbour	½M W	55 12 35 N	06 40 48 W

APPENDIX 4—*continued*

Place	Way Point Positions	Way Point	
River Bann Entrance	½M N	55 10 82 N	06 46 60 W
Lough Foyle Whistle Buoy	½M S	55 14 80 N	06 52 50 W
Inishtrahull Lt.	1M S	55 24 82 N	07 14 55 W
Malin Head	1M W	55 22 50 N	07 25 70 W
Fanad Head Lt.	1M N	55 17 59 N	07 37 85 W
Melmore Head Lt.	1M N	55 16 10 N	07 46 85 W
Horn Head	1M N	55 14 70 N	07 59 00 W
Inishbeg Island	1M N	55 13 40 N	08 09 62 W
Tory Island	1M N	55 14 37 N	08 14 90 W
Bloody Foreland Lt.	1M N	55 10 50 N	08 17 00 W

APPENDIX 5
Weather Forecasts and Marine Radio Services

Radio Telefis Eireann (RTE) gives forecasts for all coastal waters at 0633, 1253, 1823, 2355 civil time. These are broadcast on RTE Radio 1 566 kHz. They include shipping forecasts for coastal waters all round Ireland and for the Irish Sea. They are broadcast on 567 kHz and on VHF 90·4 mHz (S half of Chapter I), 89·1 mHz (N half of Chapter I and Chapter II), 97·0 or 91·9 mHz (Chapters III and IV); however on VHF there may not be a forecast at 1823. Gale warnings are broadcast at the first programme junction after receipt.

    Central Forecast Office gives forecasts on request. Tel. (01) 424655.

    British Broadcasting Corporation (BBC), Radio Ulster, gives a detailed forecast for the Northern Ireland coastal waters at about 0005 or 0010 after the midnight news. It is broadcast on 1341 kHz and on VHF 92–95 mHz.

    Aldergrove Met Office at Belfast Airport also gives local forecasts on request; phone (08494) 22888 and ask for Forecasting Office. *Coast guards*. Any manned CG station will give a local forecast on request.

VHF/MF Broadcast Services

Traffic lists, Navigational Warnings, Gale Warnings, Decca Warnings and Weather Forecasts are broadcast on the Coast Stations Working Channel/Frequency at scheduled times GMT after a preliminary announcement on Channel 16 VHF and 2182 kHz MF.

MALIN HEAD CONTROL. Tel. (077) 70103. Telex. 42072 MALR EI

MALIN HEAD RADIO VHF Ch 23 C MF 1841 kHz A	DUBLIN RADIO VHF Ch 73 C
GLENHEAD RADIO VHF Ch 24 C	BELMULLET RADIO VHF Ch 83 C

VALENTIA CONTROL. Tel. (0667) 6109. Telex. 73968 VALR EI

DUNGARVAN RADIO VHF Ch 83 D	ROSSLARE RADIO VHF Ch 23 D

For calling and answering use Channel 16 VHF and 2182 kHz MF to call the nearest station to your own position. The control centre will answer on the same channel or frequency. Working channels VHF, frequencies MF and broadcast group schedules are shown under each station.

Broadcast Group	Traffic Lists	Navigation Warning	Weather Bulletin	Gale Warning	Decca Warning
A	0103 1503 0503 1703 0903 1903 1103 2103 1303 2303	0033 0433 0833 1233 1633 2033	No Service	No Service	(Note 1)
C	0103 1503 0503 1703 0903 1903 1103 2303	0033 0433 0833 1233 1633 2033 (Note 5)	0100 1300 0400 1600 0700 1900 1000 2200	0030 0630 1230 1830 (Note 3)	(Note 1)
D	0333 1533 0733 1733 0933 1933 1133 2133 1333 2333	0233 0633 1033 1433 1833 2233	0100 1300 0400 1600 0700 1900 1000 2200 (Note 5)	0030 0630 1230 1830 (Note 5)	(Note 1)

NOTES

1. Decca Warnings are broadcast on receipt and repeated at three minutes past the next hour and again one hour later.

2. Gale Warnings are broadcast on (MF) at the end of the first silence period after receipt and repeated at the next one of the following times 0303 0903 1503 2103 or, if the first broadcast is at a scheduled time, the message is repeated at the end of the next silence period.

3. Gale Warnings are broadcast on (VHF) on receipt and repeated again at the next one of the following times 0030 0630 1220 1830 or, if the first broadcast is at a scheduled time, the message is repeated one hour later.
N.B. Times one hour earlier when DST is in force from last Sunday in March to 4th Saturday in October.

4. Gale Warnings, if in force, general synopsis and area forecasts for SHANNON and FASTNET valid for 24 hours from the time of issue. (Issued by the UK Met. Service Bracknell).

5. Gale Warnings, if in force, general weather synopsis and detailed weather forecasts for Irish coastal waters, within 30 nautical miles of the coastline and for the Irish Sea. (Issued by the Irish Meteorological Service.)

NOTE: Schedule times are one hour earlier when DST is in force from last Sunday in March to 4th Saturday in October.

Other Forecasts:

(1) A forecast is given after RTE 1 television evening news at about 2115. This time may differ with special programmes. It includes weather maps, satellite photo and forecast. It is very good value and can usually be obtained ashore in an hotel or pub.
(2) Shannon Airport Met. Office (061) 61333 (Aviation only).
(3) Cork Airport Met. Office (021) 965974.
(4) South Munster Weather (021) 964600.
(5) North Munster and South Connaught Weather (061) 62677.
(6) Leinster Weather (01) 425555.
(7) North Connaught/Co Donegal (071) 69111.

Malinhead Radio Station. A Radiotelephone service, with facilities for connection to subscribers ashore, is now available through Malinhead Radio to yachts with suitable radio equipment. Call 2182 kHz, on which the station answers and will state working frequency either 1841 or 2593 kHz.

Marine Radio Beacons

Name	Range	Freq kHz	Signal		Mins past hour	
Tuskar Rock	50 M	296·5	TR	— · — ·	05	
Skerries (Wales)	50 M	301·1	SR	· · · · — ·	00	and every 6 mins
Wicklow Head	70 M	301·1	WK	· — — — · —	02	
Craigneish (IOM)	50 M	301·1	CN	— · — · — ·	03	
Point of Ayre (IOM)	50 M	301·1	PY	· — — · — · — —	04	
South Rock LV	50 M	301·1	SU	· · · · · —	05	
Kish Bank	20 M	312·6	KH	— · — · · · ·	00	every 1 min
Mew Island	50 M	294·2	MW	— — · — —	01	
Altacarry Head	50 M	294·2	AH	· — · · · ·	02	every 6 mins
Barra Head (Hebrides)	70/200 M	308	BD	— · · · — · ·	00	
Tory Island	70/100 M	308	TY	— — · — —	01	every 2 mins

All these stations are A–2★ transmission. During recognition BFO Off. During DF transmission BFO On or Off.

Radio Beacons for Aircraft

Name		Signal		Freq kHz	Lat	Long
Killiney		KLY	— · — · — · · — · — —	378	53°16½'N	06°07'W
Rush		RSH	· — · · · · · · · ·	326	53°31½'N	06°08'W

All beacons A0A2 transmission. During recognition BFO Off. During transmission BFO On. Beacons operate continuously.

APPENDIX 6
Port VHF Radio Stations

Port	Channel	Times	Call Signs
Rosslare	16/14/12/6	24 hrs	Rosslare Harbour
Wexford Boat Club	16	Limited	Wexford Boat Club
Courtown	16/8	Limited	Courtown Sailing Club
Arklow	16	24 hrs	Arklow Harbour
Wicklow	16/14	24 hrs	Wicklow Harbour
Dun Laoghaire	16/14	24 hrs	Harbour Office
Royal St. George	16/37	Limited	Royal St. George
Dublin	16	24 hrs	Dublin Harbour
Howth Marine	37	24 hrs	Howth Marina
Malahide	16/37/83	Limited	Malahide Yacht Club
Drogheda	16/11	24 hrs	Drogheda Harbour
Dundalk	16/14	Working days	Dundalk Pilots
Greenore	16	Working days	Greenore Harbour
Warrenpoint	16/14	24 hrs	Warrenpoint Pilot
Kilkeel	16	24 hrs	Kilkeel Harbour Master
Ardglass	16/14/12	24 hrs	Ardglass Harbour
Strangford	16	Office hours	Ferry Terminal
Portavogie	16/14	24 hrs	Portavogie Harbour
Donaghadee	16/08/06	Limited	Donaghadee Harbour
Bangor Marina	16/37/80	24 hrs	Bangor Marina
Belfast	16/12/11/10/08	24 hrs	Belfast Harbour Radio
Carrickfergus Marina	16/37	24 hrs	Carrickfergus Marina
Larne	16/14	24 hrs	Larne Harbour
Portrush	16/14	24 hrs	Portrush Harbour
Coleraine Marina	16/37	24 hrs	Coleraine Marina
Londonderry	16/14	24 hrs	Foyle Pilots

APPENDIX 7
Marine Rescue and Co-ordination Centre

This service covers, as far as this book of Sailing Directions is concerned, the area from Carnsore Point to Carlingford Lough and from Lough Foyle to Bloody Foreland. The Northern Ireland coast is covered by H.M. Coast Guard; see appendix 8.

Marine Rescue Coordination Centre (MRCC) Shannon is the Coordination Centre for the entire Shannon SAR Region.

Telephone numbers: (061) 61219/61969. Fax (061) 361623. Telex 72162 MRCC EI.

In SAR situations, the Centre utilises lifeboats of the RNLI, Cliff and Coastal Rescue Service Units, Irish Air Corps helicopters or fixed wing aircraft, Irish Naval vessels, Coastal Garda (Police) Units, and fishing vessels and shipping in the area of the incident. Personnel of the Commissioners of Irish Lights on manned lighthouses also participate in SAR by providing visual or communication assistance to MRCC.

MRCC has direct telephone contact with H.M. Coastguard at Swansea, the U.K. liaison station, if U.K. SAR assistance is required in the Irish SAR Region.

MRCC Shannon organises passage surveillance on pleasure craft intending to make coastal voyages or bound for foreign destinations.

List of Cliff and Coastal Rescue (CCRS) Units below. All units use specialised cliff climbing equipment, and hand-held radio transceivers and inflatable boats are available at some stations.

Carnsore Point	(053) 31102
Rosslare	(053) 32102
Curracloe	(053) 37174
Morris Castle	(053) 30129
Courtown	(055) 25156
Arklow	(0402) 32430
Wicklow	(0404) 67310
Greystones	(01) 874228
Dun Laoghaire	(01) 809641
Skerries	(01) 491228
Clogher Head	(041) 22225
Greenore	(042) 73550

Greencastle	(077) 81100
	(077) 81506
Tory Island	(074) 35512
Mulroy	(074) 55296

145

APPENDIX 8

H.M. Coastguard—Northern Ireland and Royal National Lifeboat Institute

H.M. Coastguard is the co-ordinating authority for search and rescue at sea. Its headquarters in Northern Ireland is Belfast Marine Rescue Sub Centre at Orlock Head, near Bangor, telephone Donaghadee (0247) 883184. This station is the only one in Northern Ireland maintaining a 24 hour watch. It has remote VHF aerials and can accept VHF calls on Channel 16 from almost anywhere off the Northern Ireland Coast. Having received a call from a yacht they will request it to transfer to Channel 67.

It is suggested that small craft owners and users who sail off Northern Ireland should obtain from their local CG station (or from YCs or marinas in Northern Ireland) a "Safety Scheme Card", fill in details of their craft on it and return it to Orlock Head Station. This helps the CG to identify the vessel if it is reported overdue or in distress.

Shoreline Membership of RNLI

In 1990 Irish lifeboats launched 274 times and saved 68 lives. Over half of all RNLI launches are made to people who put to sea for pleasure.

The RNLI was formed in 1824 for the preservation of life from shipwreck, not to act as a maritime AA! It therefore seems proper that yachtsmen should contribute handsomely towards a service which yearly costs almost £2·7m in Ireland alone. RNLI SHORELINE was formed with the purpose of appealing bluntly and specifically to individuals who, however experienced they may be as sailors, know well that a time could come when their lives would be at risk in waters protected by a lifeboat.

Yachtsmen sometimes advance criticism that, if they get into trouble and receive the services of a lifeboat, then salvage will be claimed by the crew. Although lifeboatmen, like other seafarers, have the undoubted right to claim salvage, the number of occasions on which this happens can be discounted—certainly in so far as yachts and small boats are concerned.

The Committee of the Irish Cruising Club strongly recommends members and other users of this book to join RNLI SHORELINE if they have not already done so. A membership form is on the inner back sheet of the dust jacket.

If sailing outside UK waters you are recommended to contact your nearest CG station before departure, i.e., Belfast Coastguard or Orlock Head if leaving from Northern Ireland.

Radio. Your safety will be improved if your craft has VHF radio enabling you to pass distress, urgency and safety messages (including your position reports) direct to the CG. Yachts fitted with MF radio transceivers only, or when outside coastal VHF range, should contact the PO Coast Radio Stations periodically to report their position which can be transferred to the CG if necessary.

In emergency circumstances it is good seamanship to offer to try to relay messages to the Coastguard if it is quite obvious that the recipient is not hearing. In these cases messages should be prefixed "Coastguard, Coastguard this is Yacht Alpha—I relay for Yacht Bravo", this lets all parties know that you are acting as a link.

More detailed information is obtainable free from any CG station.

Royal National Lifeboat Institution

Telephone numbers—dialling codes are appropriate to the county in which the station is located.

Lifeboat Station	Honorary Secretary	Deputy
Rosslare Harbour	(053) 58836	(053) 58849
Arklow	(0402) 32901	(0402) 32727
	(0402) 32001 Office	(0402) 32001 Office
Wicklow	(0404) 67321	(0404) 67556
	(0404) 68104 Office	(0404) 67455 Office
Dun Laoghaire	(01) 802879	(01) 841691
Howth	(01) 323524	(001) 322871
	(01) 322141 Office	
Clogher Head	(041) 22225	(041) 22600
Newcastle	(03967) 78429	(03967) 22441
Donaghadee	(0247) 883253	(0247) 883253
	(0232) 325465 Office	(0247) 225265 Office
Portrush	(0265) 823216	(0265) 823265

Inshore Lifeboats	Honorary Secretary	Deputy
Courtown	(055) 25437	—
	(055) 21222 Office	—
Skerries	(01) 490579	(01) 492272
	(01) 322735 Office	—
Kilkeel	(06937) 63317	(06937) 62287
	(06937) 62112 Office	(06937) 62497 Office
Portaferry	(02477) 28318	(02477) 28414
Bangor	(0247) 882330	(0247) 468555
	(0247) 270807 Office	
Red Bay	(02667) 71218	(02667) 71722
Lough Swilly	(077) 60202	—
	(0504) 261810 Office	—

Notes: (1) The Hon. Secretary of a lifeboat station is the launching authority; the DLA is his deputy. (2) Full details of lifeboat telephone numbers can be found in Parts I and II of the Irish Telephone Directory under "LIFE SAVING SERVICES" and in the Northern Ireland Telephone Directory under "LIFEBOAT". (3) Communications: Lifeboats can communicate on 2182 kHz and on Channels 16, 6 and 67 VHF/RT.

Principal Lights

Light On in Fog, marked "On," as exhibited during daylight when the fog signals are sounded, or in the case of lights without fog signals then in periods of poor visibility.

RANGE—Luminous range is the maximum distance at which a light can be seen at a given time, as determined by the intensity of the light and the meteorological visibility prevailing at that time; it takes no account of elevation, observer's height of eye or the curvature of the earth.

Nominal range is the luminous range when the meteorological visibility is 10 sea miles.

The ranges included in the List of Lights are those published by the competent authority.

Geographical range is the maximum distance at which light from a light can theoretically reach an observer, as limited only by the curvature of the earth and the refraction of the atmosphere, and by the elevation of the light and the height of eye of the observer of two metres in this table.

Name	Lights in fog	Character and colour	Period secs	Elev m	Range miles Nom	Range miles Geo	Fog signal	Type and height of lighthouse
Tuskar	On	Q (2) W	7.5	33	28	14	Horn (4) 45 secs	Wh Tr 34 m Racon
Rosslare		Fl WRG	5	15	13/10	10		Red 5m tower on pier
South Arklow		Fl (2)	12	12	16	10	Horn Mo (A) 30s	Lanby Racon
Arklow Harbour		Fl WR	6	10	13	9		Steel tower 6m on S pier
Wicklow Head		Fl (3)	15	37	26	15		Wh Tr 14m
Wicklow Harbour		Fl WR	5	11	6	· 6		Wh Tr on E pier
Codling		Fl	4	12	16	10	Horn 20s	Lanby
Kish Bank		Fl (2)	30	29	28	14	Horn (2) 30s	Wh Tr, red band, 31m C Radio Beacon and Racon
Dun Laoghaire		Fl (2)	15	16	22	11	Dia 30s Bell (1) 6s	Stone tower 12m on E pier
Poolbeg		Oc (2) R	20	20	15	12	Horn (2) 60s	Red Tr 20m

Name	Lights in fog	Character and colour	Period secs	Elev m	Range miles Nom	Range miles Geo	Fog signal	Type and height of lighthouse
Bull		Fl (3) G	10	15	15	11	Bell (4) 30s	Bl Tr 15m
Baily		Fl	20	41	27	16	Dia 60s	Granite Tr 13m
Howth		Fl (2) WR	7.5	13	17/13	13	·	Wh Tr 13m on E pier
Rockabill	On	Fl WR	12	45	23/19	16	Horn (4) 60s	Wh Tr, black band, 32m
Balbriggan		Fl (3) WRG	20	12	13/10	10		Wh Tr 16m on pier
Boyne L Lts		Oc	12	8/12	15/17	9		In line 248°
Pile (Dundalk)	On	Fl WR	15	10	21/18	9	Horn (3) 60s	Wh house on red piles
Haulbowline	On	Fl (3)	10	32	20	14	Horn 30s	Stone tower 34m
Carlingford L Lts		Oc	3	7/12	11	8		In line 310°
St. John's Point	On	Q (2)	7.5	37	23	15	Horn (2) 60s	Bl Tr, yellow bands, 40m
South Rock LV		Fl (2) R	30	12	20	10	Horn (3) 45s	Red lightship Racon
Donaghadee		Iso WR	4	17	18/14	11		Wh Tr on S pier
Mew Island		Fl (4)	30	37	30	15	Dia (4) 30s	Bl Tr, white band, 37m C Radio Beacon
Black Head		Fl	3	45	27	17		Wh Tr 16m
Ferris Point		Iso WRG	10	18	17/13	11	Dia 30s (Barr Point)	On watchroom on tower
Chaine Tower		Iso WR	5	23	11	11		Grey Tr 24 m
Maidens		Fl (3)	20	29	23	14		Wh Tr, black band, 23m
Rue Point		Fl (2)	5	16	14	11		Wh Tr, black bands, 11m
Rathlin East Altacarry Head		Fl (4)	20	74	26	20		Wh Tr, black band, 27 m C Radio Beacon
Rathlin West The Bull	On	Fl R	5	62	22	19	Horn (4) 60s	Lantern at base of white tower
Inishowen	On	Fl (2) WRG	10	28	18/14	14	Horn (2) 30s	Wh Tr, 2 black bands, 23m
Inishtrahull		Fl (3)	15	59	25	18		Wh Tr 23m Racon
Fanad Head		Fl (5) WR	20	39	18/14	16		Wh Tr 22m
Dunree Head		Fl (2) WR	5	46	12/19	9		House

Name	Lights in fog	Character and colour	Period secs	Elev m	Range miles Nom	Range miles Geo	Fog signal	Type and height of lighthouse
Tory Island		Fl (4)	30	40	30	16	Horn 60s	Bl Tr, white band, 27m C Radio Beacon

CHAPTER V only.

Name	Lights in fog	Character and colour	Period secs	Elev m	Range miles Nom	Range miles Geo	Fog signal	Type and height of lighthouse
Coningbeg Lt F	On	Fl (3) W	30	12	24	10	Horn (3) 60 secs	Red hull and tower lantern amidships Racon
Hook Head	On	Fl W	3	46	24	16	Horn (2) 45 secs	Wh Tr 35m 2 black bands Racon
Dunmore East		L Fl WR	8	13	R9 W12	10		Stone Tr 16m on pier

APPENDIX 10

Places where a Yacht might be left unattended

The following list of places where a yacht may be left unattended or the names of people who are mentioned would give good advice on the subject.

Also most of the yacht clubs mentioned in Appendix 17 are able to find someone with good local knowledge.

Wexford	Sailing Club (053) 22039
Arklow	John Tyrell (ICC) (0402) 2452 or 2492
Dun Laoghaire	Advice from Secretaries of main Yacht Clubs—see list
Howth	In Marina—Rupert Davies—Manager (01) 322141 (Y.C.), (01) 392777 (Marina)
Malahide	Kevin Bryan, Fingal Sailing School (01) 451979
Bangor Marina	Andrew Jaggers—Manager (0247) 453297
Cultra—RNIYC	Dermod Davy (02317) 2287
Carrickfergus Marina	John Fayre—Manager (09603) 66666
Carnlough	Mr. Linton—Harbour Master (0574) 84486
Portrush	Bill Todd—Admiralty Chart agent on quay (0265) 824176
Coleraine Marina	Ronnie McGeagh (0265) 44768
Culmore	Ferrymen
Fahan	Lough Swilly YC boatman
Ramelton	L. Turner & Son Boat Yard
Mulroy	Wallace Clark, ICC (0648) 457818

APPENDIX 11

SAILING ROUND IRELAND

Ireland is ideal for sailing round. Doing so is difficult enough to be interesting and yet the distance of 681 miles fits well into a cruising holiday of two or three weeks. It would be impossible to explore all the many anchorages in any one year, however one rapidly becomes fascinated by the wonderful scenery and the excellence of the sailing. The numbers circumnavigating increase year by year, and more yachts are now to be found using the west coast anchorages as their base. An increasing number of members of the Irish Cruising Club come from the more remote areas and are always ready to give assistance in every possible way to visiting yachtsmen. A list of port members, giving their addresses and telephone numbers, is available from Mrs Barbara Fox-Mills, The Tansey, Baily, Co. Dublin.

Time. Yachts cruising normally, anchoring for the night with only occasional longer passages, seldom take less than 21 days from an Irish port or a couple of days more from the west of England. It can be done in less time, but this means by-passing a very high proportion of the attractive parts. Anyone who can afford the time could easily spend two months circumnavigating without seeing everything.

Which way round? The majority of Irish-based boats have gone anti-clock and the English ones clockwise. Analyses of wind records coast by coast for June and July show a variation of only 3% for clockwise and anti-clockwise passages; so in an average year it does not matter from a wind point of view which way you go in these the two most popular months. Allowing for the fact that it is easier to beat on the east coast where there is less swell than on the west, a clockwise passage in July offers the best statistical chance.

The chief consideration is your home port or starting point. The west coast is the least known and most interesting and it is a sound principle to begin by heading for whichever end of it is nearest. Some people may prefer to get half way round as quickly as possible and leave the part they want to visit individually, in which it is all too easy to stay longer than intended, until the second half of the cruise.

Boats from the south of England or the Bristol channel should find clockwise best, but may leave the decision until they see what winds blow as they make the passage up and head for the Tuskar or Fastnet accordingly. For Clyde, Liverpool and Welsh boats the same consideration as for Irish ones would apply.

The Kenmare-Bantry area has always been popular with yachts from Cork and the south of England. Roundstone-Kilkieran, and also in good weather Achill-Slyne are both magnificent cruising grounds, but unfortunately not places to dally in, unless you have plenty of time, say four weeks at least for an Irish-based boat. Aranmore area, also Lough Swilly, are other little known but most attractive places, and if keen to see a bit of these parts, go clockwise.

General. Some yachts have been round under sail alone, but this is not recommended, for a good engine is of much greater value on the exposed coasts than say in the Irish Sea. On the west coast particularly, a large swell and awful sea can persist long after the gale which caused it has ceased, shaking any wind there is out of the sails and making for miserable conditions aboard a pure sailing vessel.

Much time can be absorbed in the west getting stores; the nearest town is often a couple of miles or more from the anchorage; water and fuel likewise, so ship as much as you can before starting, and top up when opportunity offers.

Have two good anchors plus a spare, and plenty of chain, warps and fenders. On the west you will be relying almost entirely on natural anchorages, as opposed to largely man-made ones on the east coast. But if you have good enough gear to lie alongside a rough pier in a bit of swell without damaging the boat, it may save lot of dinghy work and wettings.

Unless you have time to spare keep to the islands as much as possible. You will almost invariably be in a much better position to take advantage of the next day's winds if you bring up in the roads at, for example, Gola, Inishkea or Turk, than in the corresponding bays or anchorages of the mainland. These and several others similar are safe and comfortable anchorages more often than not in summer.

Gales. Irish Coast Pilot gives tables for their incidence and June and July both average two force 7 gale days apiece. This ties up with experiences of yachts—in a three week cruise you will almost certainly be held up once, perhaps twice, by gales lasting one or two days, but there is generally warning and nearly everyone has managed to get shelter before the blow really developed. To be sure of getting forecasts on the west coast you should have a good set and a long vertical aerial; but it is also very important to watch the sky and the barometer for it is a fact that the forecast warning is often received subsequent to the gale. R.T.E. shipping forecasts apply to Irish coastal waters and so are more likely to be accurate for the coastal cruiser than the B.B.C. shipping forecasts which refer to much wider areas of open sea.

Fog. Ireland as a whole is lucky in this respect and complete days of persistent fog occur on average less than once in ten years. Fog generally only occurs with winds between SE and SW and is much less common on the west coast than elsewhere.

Sailing Directions. South and West Coast companion volume to this is published by Irish Cruising Club Publications. It may be obtained from any good chandlery, or from Mrs. Barber Fox-Mills, The Tansey, Baily, Co. Dublin or on the U.K. mainland from Imray Laurie Norie & Wilson Ltd., St. Ives, Cambridgeshire.

APPENDIX 12

Stores and Victualling

General Supplies. The two largest shopping centres are Dublin and Belfast, best visited by road or rail from adjacent marinas. On the E coasts there is no difficulty about supplies. Dun Laoghaire is probably the most popular port for stocking up, but Wexford, Arklow, Wicklow, Drogheda, Donaghadee, Bangor, Carrickfergus and Larne supply all normal needs and there are excellent shops in other places.

The N coast is more unevenly provided. The largest town, Londonderry, is rather far from the sea but may be visited by bus from Fahan in Lough Swilly. Coleraine and Moville are not so far from the main coast. Milford is 10 miles in at the head of Mulroy Lough and some distance from the anchorage there. Portrush is the only convenient town between Larne and Londonderry on the coast for supplies of all sorts. Portstewart harbour, with good shops very close, is only suitable in calm sea conditions. Limited provisions are available at Ballycastle, Greencastle, Buncrana, Rathmullan and Downings.

Gas. Calor gas is not obtainable in the Irish Republic. The same gas sold there has a totally different method for connecting its cylinder and the smallest cylinder is also higher than the Calor cylinder used in many yachts. UK yachts which use Calor should therefore bring as many cylinders as they are likely to require when sailing around the Irish Republic. However Calor Gas is widely available in Northern Ireland.

Fuel. Is generally available quite close to most of the anchorages and moorings mentioned in the text and at all marinas; however after passing Malin Head going westward it does become more difficult as some supplies are rather far from landing points. Keep tanks well topped up.

Alcohol is very expensive in the Republic of Ireland, so visiting yachtsmen would be well advised to bring their full allowances of Duty Free. Particular attention is drawn to the rules regarding allowances of duty free spirits and tobacco when transiting between the Republic of Ireland and Northern Ireland and vice-versa, until 1993. The cost of alcohol in Northern Ireland is similar to the rest of U.K.

APPENDIX 13

Repair Facilities

These are listed along the coast from the SE corner of Ireland under various categories. As a yacht gets farther to the W along the Donegal coast the number of facilities dwindles as the area gets more remote. In cases of emergencies most of the Hon. Secretaries of the various yacht clubs listed in Appendix 17 should be able to provide suitable names or advice. The list is by no means complete, however by consulting Golden Pages telephone book in the Republic of Ireland and Yellow Pages in Northern Ireland one should be able to find help.

Boat Builders and Repairers
Arklow: John Tyrell Ltd (0402) 2452 or 2492.
Wicklow: Wicklow Marine Services Ltd (0404) 68408.
Dun Laoghaire: J. Brennan (01) 805308.
Malahide: Malahide Boat Yard Ltd (01) 450303.
Kilkeel: McCartan Boatyard Ltd (06937) 62565.
Strangford Lough: W. Smith, Whiterock.
Portavogie: James Mahood (02477) 71262.
Bangor: Bangor Shipyard Ltd (0247) 270939.
Carrickfergus: WW Marine Ltd (09603) 69895.
River Bann: Coleraine Marina (Travel Hoist) (0265) 44768.
Lough Swilly: L. Turner & Son, Ramelton.

Marine Engineers
Dublin: Alexander Engineering (01) 749904.
　　　　 Liffey Marine Engineers Ltd (01) 744729.
Kilkeel: A. Annett & Sons (06937) 62208.
Donaghadee: Barclay Marine Services (0247) 888606.
Bangor: Bangor Marine Services (0247) 452224.
Belfast: Robert Craig & Sons (0232) 232971.
Coleraine: Tony's Marine Services (0265) 56422.

Electronic and Electrical Repairs
Dublin: All weather Radio and Repairs Ltd (01) 713655.
　　　　 Irish Marine Electronics (01) 786400.
　　　　 Marconi International (01) 749157.
　　　　 Western Marine Ltd (01) 800321.
　　　　 Racal Marine Ltd (01) 776698.
Bangor: Offshore Electrics (Marine) B&G (0247) 469027.
Belfast: Belfast Lough Marine Electronics (09603) 65565.
　　　　 QIK Electronics Ltd (0232) 760660.

Sailmakers
Bray: Sterling Sails Ltd (01) 862257.
Dun Laoghaire: Downer International Sails Ltd (01) 804286.
Dublin: Allweather Marine Ltd (01) 713655.
        Watson & Jameson Ltd (01) 326466.
Strangford Lough: John McWilliam (0238) 542300.
                Ocean Sails Ltd (0247) 874555.
                Sketrick Marine Centre (0238) 541400.
Belfast: E. A. Gaw (0232) 791975.
        James Tedford & Co Ltd (0232) 326763.

Outboard Engines
Dalkey: Killen Marine (01) 853908.
Dublin: Allweather Marine Ltd (01) 713655.
        Windmill Leisure & Marine (01) 772008.
Strangford Lough: Albert Clark (0247) 872325.
Donaghadee: Barclay Marine Services (0247) 888606.
            Outboard Services (0247) 816878.
Larne: Michigan Propellers (0574) 77350.
       M. G. Stitt (09603) 82278.
Belfast: Robert Craig & Sons Ltd (0232) 232971.

Yacht Chandlery is now widely available all along the coast covered by these directions. Consult Yellow/Golden Pages telephone directory or enquire from local yacht club if you are in need.

APPENDIX 14

CUSTOMS REQUIREMENTS

Yachts should preferably make their first call at one of the following places where there are Customs posts (though some of them are not constantly manned): Dunmore East, Waterford, New Ross, Dungarvan, Cobh, Cork, Kinsale, Baltimore (summer months only), Crookhaven, Bantry, Castletownbere, Cahirciveen, Fenit, Kilrush, Foynes, Limerick, Galway, Westport, Sligo and Killybegs. Clearance is also readily obtained at Crosshaven and in fact yachts are permitted to make their first call anywhere. On arrival yachts should hoist flag Q (or show red over white by night). If a Customs officer does not appear soon the owner or skipper should go ashore and report; if no Customs officer is available he should report the yacht's arrival at the nearest police station.

Details of requirements are set out in Customs Notice No. 93, obtainable from the Revenue Commissioners, Dublin Castle, Dublin 2. Customs Officers have a list of dutiable, restricted and prohibited articles, which must be declared. Reasonable quantities of alcohol for use aboard are permitted. Persons whose normal residence is outside the State may temporarily import for a period not exceeding twelve months a pleasure boat which they use for their private or business use, without payment of import charges. Information regarding temporary importation is contained in Notice 1795 which may be obtained from Division 1, Office of the Revenue Commissioners, Dublin Castle, Dublin 2.

Customs requirements in the case of yachts are framed with a view to causing the minimum of inconvenience to owners. The Commissioners rely on owners and masters to take such measures as may be necessary to prevent the irregular landing from, or shipment on, their vessels of any dutiable, prohibited or restricted articles. A yacht used in connection with traffic in prohibited or uncustomed goods is liable to forfeiture, and the owner and master to heavy penalties.

NORTHERN IRELAND

The correct procedure for all yachts arriving in Northern Ireland ports from the Republic of Ireland or the Continent is to contact the Coast Preventive Man, who will arrange clearance with the nearest Waterguard Officer.

If the Coast Preventive Man cannot readily be contacted, telephone the nearest Waterguard Office. Their phone numbers are: Belfast 752511/3, Coleraine 44803, Larne 70340, Londonderry 261937 or 362273, Warrenpoint 72544. Alternatively phone the Waterguard Office from the last Republic port, naming the port and estimated time of arrival in Northern Ireland.

It is the responsibility of the Master or owner to advise the Waterguard Officer of the vessel's arrival in Northern Ireland. At some places, the harbour master or H.M. Coastguard will assist in this.

The method of dealing with Republic of Ireland yachts on passage from one Republic of Ireland port to another via Northern Ireland varies according to the anticipated stay in Northern Ireland.

APPENDIX 15

List of Places to Visit

From time to time yachts get held up by bad weather, have to wait at anchor or in port for crew changes, or just want to stop sailing for a day or two. The list below, by no means exhaustive, gives some ideas for places to see and visit ashore, it is primarily directed towards overseas visitors to our shores. All the places can be easily reached from the anchorages mentioned either by walking, public transport, or short taxi journeys. Some areas, such as the Mourne Mountains, can be reached from a number of places, so a look at the chart should solve any possible doubts about which suits best.

Wexford: National Heritage Park; Wildlife Bird Sanctuary.
Dun Laoghaire: National Maritime Museum; easy access to historic Dublin.
Howth: Easy access to historic Dublin.
Malahide: Castle open 10 am–8 pm.
Drogheda: Boyne Valley, historic interest.
Kilkeel: Silent Valley Dam; Mourne Mountains for walking.
Annalong: Old Corn Mill; Mourne Mountains for walking.
Newcastle: Forest parks (2); Mourne Mountains for walking.
Audely's Roads, Strangford: Castleward House (NT).
Kircubbin: Mountstewart Gardens (NT).
Portaferry: Aquarium.
Carrickfergus: Norman castle.
Carnlough: The Nine Glens of Antrim—walks.
Portrush: Giant's Causeway—Bushmills Whiskey Distillery (8M); "Waterworld".
Londonderry: Historic walled city.
Greencastle: Fort.
Lough Swilly: Picturesque sailing area—interesting for artists.
Mulroy Bay: Some of the finest views in Ireland—photography.
Tory Island: Celtic remains.

APPENDIX 16

Places to Eat and Drink

This is a new innovation and is therefore on trial for this edition. It must be appreciated that all those who go to sea in small ships do not have the same tastes or standards. Furthermore, hostelries open and close; their chefs move on; the proprietors change, so this list is based on pubs and eating houses that have been mentioned in members' logs, by correspondents or from local knowledge. It is primarily intended to help visitors to our shores.

Dunmore East: "The Candlelight".
Rosslare: Hotels—4.
Wexford: Large selection within walking distance.
Dun Laoghaire: Many hotels, restaurants, cafes and pubs.
Howth: "King Citric", Russell's Hotel.
Malahide: Hotels, restaurants and pubs.
Drogheda: Hotels, restaurants and pubs.
Dundalk: Hotels, restaurants and pubs.
Kilkeel: Kilmorey Arms.
Annalong: Good pub on quayside.
Ardglass: "The Waters Edge".
Strangford Village: "Lobster Pot", "Cuan" bar.
Killyleagh: Hotel.
Whiterock: "Balloo House" (1½M); "Daft Eddie's"—Dinghy.
Portaferry: Portaferry Hotel, "The Scotsman".
Donaghadee: Pubs and cafés.
Bangor: Many types of restaurants, hotels and cafés.
Cultra: Culloden Hotel (½M).
Holywood: Pubs and cafés.
Carrickfergus: "Dobbins Castle", pubs and cafés.
Larne: "Olderfleet Arms".
Carnlough: "Londonderry Arms".
Portrush: "The Ramore" and pubs.
Coleraine: Hotels, restaurants, cafés about 1½M from marina.
Greencastle: Fort Hotel.
Rathmullan: Rathmullan House Hotel; Fort Royal Hotel—Dinghy.
Fannys Bay—Mulroy: Carrigart Hotel (2½M).
Downings: Hotels.
Marblehill: Hotel.
Tory Island: Club.

APPENDIX 17

List of Yacht Clubs along the Coast

This is by no means an exhaustive list, however it includes those yacht clubs who replied to a recent circular. It gives their proper name, the name of the hon. secretary and his/her telephone number together with a brief outline of the facilities available. The names of the Commodores have been omitted as the holders of high office change more frequently than the hon. secs. About six yacht clubs along this coast have permanent secretaries and these are marked with an asterisk. Telephone codes apply to the county in which the club is situated.

VM = visitors' moorings; AB = alongside berths; S = showers; M = meals; B = bar; F = fuel; W = water (some amenities have limited opening times).

Arklow Sailing Club, Arklow—W. J. Brown. VM; S; W.

Courtown Sailing Club, Courtown—Jan Cullen (055) 25307. AB; S; F; W.

*National Yacht Club, Dun Laoghaire—R. Wharton (01) 805725. AB; S; M; B; F; W.

*Royal St George Yacht Club, Dun Laoghaire—P. J. O'Reilly (Sec.) (01) 801811. VM; S; M; B; F; W.

*Royal Irish Yacht Club, Dun Laoghaire—Sarann Smith (Sec.) (01) 809452. VM; S; M; B; F; W.

Clontarf Yacht and Boat Club, Dublin Bay—Paul Smyth (01) 332691. VM; S; B; F; W.

*Howth Yacht Club, Howth—Brendan Connor, Rupert Jeffers (Sec.) (01) 322141. VM; AB; S; M; B; F; W.

Malahide Yacht Club, Malahide—Robert Barker (01) 453372. VM; S; M; B; F; W.

Dundalk Sailing Club, Dundalk—Anne Deaney (042) 73238. S; M; B; F; W.

Newcastle Yacht Club, Newcastle—Tony Dickinson (03962) 22518. W.

Quoile Yacht Club, Strangford Lough (0396) 612256. VM; AB; S; B; W.

Killyleagh Yacht Club, Strangford Lough—James Ferris (0396) 828250. VM; S; B; F; W.

East Down Yacht Club, Strangford Lough—V. Care (0396) 828375. VM; AB; S; B; W.

Strangford Lough Yacht Club, Strangford Lough—Hugh Strain (0396) 541202. VM; AB; M; S; B; W.

Down Cruising Club, Strangford Lough—Colin Erskine (0238) 541663. VM; AB; S; B; F; W.

Newtownards Sailing Club, Strangford Lough—S. Wilson (0247) 813426. VM; S; B; W.

Ballyholme Yacht Club, Belfast Lough—E. F. Mayne (0247) 454768. VM; S; M; B; F; W.

*Royal Ulster Yacht Club, Belfast Lough—T. O'Hara, Valerie Boyd (Sec.) (0247) 270568. AB; S; M; B; F; W.

*Royal North of Ireland Yacht Club, Belfast Lough—D. W. McMeekin, Gerry McMullen (Sec.) (0232) 428041. VM; S; M; B; F; W.

Holywood Yacht Club, Belfast Lough—A. Fusco (02317) 3345. S; B.

East Antrim Boat Club, Larne—Mrs L. Stewart (0574) 77204. S; B; F; W.

Portrush Yacht Club, Portrush—Perry Donaldson. VM; AB; S; M; B; F; W.

Coleraine Yacht Club, Coleraine—Robin McKelvey (0265) 44503. S; B; F; W.

APPENDIX 18
Irish words occurring in place names

A knowledge of the commonest of the following, colours in particular, often helps with identification, eg, Carrickglass—Green Rock (generally one with grass on top). Carrickbwee—Yellow Rock, Freaghillaun—Heather Isle.

Ail, alt—Cliff, height.
Aird, ard—Height, high
Ane—Birds (Illaunnane)
Anna, annagh—Marsh
Aran—Kidney
Ath—a ford (Athlone)

Bal, bally—Town
Ban (gen plur)—Woman
Barnog, barnagh—Barnacle (Inishbarnog)
Barra—Sandbank, or head
Ban, bawn—Fair, whitish
Bel, beal—Mouth: hence strait (Bealadangan, Belmullet)
Beg—Little
Ben, bin, binna—Hill
Bo—Cow: hence sunken rock
Boy, bwee—Yellow
Brack, breaga—Speckled
Brad, bradan—Salmon
Breole, breel—Cormorant
Bullig—Belly: hence shoal or rounded rock, hence breaker
Bun—End. River mouth

Caher—Fort
Camus—Bay or River Bend (Cambridge)
Carrick, carrig, cloy, clough—Rock (Portacloy, rocky port)
Cladach, Chaddy, Choch—shore (Cloghane)
Cloon, lon—Meadow
Coor, cuar, cour—Foam (Couraghy)
Cor, car—Small Hill
Corr—Sand eel
Corraun, corran—Reaping hook, hence curved point
Cuan, coon—Harbour, particularly a winding bay
Cul, cool—Recess
Cowan (cf gamhain)—Seal (Co Donegal)

Derg, dearg—Red
Derry—Oakgrove
Dillisk, dulk dulse—Edible seaweed
Drum—Hill, ridge (Drumbo)
Duff, duv, dhu, dubh—black
Dun, doon—Fort

-een—Small

Ennis—Island
Fad, fadda—Long (Carrickfad)
Fan—Slope
Fin—White
Freagh, free—Heather (Inishfree, Freaghillaun)

Gall—Stranger
Garv, gariff—Rough
Glas, glass—Green (Glassilaun)
Glinsk—Clear water
Gola, gowla—Fork (Inishgowla)
Gore, gobhar, gower—Goat

Gorm—Blue
Gub—Point of land

Hassans—Swift current, waterfall or stoats

Inish, innis, inis, illaun—Island
Inver—River mouth

Keel, keal—Narrow place, sound
Keragh, keeragh—Sheep (Inishkeeragh)
Kill—church or cell (Killybegs)
Kin, ken—Head, promontory
Knock—Hill

Lag, log—Hollow
Lahan—Broad
Lea—Grey
League, legaun—Pillar stones (Slieve League)
Lenan, leenan—A weed covered rock
Lis—Ancient fort
Long, luing—A ship (Annalong)
Maan—Middle (Inishmaan)
Maghera, magher—Plain
Maol, mwee—Bare (Mweelaun, bare islet)
Mara—Of the sea
More, mor—Big (Dunmore)
Muck—Pig
Murren, murrisk—Place of sea grass or low lying seashore

Og—Young
Ooey, owey—Cave

Partan, portaun—Crab (Carrickaportaun)
Pool—Hole or pool

Rannagh, ranny, rin run, rue, rush, ros—Point
Roe, ruadh—Red
Ron, roan, rone—Seal (Roancarrick, Roaninish)

Sal, salia—of the sea, hence salty
Scolt—Split, rocky gut
Scrow, scrah, scraw—Boggy, grassy sward
Slieve—Mountain
Slig—Shells (Sligo)
Stag, stac, steuc, stook—High rock

Tawney—Low hill
Thangy—Rock or bank (Usually underwater)
Tigh, Ti—House (Tinabinna)
Tir—Land (of)
Tober—Well
Togher—Causeway
Tor—Tower, pointed rock
Trusk—Codfish
Tra, traw—Strand (Tramore)
Turk—Boar
Turlin—Boulder beach

Vaddy, maddy—Dog
Vad, bad—Boat
Vore—Great ("more" changed by aspiration)

Will, whill, wheelaun—Seagull

APPENDIX 19

Abbreviations used in this volume

Aero	(*light*) for aircraft	ICC	Irish Cruising Club
Al	(*light*) alternating	ICP	Irish Coast Pilot
B	black	IQ	interrupted quick
Bn	beacon		flashing
BBC	British Broadcasting Corporation	Iso	(*light*) isophase
BST	British Summer Time	kHz	kilohertz
Can	can red buoy	kn	knot or knots
CB	centre board	Lanby	large automatic
CG	Coast Guard		navigational buoy
C/S	Call sign	LAT	lowest astronomical tide
CO	Commanding Officer	LFl	(*light*) long flash (2s)
Con	conical green buoy	LOA	overall length (of vessels)
Card	cardinal (mark)	LV	light vessel
CQR	type of anchor	LW	low water
derv	diesel oil for road vehicles	LWN	low water neaps
Dia	(*foghorn*) diaphone	LWS	low water springs
DST	Double Summer Time	LWOST	low water ordinary
E	east (*see next page*)		spring tides
EC	early closing	max	maximum
elev	elevation	m	metre or metres
ESB	Electricity Supply Board	M	miles
F	(*wind*) force	MHWS	mean high water
F	(*light*) fixed		springs
Fl	(*light*) flashing	MHWN	Mean high water neaps
F Fl	fixed and flashing	MLWM	mean low water neaps
Fl (2)	group flashing	MLWS	mean low water springs
G	(*light*) green	MTL	mean tidal level
GMT	Greenwich Mean Time	Mo	morse code
Hbr	harbour	N	north (*see next page*)
Hon Sec	Honorary Secretary	N	number
HM	Harbour Master	NB	note well
hrs	hours	NT	National Trust
HQ	headquarters	Obsc	obscured
HT	high tension cable	Oc	(*light*) occulting
HW	high water	Or	(*light*) orange
HWN	high water neaps	PO	post office
HWS	high water springs	Qk	(*light*) quick (1s)
HWOST	high water ordinary spring tides	R	Royal, (*lights*) red
IALA	International Association of	RTE	Radio Telefis Eireann
	Lighthouse Authorities	Rly	railway

RNLI	Royal National Lifeboat Institution			UK	United Kingdom		

RNLI — Royal National Lifeboat Institution
S — south (*see next page*)
s — second, seconds
SC — sailing club
SS Co — steam ship company
St — Saint
st — starboard
T — T-shaped road junction
Thur — Thursday

UK — United Kingdom
vert — vertical
vis — visible, visibility
VHF — very high frequency
VQ — (*light*) very quick ($\frac{1}{2}$s)
W — west (*see opposite page*)
W — (*light*) white
Wed — Wednesday
Y — yellow

Cardinal points N = north, S = south, E = east, W = west

The old 32 compass card points, 11¼° apart; directions shown below to the nearest or lesser degree.

N	360°	E	090°	S	180°	W	270°
N by E	011°	E by S	101°	S by W	191°	W by N	281°
NNE	022°	ESE	112°	SSW	202°	WNW	292°
NE by N	034°	SE by E	124°	SW by S	214°	NW by W	304°
Ne	045°	SE	135°	SW	225°	NW	315°
NE by E	056°	SE by S	146°	SW by W	236°	NW by N	326°
ENE	067°	SSE	157°	WSW	247°	NNW	337°
E by N	079°	S by E	169°	W by S	259°	N by W	349°

N quarter means directions between NW and NE.

N as well as north may mean northern, northward, or northerly, and other abbreviations are similarly used. The full cardinal point words are only used in names, eg South Rock, North Channel.

Lights and foghorns. The abbreviations are included in the above list. Some speciments of their combinations are explained below.

2 FG (vert) — two fixed (continuous) green lights one above the other.

Q — continuous quick white flashes, about every second.

Fl 30s — a white flash every half minute.

Fl (2) WRG 20s — two flashes repeated every 20 seconds, white red and green in different sectors which would be described afterwards.

Iso 4s — white light for two seconds and eclipse for two seconds.

Oc R 10s — red light for 8 seconds followed by eclipse for 2 seconds.

Aero Alt Fl WG 7½s — light for aircraft, alternative white and green flashes, 7½ seconds from one white flash to the next white flash.

V Q (6) + LFl 10s   six very quick white flashes (3 seconds) followed immediately by a long white flash (2 seconds), then a 5 second eclipse (S Cardinal buoy light).

Dia (4) 60s   Four low-pitched sounds from a diaphone at one minute intervals.

Admiralty Chart Number 5011, now in book form, edition 5, is a very useful guide to all symbols and abbreviations used on their charts. It is regularly updated by Admiralty Notices to Mariners, Small craft edition published four times a year in February, May, July and September.

APPENDIX 20

Conversion Tables

In the first three tables metres are converted to the nearest inch, ¼ fathom or yard; in the right-hand table feet are converted to the nearest 0.1 metre. Exact equivalents are as follows: 1 metre = 3·28084 feet. 1 foot = 0·3048 metres. For readers unfamiliar with local units: 12 inches = 1 foot. 3 feet = 1 yard. 2 yards = 1 fathom. The Nautical Mile ("mile" in the text) is 6,080 feet, about 1,853 metres; it is the average local Sea Mile which is a minute of latitude and therefore variable. The cable is one tent of a Nautical Mile, approximately 203 yards or 185 metres, usually thought of as 200 yards, ¾ cable = 139 m. ½ cable = 93 m. ¼ cable = 46 m.

Metres	Ft. inches	Metres	Fathoms	Metres	Yards	Feet	Metres	Feet	Metres
0·1	4″	2	1	10	11	1	0·3	30	9·1
0·2	8″	3	1¾	15	16	2	0·6	31	9·4
0·3	1′	4	2¼	20	22	3	0·9	32	9·7
0·4	1′ 4″	5	2¾	25	27	4	1·2	33	10·1
0·5	1′ 8″	6	3¼	30	33	5	1·5	34	10·4
0·6	2′	7	3¾	35	38	6	1·8	35	10·7
0·7	2′ 4″	8	4¼	40	44	7	2·1	36	11·0
0·8	2′ 7″	9	5	45	49	8	2·4	37	11·3
0·9	2′ 11″	10	5½	50	55	9	2·7	38	11·6
1·0	3′ 3″	11	6	55	60	10	3·0	39	11·9
1·1	3′ 7″	12	6½	60	66	11	3·3	40	12·2
1·2	3′ 11″	13	7	65	71	12	3·7	41	12·5
1·3	4′ 3″	14	7¾	70	77	13	4·0	42	12·8
1·4	4′ 7″	15	8¼	75	82	14	4·3	43	13·1
1·5	4′ 11″	16	8¾	80	87	15	4·6	44	13·4
1·6	5′ 3″	17	9¼	85	93	16	4·9	45	13·7
1·7	5′ 7″	18	9¾	90	98	17	5·2	46	14·0
1·8	5′ 11″	19	10½	95	104	18	5·5	47	14·3
1·9	6′ 3″	20	11	100	109	19	5·8	48	14·6
2	6′ 7″	21	11½	110	120	20	6·1	49	14·9
3	9′ 10″	22	12	120	131	21	6·4	50	15·2
4	13′ 1″	23	12½	130	142	22	6·7	51	15·5
5	16′ 5″	24	13	140	153	23	7·0	52	15·8
6	19′ 8″	25	13¾	150	164	24	7·3	53	16·1
7	23′	26	14¼	160	175	25	7·6	54	16·5
8	26′ 3″	27	14¾	170	186	26	7·9	55	16·8
9	29′ 6″	28	15¼	180	197	27	8·2	56	17·1
10	32′ 10″	29	15¾	190	208	28	8·5	57	17·4
		30	16½	200	219	29	8·8	58	17·7

General Index

Bold numerals refer to the numbers of photographs